3/90

Rich

Best to you...

[illegible]

Phil 2:2

[illegible]

Money & Your Marriage

Russ Crosson

Foreword by
RON BLUE

WORD PUBLISHING
Dallas · London · Sydney · Singapore

To Clark, Reed, and Chad
my posterity!

MONEY AND YOUR MARRIAGE

Library of Congress Cataloging in Publication Data

Money and your marriage
Crosson, Russell, 1953–
Money and your marriage / Russell Crosson.
p. cm.
Bibliography: p.
1. Marriage—United States. 2. Married people—United States—Finance, Personal. 3. Finance, Personal—Religious aspects—Christianity. I. Title.
HQ734.C95 1989
332.024′0655—dc20 89-14649
CIP

ISBN 0-8499-0683-0

9 8 0 1 2 3 9 AGF 9 8 7 6 5 4 3 2 1

Printed in the United States of America

Contents

Foreword

This book is informative, decisive in its advice, but, better yet, extremely practical. It identifies the primary communication problems and gives practical advice on how to solve them. I recommend this book to anyone who, first of all, desires to communicate, and, second, desires to communicate specifically about financial issues.

My wife, Judy, and I have been married for almost twenty-five years. We have had the privilege of raising five children during that time, and I have had the opportunity to be involved in giving financial counsel and advice throughout my entire professional life. Given these facts, it would be easy to assume that we would have little to learn from Russ and Julie Crosson who have been married many years less than we have. Quite the contrary is true.

Judy and I have observed that the outstanding characteristic of Russ and Julie's lives—individually and as a couple—is that they take the Word of God seriously. Many people know the Word of God and can talk about it, but few can consistently model it. We have been impressed over the ten years that we have observed their marriage that they are a couple that we can learn a great deal from, especially as marriage relates to effective husband/wife communication.

My experience is that effective communication about financial issues is extraordinarily difficult. The primary reason for the difficulty is that every financial decision is ultimately a priority decision. Two people in a marriage relationship will, without exception, have differing priorities. Unless there is a commitment to communication and a methodology for communication, there will almost certainly be conflict. Russ and Julie have identified the problems that commonly come up in handling money topics. More importantly, they have illustrated in this book their plan for communication. I have seen this plan worked out effectively in their own marriage.

Ron Blue

Acknowledgments

To write a book on marital harmony and money management is indeed a challenge and one that would have been impossible were it not for my relationship with Julie, my bride of ten years. Her love for God and unwavering desire to be a godly help-meet have enabled us, as a couple, to experience and live out firsthand the financial principles and thoughts shared throughout this book. I am extremely grateful for her and her constant support and encouragement. I am committed to her for the rest of my life. We are both grateful for the saving work Christ has done in our lives without which the power and ability to live out these truths would be impossible.

I owe a special debt of gratitude to Charles and Peggy McCreight who, along with the young couples in their church in Sumter, South Carolina, provided the forum where this material first came together. Charles and Peggy encouraged Julie and me and prayed for us constantly as we undertook the challenge of this project.

Ron Blue gave me the opportunity to work with couples in the financial arena when he hired me nine years ago. His confidence in me then and constant support and counsel throughout the years has been invaluable. Financial insights gleaned from Ron as well as my other partners at Ronald Blue & Co. are woven throughout this book, and for them I am grateful.

The couples who read the initial manuscript and offered valuable input have had a tremendous impact on the finished product—Elaine Franklin, Scott and Candy Houser, Cheron Lucy, and Bradley Fulkerson deserve a special thanks.

To our parents, Bert and Jan Harned and Lon Dean and Barbara Crosson, we are forever grateful. They modeled harmonious marriages and the proper way to handle finances for us. They have been and continue to be an inspiration to Julie and me.

A special thanks to Lisa Pate, Karen Kreiner, and Kelly Nottingham for their countless hours of typing and responding to my time demands as this book came to completion.

We would also like to thank Candy Houser, Georgia Spearman, Carol Crosson, and Heidi Andrews for watching our "posterity" while we finished the book.

Introduction

"We've been married fifteen years," Bob began. "It seems that no matter how hard I work or what I make, our finances are always a source of conflict. I used to be an executive with a large retail company before going to work as a sales rep three years ago. I just couldn't seem to make enough money in my previous job, and the sales job allowed me more potential to increase my income. Sally has been at home most of the time during the fifteen years, though she did work off and on in the early years when we needed additional income."

"I've worked some through the years to help make ends meet," interrupted Sally. "I have my RN and do enjoy working, and it does give me some fulfillment. As a matter of fact, I am considering going back again, but Bob really doesn't want me to."

"I work hard," continued Bob, "and make a decent income. I guess that is why we wanted to talk to a financial consultant like you. I make enough income that we shouldn't have any financial problems. Just last night we argued again about the debt on our credit cards. I tried to explain . . ."

"Tried to explain like you always do," Sally broke in. "Whenever I ask him about the debt we have, he just explains to me that debt is normal. That everybody uses it and that I shouldn't worry about it. Well, I did okay when he took out the second mortgage on the house . . . even though I told him I didn't like it. But when the credit card balances got back up to $5,000, I had had enough. He just doesn't seem to understand how I feel about debt. I don't like it."

"The second mortgage was good planning," countered Bob. "It allowed me to consolidate some other loans and keep the interest deductible."

"That is beside the point," chided Sally.

"She is probably right. I guess I don't understand how she feels about debt," Bob said. "To me, using debt is the way for a man to get ahead and increase his financial position. My dad used debt, and that is what I learned in business school. All I'm trying to do is get us ahead financially and make it easier for Sally and the kids."

"It would be easier for us if you were around some," fumed Sally. "Ever since you've taken that new sales rep job, you're never home. What good does it do to make more money if you aren't around? You're more concerned about your job and making investments and watching after them than you are about what we need as a family."

"I don't know how you can say that," retorted Bob. "One of the reasons I have made those investments is to be able to provide more for you and the kids. To me, they *are* what you need."

"Oh? I'm sure I needed that real estate deal you did with that guy I didn't like. It seems to be nothing but a headache and is taking a lot of our cash right now as well as your time. I handle the books, and I know how much cash you've put into investments the past three years. What good is an IRA at 59 1/2? I'd like some cash to do some things on the house, but it is always going into some investment someplace."

"Well, if you had your way, we would spend it all right now and not save up anything," groused Bob. "Of course, that is the way your family was. They never saved a dime. At least having money in an investment is better than spending it."

"I don't want to spend it all," snarled Sally. "I just want to have some cash to do some little things around the house. If you'd listen to me and look at the books once in a while, you'd see how tight the month-to-month cash really is. Of course, you don't buy the groceries or the kids' clothes, so you don't have any idea how much it costs to run this place."

"I'm sure I give you enough money to meet the needs," said Bob flatly.

"How do you know? We never talk about it!" exclaimed Sally.

"Well, when I do talk to you, you don't seem to understand," exclaimed Bob. "You never seem to see it my way. As you can see, Russ, we don't seem to see eye to eye on our money."

Bob was right. It was obvious that he and Sally did not see eye to eye on how they handled their money. In the discussion to this point they had displayed different perspectives on debt, investments, work, and spending level. They had brought up Sally's family and made accusations. They were obviously not in agreement regarding their finances, and it was true that neither one really understood the other, especially in regard to their finances.

Sally was trying to state her preference for communication and some guidelines from Bob. Bob, on the other hand, was trying to help her see that he was doing all that he could to provide for her. The use of debt, the long work hours, and the investments were for her. They were both trying to get the other to think the way they did regarding their money—to understand money from their perspective.

In front of me were two people who had loved each other for fifteen years. They loved each other; yet, when it came to money, they did not understand each other. The amount of money was not an issue, as it was obvious that Bob made enough money to provide for his family. Yet, this very money was a source of conflict in their marriage. Why was it a source of conflict? Why did Bob and Sally have so much trouble communicating about money? Why didn't they seem to see eye to eye? Is it possible for them to see eye to eye? To answer these questions and others is the purpose of this book.

As I have consulted with couples I have found the above scenario far too common. Although money can provide tremendous freedom and be used to do great and noble things for the Kingdom of God, in many marriages it is a source of friction, frustration, and anxiety. As a matter of fact, various sources show that 50 percent of all marriages end in divorce, and 80 percent of those are the result of money problems. It is my observation that there are three underlying reasons money causes so many marriage problems.

INCORRECT THINKING

First of all, we do not think correctly about money or our marriages. Society has influenced our thinking in these two areas, so much so that we believe what the world says to be true rather than what God says to be true. Let me illustrate:

• The world says that money is the key to happiness. That we believe this is evidenced by the priority we put on making money. It consumes the majority of our day and the majority of our thinking. Money, however, does not make us happy. In the most affluent country in the world, we see individuals and families who have all the material trappings they could ever desire and yet they are not happy. The truth is that we are truly happy only as we are rightly related to Jesus Christ (John 10:10).

• The world says that the accumulation of money meets our needs and gives us worth, acceptance, and significance in life. This is evidenced by our pursuit of money and our lack of devotion to our marriages, our children, and our God. We sacrifice our families and marriages and relationship with God on the altar of money. The truth is that our worth is a function of who we are in Christ and not what we own materially (Luke 12:16–21). The truth is that our children, and not the things we can buy with money, are what will last (Ps. 37:37–38; Eccles. 5:15). The truth is that we are most fulfilled and our self-worth most esteemed as we enjoy a harmonious, loving marriage relationship with the spouse of our youth (Eccles. 9:9).

• The world says that the ultimate end in life is to achieve ease, comfort, and pleasure and that money is the ticket to get there. We believe it, as evidenced by how we set our priorities and by our insatiable desire to get ahead at all costs. We put a premium on being able to "arrive" and use words like "retire" and "make it." The truth, however, is that the more a person has, the more he wants. "He who loves money will not be satisfied with money" (Eccles. 5:10). The truth is that the ultimate end in life for fulfillment is to learn to be content and enjoy the process without seeking to arrive (Phil. 4:11). The truth is that we will have trials and tests (1 Thess. 3:3). Ease, comfort, and pleasure are not promised by God.

• The world says that the purpose of our marriage relationship is to meet *our* needs and make *us* happy. That "*me*" is who is important. We feel our spouse is there only to meet our needs and assist us in our never-ending pursuit of ease, comfort, and pleasure. This is evidenced by the rampant divorce rate in this country. Once our needs cease to be met the way we feel they should be, we try another spouse. The truth is that our marriage relationship was ordained by God for man to be fulfilled (Gen. 2:18) and to enable man and woman to become more like Him. It was intended by God to be for life, as He hates divorce (Mal. 2:16).

This incorrect thinking has caused many couples to lose perspective and, as a consequence, put their marriages at risk. Perspective is simply keeping things in proper relation one to another and thinking correctly. In this case, the key is keeping money and our marriages in proper relation to each other and thinking correctly about them. That means thinking about them the way God thinks about them.

Lack of Communication

The second basic problem is lack of communication. Communication occurs when each spouse has listened and fully comprehended what the other has said and understands how the other feels and why. As couples, we seem to have a very difficult time communicating, especially in this area of money. In most cases, we don't understand what our spouse is saying, let alone know why they feel the way they do about money. We don't take time to find out each other's goals and thoughts about money. Bob and Sally were talking, but there was no real communication taking place. They had not taken time to really understand each other in the financial area of their lives.

Julie and I have found that it is difficult to set aside time to communicate about money. It takes a lot of time to discuss budget amounts, develop a workable cash control system, talk about investments and insurance and wills, and so on. Although it does take significant time, we have determined that our marriage is important enough to take the time. Hopefully, as you read this book you will come to the same conclusion.

No Game Plan

The last problem is a result of having no predetermined game plan. No one would start out on a vacation without a map and a destination and a plan as to where they were going. Yet, we start out in our marriages without a plan for dealing with money. It is important for us to have a *pre*-determined plan in order to avoid the tensions that spring up when we get in the middle of the conflict. It is too late if we wait until the conflict arises to try to figure out what to do. As couples, we need to agree *beforehand* what our plan for handling money is and how we will handle conflicts when they arise. This will enable us to turn the conflict into a positive experience rather than a potential marriage breaker.

OBJECTIVES OF THE BOOK

The purpose of this book is to provide insight to help you overcome the potential marriage conflict that can occur as a result of money. To do this, chapters 1–3 will take a look at the *general* purpose of money and of marriage and the reasons for conflict to assist you in beginning to *think correctly* about these areas.

In chapters 4–14 I will look at *specific* areas of money management where conflict can occur, such as work, income, living expenses, budgeting, debt, investments, giving, wills, and insurance. We will look at why *communication* is so difficult and develop a *game plan* to promote it in each of these specific money areas. In these chapters we will also look at specific financial steps that couples can take in each of the areas mentioned to promote harmony in the marriage.

It is my sincere hope that as you read this book you will gain a fresh perspective on money and your marriage. With that perspective, I trust, you will have a better appreciation of why money has so much potential for destroying marital harmony and unity. I hope you will conclude, as Julie and I have, that your marriage is very special and worth great effort on your part to keep it harmonious and unified. We have found the following verses to be a great source of motivation to us to put forth the necessary effort for the desired end of harmony and unity:

> To sum up, let all be *harmonious,* sympathetic, brotherly, kindhearted, and humble in spirit; not returning evil for evil, or insult for insult, but giving a blessing instead; for you were called for the very purpose that you might inherit a blessing.
>
> 1 Pet. 3:8–9

> . . . being of the same mind, maintaining the same love, *united* in spirit, intent on one purpose.
>
> Phil. 2:2

Russ Crosson

Part 1

Getting Proper Perspective

In Part 1 we will look at the truth from God's Word regarding money, marriage, and the sources of conflict. Truth is defined as that which is fact and reality. It is paramount, I believe, that we look at reality from God's viewpoint. For too long we have believed the world's view of reality about our marriages and our money.

It is my intention in this part of the book to develop for you a picture of God's best for your marriage as it relates to your money. I want to give you a baseline to be able to deal with the specific money issues shared in Part 2. The thoughts I will share come not only from a practical and literal look at God's Word but also from observations gleaned in consulting hundreds of couples, the research of others who have written on this topic, and the experience of seeing these truths work in my marriage to Julie.

As you ponder the thoughts shared in these chapters, may you be motivated to study God's Word for yourself and seek Him in order to have the best marriage possible.

Chapter 1

The Purpose of Money

Money. There isn't a day that goes by that most of us do not think about, work for, or use money. Money is one of those "things" in our life that cause mixed emotions. On the one hand, we cannot function without it in our society; on the other hand, if we're not careful, it will consume us. But what is the truth about it? What is it anyway? Why do we have it? How do we get it? Is it really worth all the time and effort we spend trying to make it? How should we spend it? Is it really critical for my self-image and who I am? How should I think about money? Do people (even well-meaning Christians) evaluate me on the basis of how much money I have?

The purpose of someone or something is the end or aim that that person or thing is here to accomplish. What is the end or aim of money? What is its ultimate purpose? I am convinced from my time working with hundreds of couples that if you can come to grips with the real purpose of money and with the truth about it from God's perspective, your marriage will benefit greatly. Let's look, then, at the purpose of money—what it is and what it is not.

What Money Is Not

When I was a young boy, I was involved in a small business. As a part of my 4-H club project I had a flock of sheep. By buying and selling the lambs as well as showing them at the county fair I was able to generate a profit and have some money in my pocket. I remember walking around the fairgrounds with a feeling of confidence and self-worth as a result of the money in my pocket. I felt good about myself. But what if I didn't have the money? How did I feel then?

One time I lost some of my money at the county fair. My feeling of confidence and self-worth was damaged as my money dwindled away. I began to feel worse about myself. But was I really any different then than when I had the money?

As I reflect on that time in my youth I realize that I had already believed the lie of the world that my value and worth as a person had something to do with the amount of money I had. Like so many others, I did not know the truth about money. How does the Bible view money? Let's look at that now.

MONEY IS NOT A COMPONENT OF SELF-WORTH

The first thing that we must understand is that *money is not a necessary component of self-worth.* If I do not accept this truth, then my self-worth will vacillate depending on my income and net worth. I will tend to feel that I am worth something only if I make a certain amount of income. This thinking goes totally contrary to what the Scripture says about who we are in Christ and about the source of our income.

We do not need to look very far in Scripture to see how valuable we are. In Gen. 1:26–27, we see God, the creator of the universe, considering man of such value and worth that He created him in His own image and according to His likeness. In Psalm 8 we read:

> When I consider Thy heavens, the work of Thy fingers,
> The moon and the stars, which Thou hast ordained;
> What is man, that Thou dost take thought of him?
> And the son of man, that Thou dost care for him?
> Yet Thou hast made him a little lower than God,
> And dost crown him with glory and majesty!
> Thou dost make him to rule over the works of Thy hands;
> Thou hast put all things under his feet.

In the New Testament we see that we are His workmanship —hand-fashioned by God Himself (Eph. 2:10). We also see the ultimate expression of our worth to Him in John 3:16, "For God so loved the world, that He gave His only begotten son, that whoever believes in Him should not perish, but have eternal life." That means we are worth an incredible amount to God. Yet we typically evaluate another person's "worth" by how much money that person accumulates or earns. Money is all too often a concrete standard of merit used in rating ourselves with others. "Our very wording betrays us: 'How much is he/she *worth?*' we ask."[1]

Bill Gillham has made a list of scriptural truths about you and me as Christians. We are seated in the heavenlies; joint heirs with Christ; we are near to God; we are a new creature; we are liberated; we are complete in Him; and on and on.[2]

It is clear that my value, my merit, my excellence, has nothing to do with money (my net worth or the income I earn). It has everything to do with who I am in Christ and what God says about me. You and I have a choice. We can believe what God says or what the world says. God says that I am valuable whether I have much or little money.

It is critical for the health and harmony of our marriages that we detach our self-worth from money. This is especially true for husbands. Scripture tells us, as husbands, in Ephesians 5 that we need to love our wives as our own bodies. I need to love myself and have a good self-image if I'm to love my wife the way God intends for me to. If I allow money to be a factor in my self-image, I run the risk of having my love and devotion to my spouse vacillate with my income. I cannot afford to take the risk if I want harmony in my marriage.

MONEY IS NOT A REWARD FOR GODLY LIVING

The second truth about money is that it is not necessarily a reward and guaranteed outcome of godly living. Some would have us believe that if we live obediently to God and do what He says we will be blessed financially (1 Tim. 6:5b). Nothing could be further from the truth.

To prove the fallacy of this thinking one need only look at the contrast of two godly men in Scripture. On the one hand you have Abraham, who was extremely wealthy (Gen. 13:2) from a material standpoint, and on the other hand Paul, who at times had to be supported financially and basically had no worldly goods (1 Cor.

4:11 and 2 Cor. 11:9). They were both godly men who were obedient to God; yet, one had material blessings and the other did not.

Also, as we study Scripture we see that the reward for godly living takes on many forms other than money. Proverbs 10–18 contrasts the godly with the ungodly. We see such terms as "health," "long life," "wisdom," "guidance," "deliverance," "peace," "pleasant ways," and "life" used to denote the rewards for godly living. To think correctly about money we need to realize that although God does work on a rewards system (we *will* receive rewards as a result of our obedience during our sojourn here on earth; 1 Cor. 3:10–15), the rewards are not necessarily financial or material or even in our time frame.

We see the issue of timing and rewards illustrated in Hebrews 11 where we read of men and women who were unarguably the most godly who have ever lived. Yet, "all these died in faith, without receiving the promises, but having seen them and having welcomed them from a distance . . ." (v. 13), and "all these, having gained approval through their faith, did not receive what was promised" (v. 39).

If we continually make the mistake of assuming money will be the guaranteed result of godly living, we run the risk of drawing wrong conclusions about our spiritual condition. We may feel we do not have enough faith because we have not been blessed financially or within the time frame we feel is reasonable. We can become angry at God because we have done our part but do not seem to have financial blessings. Money is an incorrect barometer of our spiritual health. If we focus on financial blessings, we may totally miss all He *is* doing for us. We need to listen closely to God's Word and not to the world.

We need to be faithful to manage wisely the money God entrusts to us—that is stewardship. But our faithfulness is no guarantee that we will have a lot of money. I have observed that many Christian marriages have dramatic ups and downs because of a wrong expectation that more money is the guaranteed result of faithfulness and obedience.

MONEY IS NOT A GUARANTEE OF CONTENTMENT

The third fact about money is that it is not a guarantee of contentment. Contentment is defined as being satisfied with one's circumstances; not complaining; not craving something else; and having a mind at peace. I am convinced that contentment as just defined has nothing to do with money. A person may have a lot of money or a little bit of money and still miss the whole point of contentment. He can complain whether he has a little or a lot. He can be covetous just as easily with a lot of money as with a little.

In Eccles. 5:10 Solomon wrote, "He who loves money will not be satisfied with money, nor he who loves abundance with its income. This too is vanity." Contentment has nothing to do with money. It is a *learned* response. Paul in Phil. 4:11–12 stated this very clearly: "Not that I speak from want; for I have *learned* to be content in whatever circumstances I am. I know how to get along with humble means, and I also know how to live in prosperity; in any and every circumstance I have learned the secret of being filled and going hungry, both of having abundance and suffering need."

The secret that Paul was alluding to was a result of learning to think right about money and God. Contentment is learning to see money as God sees it and nothing more. It is also learning to see God for who He is. He is the bedrock of our contentment. I like what Major Ian Thomas says: "All you need is what you have; what you have is what He is; You cannot have more; and You do not need to have less."[3] Only as I realize that He is sovereign and providentially in control of my earthly lot (my vocation and income) can I truly be content. Only as I learn to trust Him can I have contentment. Only as I realize that the creator God of the universe loves me and has my best interests at heart can I be content.

Contentment really is a spiritual issue and not an amount-of-money issue. God is always there and never changes. He is consistent and stable. I can trust Him. What about money? Prov. 23:4–5 speaks to this when it says, "Do not weary yourself to gain wealth, cease from your consideration of it. When you set your eyes on it, it is gone. For wealth certainly makes itself wings, like an eagle that flies toward the heavens." How content can I be in something that flies away?

No principle in this book can have a greater impact on you and free you up more than this truth: *money is not the key to contentment!* Contentment has everything to do with your relationship with God and nothing to do with your money. Once you are free from the love of money and the pursuit of it, you can have a lot or a little and be content all the same. You have learned the secret to contentment at that point.

Before leaving this concept let me add a definition of "financial contentment." Financial contentment is simply *living within one's income.* How we handle what God has given us will indicate whether we have financial contentment or not. I vividly remember returning from a trip where I had met with a man who earned in excess of $600,000 a year. Instead of being content and at peace he was miserable. He had financial pressures because he was spending $100,000 more than he was making. I remember commenting to Julie that the key to contentment in one's finances was not the amount one made but rather a willingness to live within that amount. We will look at this in more detail in later chapters.

Do you feel that more money would give you contentment? If you are not content in your current financial position, you will not be content if you have more money. I have found that our marriage is most peaceful and contented when first of all we are committed to live within our income and second when we do not focus on and put our confidence in the income we do have.

MONEY IS NOT A MEASURE OF SUCCESS

To illustrate this truth consider a doctor and a teacher. Each can do an excellent job and be successful at his vocational calling, and yet the income generated can vary greatly. The doctor may earn ten times what the teacher earns and spend less time doing it. In this case, money obviously cannot be used to measure success. It is even more obvious when you consider that a doctor could do a mediocre job and still earn more than a teacher who does an excellent job. Since God has equipped each of us uniquely to do a particular one or two of the myriad of jobs that need doing upon the earth, and since each job produces a different amount of income, it is God who ultimately determines our income. My income is not so much a function of my success or failure as it is of my vocation.

I do not wish to discount that an excellent job on your part may cause you to earn more than someone else who does not work as excellently or diligently in the same vocation. My caution to you is to be careful not to think that it is *your ability* that is making you the income, that it is *your* success. Deut. 8:16–18 is clear on this point, ". . . but you shall remember the Lord your God, for it is He who is giving you power to make wealth."

If you are having difficulty accepting this principle that God is providentially in control of your income, consider the following verses: "The rich and the poor have a common bond, the Lord is the maker of them all" (Prov. 22:2); "What do you have that you weren't given?" (1 Cor. 4:7); "Every good thing bestowed and every perfect gift is from above" (James 1:17). Life is full of financial inequities, as Solomon reminds us in Eccles. 9:11–12, "I again saw under the sun that the race is not to the swift, and the battle is not to the warriors, and neither is bread to the wise, nor wealth to the discerning, nor favor to men of ability; for time and chance overtake them all."

Although the Bible tells us that the amount of money we have is from God's hand, the problem we have is that the world tells us the opposite. It tells us that a sign of success is how much money we make. However, if we look up the definition of *success* we see that we are successful if we are making progress in accomplishing our goals. Success occurs when we satisfactorily complete whatever we attempt. Money may result at the termination of our endeavor, but it should never be the standard in determining whether success has occurred.

I always had a problem getting Josh. 1:8 into perspective until I applied the correct definition of success. Josh. 1:8 says:

> This book of the law shall not depart from your mouth, but you shall meditate on it day and night, so that you may be careful to do according to all that is written in it; for then you will make your way prosperous, and then you will have success.

I am successful as I am in the process of being obedient and carefully doing all that God's Word says to do. For example, I am successful as I train and love my children (Eph. 6:4; Deut. 6:6–8), love my wife (Eph. 5:28), and work hard (Col. 3:23). This verse does not guarantee or promise financial blessings if I do what God's Word says. Rather, it frees me up to realize that I can be successful whether or not I have money. *Money is not the barometer!* A successful person may or may not have money. A person with money may or may not be a "success."

In the early 1980s a friend of mine began developing and growing a very profitable business. It soon went public, and my friend was acclaimed a success by his industry and the media.

Everybody wanted a piece of the action. His net worth was in the millions, and in the world's eyes he was a "success."

As the decade wore on, however, the business began to decline. Although my friend did all he could to keep the business afloat, it eventually went bankrupt. My friend's net worth plummeted. Is my friend still a "success"? Many would probably say no because the world's measuring stick is money and he no longer has much of it. However, I know better. During this decade my friend has made more progress in the things that are important to God than most people would ever guess. His relationship with his family and the Lord has improved dramatically. He has had significant impact on others' lives. He is still a "success." He is successful because he has made progress in accomplishing many of the goals that God says are important.

Much of the stress in our marriages is a result of using money as the measuring stick to determine whether or not we're successful. We need to remove it from the prominent place it has in our thinking because what the world is telling us is just not true.

What Money Is

According to the dictionary, money is a medium of exchange; any equivalent for commodities; something for which individuals readily exchange their goods or services; a circulating medium. It must satisfy three basic functions: It must be storable, divisible, and valuable. Money today still has the first two components, but in a practical sense it no longer has any real value.

Up until 1933 the United States held to a gold standard that required all paper money issued to be backed by a fixed quantity of gold. At any time all paper money could be exchanged for gold. At that time the real money was gold, which does have value, but paper was used as a substitute since it was more easily divisible and easier to store.

The reason the government departed from the gold standard was to allow banks and the government to inflate or deflate the money supply to smooth out the normal business cycles of inflations and retractions (booms and busts). They thought that if they could smooth out the cycles by issuing more or less credit, depending on what the economy needed at that time, there would be more consistent prosperity for all. Instead, all they have succeeded in doing is running up a multibillion dollar deficit that causes our money to be (for all practical purposes) worth very little.

Let me hasten to say that what you can buy with money has utilitarian value. The clothes you wear, your home, your investments in real property, and even your investments in credit instruments such as bonds and CDs—all these have value because they are useful to you. They help you to exist and to provide for your family and meet your needs.

The problem is that we have elevated money to something other than it is. We seem to think it is not just a medium of exchange, but power, prestige, and worth. We view it as an end rather than a means to an end. We each have a challenge to lower the rating on money.

To show just how overrated money is and how our perspective of it has totally gotten out of whack, let's look for a minute at 2 Cor. 4:18: ". . . while we look not at the things which are seen, but at the things which are not seen; for the things which are seen are temporal, but the things which are not seen are eternal." Money is a medium of exchange that we can see and touch. It is purely temporal. It does not fit at all in the list of things God says we should focus on.

What happens to all the things we can buy with money? 1 Tim. 6:7 says, "For we have brought nothing into the world, so we cannot take anything out of it either." In Eccles. 5:15 we see that nothing from the fruit of our labor (purchased with our money) can be taken with us. Ps. 49:17 continues this theme when it says, "For when he dies he will carry nothing away."

Wow! God's Word indicates that money is not eternal and that we can take none of it with us. It is clear that money is simply a medium of exchange, useful during this lifetime but of no eternal significance. Recently I saw a church billboard that said, "Your children are your only earthly possession that can go to heaven." How insightful! The same cannot be said of money. It is time we cleared up our focus on money and realized that in far too many cases we have sacrificed what really matters for that which we cannot take with us.

If in a practical sense money is a mode of exchange, what is it from God's perspective? How does He view it?

In his book *Master Your Money,* Ron Blue uses three words —tool, test, and testimony—to summarize how money is viewed by God. He says that money is a tool God uses to mold us to His image. It is a test of our faithfulness (Luke 16:11–13). And it is a vehicle that can enhance our individual testimonies; it provides opportunities for us to be salt and light to this world (Matt. 5:13–16).

A TOOL

There are countless forces God uses to mold us to His image, and money is one of them. Just as the craftsman uses the tool of his respective trade to form a final product that is pleasing to him, so does God use money (its abundance and its scarcity) to mold us and make us pleasing to Him. He did that with Paul. In Phil. 4:11–13 we learn that Paul was taught contentment by the extremes of having much (abundance) and little (scarcity).

You may be thinking that God can only use the lack of money to mold and train and form a person into His image. I can assure you that this is not the case. In my consulting I have observed that the person with wealth has to learn how to deal with greed, how to share, how to show wise stewardship, how to love and maintain relationships, how to use time wisely, how to deal with the fear of losing money, and so on. Money's use as a tool is effective at all levels of income.

A TEST

Money is also used as a test in our lives. It is a test of our faithfulness to God. In Luke 16:11–13 we read: "If therefore you have not been faithful in the use of unrighteous mammon, who will entrust the true riches to you? And if you have not been faithful in the use of that which is another's, who will give you that which is your own? No servant can serve two masters; for either he will hate the one, and love the other, or else he will hold to one, and despise the other. You cannot serve God and mammon." You notice that the verse does not say that we "should not" serve both or that we should "try not to" serve both. It says that we *cannot* serve both! Either I will serve God and use money to serve people, or I will use people to serve myself and make money for myself. Yancy adds,

"Money is far more than a question of statistics and numbers, it is a god that bids us worship it. Will I serve God or Mammon? God will never make that decision for me; it is mine alone."[4]

One way I can ensure that I am not serving money is to serve God. If I am serving God and being obedient to what He says, I cannot serve money. I would encourage you to ask this question as it relates to your marriage: Are you serving God or money? A practical way to evaluate this is to take a look at your weekly schedule.

A TESTIMONY

Finally, money is a testimony. Study Matt. 5:13–16:

> You are the salt of the earth; but if the salt has become tasteless, how will it be made salty again? It is good for nothing anymore, except to be thrown out and trampled under foot by men. You are the light of the world. A city set on a hill cannot be hidden. Nor do men light a lamp, and put it under the peck-measure, but on the lampstand; and it gives light to all who are in the house. Let your light shine before men in such a way that they may see your good works, and glorify your Father who is in heaven.

What kind of a testimony do I have with my money? Does it bring glory and honor to God? As Christians, we are not called to be better than the world when it comes to our money but rather we are called to be different from the world. Each of us needs to look at our finances and ask, what kind of a statement am I making to the world with the way I handle my money? Could anyone tell by looking at my checkbook that I was a Christian?

When we talk about being different, what does that mean? I have observed that it means such things as spending less than you make (most Americans don't do this) and limiting or avoiding altogether the use of debt. This debt issue is a real stickler because that will mean that more than likely you will live in a smaller house in a different neighborhood and drive older cars than many of your friends who have bought into the world's philosophy of using credit to have what they want *now* rather than waiting.

We as Christians must look different from the world. God uses money as a means to allow us to do that.

MONEY IS DANGEROUS

Millions of couples have money at the focal point of their marriage nearly every day. If they do not know the truth about money, the focus can be so intense that it ruins their marriages. This is why money is so dangerous. Husbands and wives let money, not marriage, dominate their relationship. We have seen that money can give us a temporary sense of self-worth and contentment; that it can be a subtle vehicle that we use to measure our success; and that it can be ignored as a medium that God uses in our life as a test, tool, and testimony. Hopefully, these thoughts about money will begin to change your thinking about it and cause you to begin to focus more on your marriage and less on your money. The next chapter on marriage will challenge you to not allow money to disrupt harmony in your marriage.

GAME PLAN

To help you put money into perspective, draw up a chart like the one below and list all the things that come to mind under each category. One column is for listing temporal things, and the other is for listing eternal things. Prayerfully make your list and then ask yourself, just how important is money? Really?

If you are like me, you will find that all the areas in your life that are really important and mean the most to you have little or nothing to do with money. You will also find that nothing related to money (except the good that comes when you give it to meet needs) is on the eternal list.

CHART 1.1

2 Cor. 4:18

"While we look not at the things which are seen, but at the things which are not seen; for the things which are seen are temporal, but the things which are not seen are eternal."

TEMPORAL	ETERNAL

Chapter 2

The Purpose of Marriage

What is the purpose of marriage? Why do we marry? It is important that we understand the answer to those two questions. Mike Mason states it well when he says, "Marriage has been devised by the Lord as a particularly gentle (but no less disciplined and effective) means for helping men and women to humble themselves and to surrender their errant wills. Even the closest of couples will inevitably find themselves engaged in a struggle of wills, for marriage is a wild, audacious attempt at an almost impossible degree of cooperation between two powerful centers of self-assertion. Marriage cannot help being a furnace of conflict, a crucible in which two wills must be melted down and purified and made to conform."[1] Nowhere is this struggle seen more vividly than in conflicts relating to money. This is why it is so critical not only to think correctly about money but also to think correctly about our marriages.

Marriage has many aims; however, four relate to this discussion. First, marriage allows us to model Christ and the church. Second, marriage is a union that allows us to model the correct male/female roles. Third, procreation is an important reason for marriage. Fourth, marriage allows us an opportunity to raise a godly posterity—children that will have an impact on the generations to come.

TO MODEL CHRIST AND THE CHURCH

In the following passage from Ephesians we see the clear calling that marriage is a model of Christ and the Church:

> For the husband is the *head* of the wife, as Christ also is the head of the church, He Himself being the Savior of the body. But as the church is *subject* to Christ, so also the wives ought to be to their husbands in everything. Husbands, *love* your wives, just as Christ also loved the church and gave Himself up for her; that He might sanctify her, having cleansed her by the washing of water with the word, that He might present to Himself the church in all her glory, having no spot or wrinkle or any such thing; but that she should be holy and blameless. So husbands ought also to love their own wives as their own bodies. He who loves his own wife loves himself; for no one ever hated his own flesh, but nourishes and cherishes it, just as Christ also does the Church, because we are members of His body. For this cause a man shall leave his father and mother, and shall cleave to his wife; and the two shall become one flesh. This mystery is great; but I am speaking with reference to Christ and the church. Nevertheless let each individual among you also *love* his own wife even as himself; and let the wife see to it that she *respect* her husband.
>
> Eph. 5:23–33 (italics added)

As someone has said, "the only Bible some people will ever read is our lives." If they are reading our marriages, what do they see? Do they want to have a relationship with God because our marriage is so attractive and works so well they can't resist it? Or do they want to have nothing to do with it? The calling of our marriages to represent Christ and the church is indeed a high one and one that we need to live up to. Let's look at this passage and reflect on the primary responsibilities of men (to love) and women (to submit and respect) if their marriage is to model Christ and the church. This does not mean that the wife is not to love or the husband not to submit or respect. Those responsibilities are not mutually exclusive. For this discussion, however, we will focus on these responsibilities as being unique to each spouse as they have been underscored in the passage above.

HUSBAND, LOVE YOUR WIFE

Men, we are instructed to *love* our wives as Christ loved the church and also as we love our own bodies. The quality of our marriages depends on our ability to love our wives to the fullest definition of the word. Using 1 Cor. 13:4–8 as our guide, let's look at how the qualities of this love will manifest themselves to our wives in the realm of finances.

1. Patient—the husband tolerates problems and is patient with his wife regardless of her behavior. He endures offense from his wife even though he feels like retaliating. He responds with patience even when she doesn't handle circumstances exactly the way he wants her to. (He takes time to explain an investment to her and doesn't explode with anger or become exasperated when she doesn't understand or agree.)
2. Kind—he is good-natured, thoughtful, gentle, and sensitive to her. (He gets her input on budget amounts.)
3. Never jealous or envious—he trusts her completely and thinks only the best of her. He always assumes her motives and intentions are right. He lets his wife know that he trusts her to spend "their" money by giving her maximum freedom in the financial budget.
4. Never rude—he is not unmannerly and is careful to avoid embarrassing her.
5. Unselfish—he does not seek his own convenience and rights but rather looks out for her best interests and is concerned about her. (He meets her needs financially.)
6. Not irritable or touchy—he keeps his temper and exhibits self-control. (When she spends money in a way he doesn't understand, he talks it over with her in a controlled, calm manner.)
7. Never holding a grudge—he does not keep score and return evil for evil (1 Pet. 3:9). He forgives and forgets. (If she blows the budget one month, he does not withhold money from her the next.)

8. Rejoicing in right—he exults in his wife's successes and is never glad about her misfortunes. He encourages her when she is down. (He encourages her and compliments her for the fine job she does with the budget day in and day out.)
9. Loyal and dependable—he is faithful to her, and she knows she can always count on him. He is never on and off. He is stable and consistent. (He is always sensitive to communicate with her at all times, not just when he wants something. He does not vary the monthly budget amounts that she is responsible for without seeking her input and understanding.)

If we love our wives with the *agape* love that God requires in all areas, including the financial area, it will promote stable, positive self-esteem and confidence in them and go a long way toward promoting harmony in our marriage. Men, the key to harmony is love. You may be thinking that you cannot show love the way I've illustrated in the financial area. You may feel right now it is too much to communicate with your wife about the budget or investments or to give her maximum freedom with your finances. This book is for you. Keep reading.

WIFE, SUBMIT TO AND RESPECT YOUR HUSBAND

Women, your part in ensuring that your marriage models Christ and the church is to *respect* your husband and *submit* to him. These words are not especially popular in today's society. "Me submit and respect him?" is too often the question in a woman's mind. The issue, however, is not what the world says but rather what God says.

Submission is simply understanding God's order and fitting into that order (1 Cor. 11:3; illustrated in chart 2.1). It is yielding to God's design for marriage. It is interesting that men have responsibility both ways. Not only are they to love their wives, but they are told to likewise submit and understand their wives (1 Pet. 3:7). A spirit of graceful submission is required on the part of each spouse, and there can be no peace and harmony without it. The response of one spouse is not dependent on the other. No matter how our spouse responds, we are responsible to respond the way

God instructs us. "So then each one of us shall give account of *himself* to God" (Rom. 14:12).

Mutual submission can be illustrated in the living expense area of one's finances. The wife should submit and live within the income allocated to her for living expenses by her husband. The husband should listen to and give deference to his wife's desires as to the appropriate amounts in the various living expense categories. We will see how this is worked out in more detail in chapter 9.

Suffice it to say that the critical ingredient on the part of the wife is her attitude. Submission is an attitude and view of life that is consistent with God's view:

> In the same way, you wives, be submissive to your own husbands so that even if any of them are disobedient to the word, they may be won without a word by the behavior of their wives, as they observe your chaste and respectful behaviors.
>
> 1 Pet. 3:1–2 (NASB)

> to be self-controlled, chaste, homemakers, good-natured (kind-hearted), adapting and subordinating themselves to their husbands, that the word of God may not be exposed to reproach—blasphemed or discredited.
>
> Titus 2:5 (Amplified)

Respect is the other responsibility of the wife in the marriage relationship. What that word entails is best summed up in 1 Pet. 3:2 (Amplified), "When they observe the pure and modest way in which you conduct yourselves, together with your reverence [for your husband. That is, you are to feel for him all that reverence includes]—to respect, defer to, revere him; [revere means] to honor, esteem (appreciate, prize), and [in the human sense] adore him; [and adore means] to admire, praise, be devoted to, deeply love and enjoy [your husband]."

Financially, this means that a wife defers to her husband, honors him, and respects his wishes and decisions concerning how she spends money. She makes sure that she always asks or thinks, "What does *he* want me to do with *our* money?"

If our marriages are to model Christ and the church, then men must love their wives with *agape* love and wives must respect and submit to their husbands. If husbands and wives will focus on these responses and spend time cultivating them, their marriages can be enhanced tremendously. It will take time, but what a reward for the time spent! "There is no work more important than the work of relationship and no relationship more important than one's marriage."[2]

TO MODEL CORRECT ROLES

Not only do we have the responsibility in our marriages to model Christ and the church but also to model the roles (or job descriptions) God has laid down for us in Scripture. As hard as some have tried to make male and female alike, they just cannot do it. Even the renowned anthropologist and notorious feminist Margaret Mead concluded from all of her studies that gender role differentiation is a common condition in all cultures.[3] Let's look at how men and women are different and how our roles are different to better understand how our marriages were intended by God to look and function. This understanding will help us as we look in later chapters at the potential financial conflicts that can occur in the marriage relationship.

MAN'S JOB DESCRIPTION

As we saw in the Ephesians passage, a man is to love his wife but also to be her *head.* The concept of *headship* is also found in 1 Cor. 11:3 (chart 2.1): "But I want you to understand that Christ is the head of every man, and the man is the head of a woman, and God is

CHART 2.1

1 Cor. 11:3
"But I want you to understand that Christ is the head of every man, and the man is the head of a woman, and God is the head of Christ."

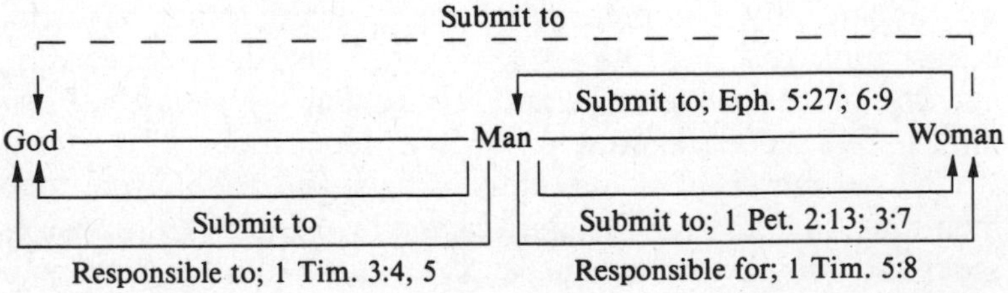

the head of Christ." The Greek word translated "head" is *kephale.* It means "prime source" or "chief cause." Headship means the man is the prime authority in his family. He is God's representative in the home. He supervises the family and makes sure it is progressing in the right direction. He provides leadership for the family.

James Dobson points out that, "God holds men accountable for leadership in their families. The primary responsibility for provision of authority in the home has been assigned to men."[4]

We see this position of responsibility and headship illustrated clearly in the story of Eli in 1 Samuel 2. Obviously, Eli was married, as he had two sons. His sons were worthless men and did not know the Lord (v. 12). I find it interesting that they were referred to as "his" sons. This is because he was responsible for his family. His wife undoubtedly took part in rearing the boys; but when the time came for God to talk to the family about the boys, it was Eli he talked to and the boys were referred to as "his sons." God talks to Eli in verses 27 to 36. He does not talk to Eli's wife or even to both of them. He declares his judgment to Eli: "And this will be the sign to you which shall come concerning *your two sons, Hophni and Phinehas:* on the same day both of them shall die" (1 Sam. 2:34, emphasis added).

In the creation account in Gen. 2:7 we find that "the Lord God formed man of dust from the ground, and breathed into his nostrils the breath of life; and man became a living being." "Then the Lord God took the man and put him into the garden of Eden to cultivate it and keep it" (v. 15). It was in the exercise of cultivating that man exhibited one of his responsibilities as the leader of the family—*provision.* He provided through cultivation and working the ground. God said in Gen. 3:17–19 that man would provide all the days of his life and that it would be hard work. Even so, he would still desire to do it. God had put that desire within him; so much so that even when God cursed the ground, man still cultivated it and worked to provide. In today's society we see this provision drive manifested in man's desire and drive to work (1 Thess. 4:11; 2 Thess. 3:12). If a man does not work, he is not to eat (2 Thess. 3:10).

The word "keep" in Gen. 2:15 refers to *protection.* Man is to protect his wife and family. He is to cover, shield, guard, and defend them. It is obvious how he does this in our society. He buys a house, a dependable car, and insurance. He makes sure his family is clothed and well fed. He puts locks on the doors of his house and, in some cases, buys a dog as protection for his family.

Another way man exercises his role of protector and provider is through his drive to subdue and control his environment. In Gen. 1:28 man was given the mandate by God to subdue the earth and rule over it. Psalm 8 declares that all created things were put in subjection to man. The drive to subdue complemented his drive to provide and protect. The evidence of this drive is found in man's efforts to find cures for disease; the development of insecticides to control pests; the development of advanced machinery to make work easier; putting men on the moon; and so on. Man spends his life trying to subdue his environment, in part to make it easier to provide. When it comes to money, this drive manifests itself in aggressive investments, long work hours, and more.

It is very clear that man has the assigned job description by God to not only love his wife but to also *lead her by protecting her and providing for her.*

WOMAN'S JOB DESCRIPTION

Woman, on the other hand, was made, according to God, because it was not good for man to be alone and because he needed a "helpmeet" (Gen. 2:18). Her job description was defined as that of companion (Gen. 2:18), helper (Gen. 2:18), nurturer (Gen. 3:20).

To fulfill her job description the wife's *primary* responsibility is *homemaking* and *mothering.* We see this clearly in the following passages:

1 Tim. 2:15	But women shall be preserved through the bearing of children if they continue in faith and love and sanctity with self-restraint.
1 Tim. 5:14	Therefore, I want younger widows to get married, bear children, keep house, and give the enemy no occasion for reproach.
Titus 2:4–5	. . . that they may encourage the young women to love their husbands, to love their children, to be sensible, pure, workers at home, kind, being subject to their own husbands, that the word of God may not be dishonored.

As a result of her job description she should concentrate first on tasks that fall into the domestic (homemaking and mothering) area before getting involved in other areas such as volunteer work, and marketplace functions (vocational employment outside of the home). We will discuss these situations in chapter 6 when we look in detail at Proverbs 31.

In summary, the universal challenge facing us as men and women today is to flesh out and model the correct roles, as laid out by God, in a very difficult society that tells us that everything is equal and 50/50. Our society tells us that there are no differences in the job descriptions for men and women in marriage. God, however, though creating us equal as male and female, designed us uniquely to fulfill respective and unique roles. (We will look at these differences in detail in chapter 3.) Today there is no area that can put more pressure on the different roles than the area of money. If we as husband and wife do not understand money and how our different perspectives affect our perception of it, much conflict can occur.

You can function and survive your marriage even if you don't order it after God's design. However, if you want ultimate harmony and effectiveness in your marriage, it is important to put it together according to God's job description for you as husband and wife.

Julie and I have found that it is important to the harmony in our marriage to encourage each other in our unique roles. Without encouragement, our role implementation becomes more difficult. May God encourage you as you seek Him and manifest the correct roles in your marriage.

To Provide for Procreation

In Gen. 1:28 we find the mandate to procreate, "And God said to them, 'Be fruitful and multiply, and fill the earth.'" Obviously, couples today take this purpose seriously—as evidenced by the children that continue to be born. Most couples, however, do not follow through on the responsibility that goes with the procreating. That is the training of the offspring. We are commanded in Scripture to train up our children in the way they should go, so when they are old they will not depart from it (Prov. 22:6). We are also told that we are to teach God's principles diligently to our children as we walk along, lie down, get up, and sit in our homes (Deut. 6:6–7). Even with these mandates we seem to be content to just let our children "grow up" like unweeded gardens. We would rather pursue money and luxury than family strength.

Children are the only investment we can make that lasts forever. They are our posterity. Yet today, even Christians are sacrificing their children on the altar of materialism. It is my strong conviction that we are to leave a godly posterity. Our children and those others we have influenced for eternity will carry on a Christian legacy.

Why do so many not develop a godly posterity? I feel it is because they shift their emphasis to prosperity.

TO DEVELOP A GODLY POSTERITY

Except for two letters, the words *prosperity* and *posterity* are the same. Though they sound alike, they are dramatically different in what they mean. Though most of us have probably not stopped to think about the meaning of these words, each of us is in pursuit of one or the other. The way we live our lives clearly demonstrates which of these two is our personal goal.

Each of us places hope in something—something of value, profit, gain, or reward to us. For example, when I was in high school, the hope of having my name and picture in the paper (I perceived that to be of value, profit, and reward to me) was a tremendous source of motivation as I worked out and trained for athletic teams. Our hope keeps our motivation alive. It incites us to action. You will never be motivated and thus disciplined to do anything unless you have hope. The key then is *what you place your hope in.*

I am sad to say that it has been my observation that most are motivated by prosperity rather than posterity. It is interesting to note, however, that those motivated by prosperity are usually driven by a mistaken concept of prosperity! Most Americans (Christians included) have defined prosperity as health, wealth, and materialism. This is not the true meaning, as we will see. Even so, with that definition in focus they subtly order their lives in the pursuit of things that God's Word tells us will not last. They will find that they climbed the ladder, but it was against the wrong wall.

This is vividly expressed in Psalm 49, which points out the plight of so many of us who have placed our hope in worldly prosperity rather than in what God says is important. Verses 11, 12, 17–20 tell us that man's "inner thought is, that their houses are forever, and their dwelling places to all generations; they have called their lands [and buildings!] after their own names. But man in his pomp will not endure. . . . When he dies he will carry nothing away; his glory will not descend after him. Though while he lives he congratulates himself—and though men praise you when you do well for yourself—he shall go to the generation of his fathers. . . . Man in his pomp, yet without understanding, is like the beasts that perish."

Eccles. 5:15 also expresses the futility of pursuing prosperity as defined by money, "As he had come naked from his mother's womb, so will he return as he came. He will take nothing from the fruit of his labor that he can carry in his hand."

It is obvious, then, that prosperity—defined by material goods, houses, buildings, etc.—will not last. Stop and think about that for a minute. The high-rise office building you are in, the mighty fortress you have built as a house, the estate you have amassed—none of it will last.

What is the correct definition of prosperity? *Prosperity is simply the state of succeeding in any good, making progress in anything desirable, not just money.* In evaluating this definition, we find that wealth, materialism, houses, boats, and other material belongings are really not the essence of the definition. Prosperity occurs when someone is making progress in the pursuit and accomplishment of a desirable end. For example, if your goal is to spend two hours a day with your children, you are *prosperous* as you accomplish that goal. You are prosperous as you do an excellent job for your employer and he says, "Well done!" Neither of these situations is directly related to money, the thing we normally think of when we use the word *prosperity.* Yet, you are prosperous as you accomplish them, since they are desirable goals and goals that God says are important (Deut. 6:6–8; Col. 3:23). As we saw in chapter 1 when we looked at

Josh. 1:8, believers can only be prosperous and successful if they are doing what God says is important. What does God say should be desirable and important goals? This brings us to the second word—*posterity.*

Your posterity is your descendants that succeed you in future generations. Though your posterity is primarily your children and will be referred to as such throughout this book I think it also can include other people whom you influence for eternity. (This is how the childless couple can have a posterity.) In Psalm 37 we see a dramatic contrast to the futility of prosperity we just looked at: "Mark the blameless man, and behold the upright; for the man of peace will have a posterity. But transgressors will be altogether destroyed; the posterity of the wicked will be cut off" (vv. 37–38). ". . . . His godly ones . . . are preserved forever; but the descendants of the wicked will be cut off. The righteous will inherit the land, and dwell in it forever" (vv. 28–29).

Isn't that something! We define prosperity incorrectly and then pursue it with all we've got, all the while worrying little about the only thing that will last—our posterity. It is quite obvious if we contrast Psalm 49 with Psalm 37 that true *prosperity* can only be developed through a righteous *posterity.* If our focus is not on developing a godly posterity, then we will leave nothing of significance to mark the generations that come after us. If you give your life in the pursuit of money and the things money can buy and neglect your posterity, you will be unable to leave a mark on the next generation. What a travesty of God's plan! Don't pursue prosperity (wrongly defined as materialism) to the exclusion of posterity.

We can leave land, expensive china, coins, gold, houses, stocks and bonds, CDs, airplanes, and so on (an estate), and we can leave a heritage—a lineage—a posterity. The paradox is that if we choose to order our lives to leave a posterity, we can also leave an estate. However, if we seek after the estate at the exclusion of the posterity, we will find at the end of our lives that the estate doesn't matter. If we do not train our children and spend time with them when it matters (when they are young), we will find, as Solomon did, that his accumulation was in vain (Ecclesiastes 2).The man who seeks only after money and accumulation and has money on the throne of his life rather than God will find that his wealth will be left to someone else. His efforts will all have been for nothing (Prov. 13:22).

I have prepared estate plans for far too many couples that for various reasons could not or desired not to leave their hard-earned estates to their children. The reasons ranged from the fact that their children were estranged, to their not being trustworthy or competent. These couples had amassed their estates to the exclusion of their children. I always wonder in those situations whether, if they had it to do over again, they would have balanced their pursuit of money and the accumulation of an estate with time with their children.

What is your choice going to be? Are you going to spend your time pursuing money (which will not last) or will you pursue the development and enhancement of a godly posterity—and thus be truly prosperous? We are each free to choose the avenue we will pursue, but we are not free from the consequences of our choice. Your posterity will last; your prosperity won't!

One Sunday, sitting in church, I ran across an interesting article in a bulletin insert that underscored the importance of focusing on a posterity. This article was so vivid and so personal to me that it sent chills down my spine.

> A Sunday school teacher, Ezra Kimball, in 1858 led a Boston shoe clerk to Christ. The clerk, D. L. Moody, became an evangelist and in 1879 awakened evangelistic zeal in the heart of Frederick B. Meyer, pastor of a small church.
>
> F. B. Meyer, preaching on an American college campus, brought to Christ a student named J. Wilbur Chapman. Chapman engaged in YMCA work, employed a former baseball player, Billy Sunday, to do evangelistic work.
>
> Sunday held a revival in Charlotte, North Carolina. A group of local men were so enthusiastic afterward that they planned another campaign, bringing Mordecai Hamm to town to preach.
>
> In the revival, a young man named Billy Graham heard the Gospel and yielded his life to Christ.[5]

In 1968, at a Billy Graham movie, I became a Christian. A mark left in 1858 is still here in 1989. I am that mark. By contrast, how many buildings built in 1858 are still standing? What an awesome thought! (Julie's spiritual heritage is also through Billy Sunday; that is how her grandfather came to Christ.)

As we conclude this chapter, it is my hope that you have a better understanding of the purpose for your marriage; that you realize how critical it is to live in harmony with your spouse; that you are committed to making your marriage work regardless of the circumstances; that, most of all, you will not allow the pursuit of money, which is a temporal tool and really "no big deal" in the scope of eternity, to destroy your marriage, which has so much ability to store up eternal treasure through your posterity. *The best thing you can do for your posterity (children) is develop a strong, loving, and harmonious marriage.*

GAME PLAN

As Julie and I have come to understand the purpose of money and some of the awesome purposes of our being married we have concluded that to leave a godly posterity is an extremely worthwhile goal to pursue during our lifetimes. To that end we have developed a "purpose statement" for our marriage. This is a statement that we use as a baseline for making decisions that come our way.

A purpose statement is simply a short sentence that summarizes in a nutshell the end or aim of your life—what you intend to do. It is the objective to be reached and accomplished.

We have found that having a written purpose statement makes it easier to stay on track. It gives us a grid to pass critical decisions through. Do we move to a new house? Where do we attend church? Do I take that job promotion? The answers to such questions are easier to arrive at if possible solutions are passed through our purpose statement grid. If they better allow us to fulfill our purpose, we may do them. If not, we may look to other alternatives.

Before you and your spouse leave this chapter, prayerfully write your purpose statement together. This will help you as you face many decisions related to money. To help you get started, here is the purpose statement Julie and I have developed:

> *It is our purpose to create an environment and multiply opportunities that will promote and enhance the development of a godly posterity.*

Let me give you an illustration of how we might use this statement. We had to make a decision about changing houses. As we weighed the pros and cons and came back to our purpose statement, we concluded that if I could reduce my commute time to work, it would give me more time to enhance my posterity—spend time with the boys and have time for Bible studies with others. Since my posterity is important then I am willing to make sacrifices on the house. Move to a smaller house to get closer to the office; sell one car to help with the down payment, etc. The purpose statement helps me focus on why I am doing what I am doing.

Your purpose statement:

Chapter 3

Reasons for Marriage Conflict

If you are like most couples, money at one time or the other has been the source of some conflict in your marriage. Conflict is defined as strife, or contention; to be in opposition one with the other; to be incompatible. As we saw in the last chapter, the purpose of our marriage is to live in harmony and unity and to develop a godly posterity.

It is important that we understand the source of marital conflict. The *real* source of this conflict is our desire to each have his or her own way (Isa. 53:6). Money may appear to be the source of this conflict, but all too often it is simply a vehicle through which the real problem manifests itself. The ultimate solution, of course, is for each spouse to walk in the Spirit and maintain a close relationship with the Lord.

In the marriage relation (1 Pet. 3:7) it is important to understand that men and women perceive money differently. These differences underlie why money is generally the avenue through which conflict arises. I like what James Dobson says in his book *Love for a Lifetime.*

> Men and women tend to have different value systems which precipitate arguments about money. My father, for example, was a hunter who thought nothing of using three boxes of shotgun

> shells in an afternoon of recreational shooting. Yet, if my mother spent an equal amount of money on a 'useless' potato peeler, he considered it wasteful. Never mind that she enjoyed shopping as much as he did hunting. They simply saw things differently.[1]

It is the purpose of this chapter to help you understand three areas where these differences are manifested. They are background experiences, different temperaments, and male/female differences. A clear understanding of these areas as they relate to money will go a long way toward promoting harmony and unity in your marriage.

BACKGROUND EXPERIENCES AND UPBRINGING

As I work with couples I find that in many cases the conflict over money is because of different backgrounds. Different experiences and family upbringing and training have caused each spouse to have different *expectations* of how to handle money.

This was vividly illustrated by a couple I counseled recently. As I talked with them it became obvious that they disagreed on the use of debt. In going over their net worth statement I casually asked them the balance of their credit card debt. When the husband responded that it was "around $3,000," his wife went into a rage. As I sat there and listened she went on and on about how she didn't want to use the credit cards, but he did, and that she couldn't understand why he used them so frequently, and that it made her nervous and upset to use them, and so on. She also explained that she was nervous about all the debt they had on their balance sheet. She just didn't understand it.

Needless to say, he retaliated with some comments of his own. He didn't see any problem in using the credit cards, since he kept the balance current most months. He also commented that debt was simply a tool to use to grow his net worth. He really didn't see any problem in debt. After all, his father had amassed a small fortune using debt.

The comment about his father gave me some insight into the problem. To see if I was correct, I asked his wife how her family used debt. She responded that they had never used debt and had always paid cash for everything. As a matter of fact, to her recollection her parents did not even have a credit card.

My assumption was correct. Although debt appeared to be the reason for the conflict, in reality their different backgrounds were the contributing factors. With our backgrounds we bring a whole set of expectations about a wide variety of things: how we handle money; how we discipline our children; our perception of work, leisure time, and so on. With expectations comes the potential for conflict.

The key to overcoming the conflict is to make sure good communication takes place between husband and wife. They need to find out what expectations are there and to then decide what decisions need to be made to promote maximum harmony. In this case, once the husband began to understand why his wife always responded to debt the way she did, he was much more sensitive to communicating with her about why he had the debt, what its purpose was, and how it would be repaid.

As you reflect on your situation you will undoubtedly find that you and your spouse have different expectations about money in many areas, such as giving, living expense level, and type of investments. You will also find differences in areas such as where you like to go to eat and where you like to shop. Your spouse may feel uncomfortable in nice restaurants and prefer the more middle-of-the-road eating places. Your spouse may like to spend more money on vacation than you do. Vacation may have been emphasized by your spouse's family, while they were really not that big a deal to your family. You may see money used more wisely in a larger house, while your spouse may rather have a smaller house and newer cars. It can go on and on. Be aware that many of these expectations are the result of the way you view money, which you learned from your parents. You will not change the background of your spouse, but you can be sensitive to it so as not to allow it to contribute to disunity in your marriage. The more sensitive you become to your spouse's ideas and the source of them, the greater the mutual understanding and harmony in your marriage. It is essential to communicate your expectations about money and make sure that any decision you make contributes to harmony.

Before leaving this concept, I must share how Julie and I became aware of the different expectations created by our backgrounds and how we learned to overcome the conflict they caused. Early in our marriage we got a chance to go to Hawaii on vacation.

While there it seemed that we were always at each other's throat. Can you believe that? In a place like Hawaii we were always having conflict. As a matter of fact, as I reflected on it, we always seemed to have conflict on our vacations. Finally, as we began to talk about it we realized that our views of vacation were totally different. To me vacation was getting away and doing nothing. My idea of a vacation was to read a good book and do as little as possible. Julie, on the other hand, looked at vacation as a time to go and do things. Thus, we had conflict because we had different expectations. Those expectations had come from our backgrounds. My family did very little on vacation, whereas Julie's family was always on the go. So without realizing it, we had each gone on vacation expecting something different out of it. We were both trying to get our expectations met and, as a result, were at odds with each other. Neither of us wanted to give up our own "rights" and expectations for our vacations.

We realized that to have harmony we needed to do two things. First, we needed to be aware that we had different expectations as a result of our backgrounds and that this could result in conflict. Second, we needed to realize that those expectations would not be a problem if we each gave up our own rights and expectations and desired above all else to meet the other's needs. This, of course, is not a natural response (naturally we each wanted our own way) and consequently we needed to trust God to do that through us. Once we understood the situation we were in, we then communicated clearly about our expectations and decided to enjoy together whatever we did. We enjoy our vacations now because we have adjusted our expectations. Our willingness to submit to each other and relinquish our "rights" has resulted in some great vacations.

DIFFERENT TEMPERAMENTS

When we first met Greg and Norma, it was difficult to understand why they were having marriage problems. He obviously loved her and the children and provided adequately for them. She was very talented and was willing to fit in with her husband's plans and desires and had stayed home to raise the children. As we spent time with them, however, we realized they did not understand or appreciate each other's different temperaments.

Norma had a high-driving, aggressive temperament by nature, and Greg was more laid-back and easygoing. It just drove her crazy that he would not be more aggressive on the job and advance up the corporate ladder more quickly. As a matter of fact, she kept after him to increase income to the point that he took on a second job as a part-time salesman. This job required him to be aggressive and schedule appointments and go, go, go—which was contrary to his temperament. As a result, the second job did not fulfill him, and it was not long before he got so frustrated that he quit.

Norma, meanwhile, could not stand it any longer. She reasoned that if Greg was not going to be more aggressive and generate more income, she would start working. She began to work at first two days a week and gradually worked up to full-time. Although she wanted to be at home with the children, she just felt she needed to work to offset what Greg was not doing. Although Greg was providing enough, he didn't seem to be aggressive enough to please her. As she worked more, Greg's self-image grew worse and worse. He wondered whether she really needed him. The harmony in their marriage eroded more and more.

Different temperaments! I have seen many times that a poor understanding of them contributes to much of the conflict in marriage. Money seems to magnify the temperament differences, especially if the husband (who, as we saw in the last chapter, is to be the provider) has a more laid-back personality and the wife (who is to be the submissive help-meet) has a more aggressive personality. Their temperaments appear to run against the grain of the job description God has given them. Temperament type, however, does not change the job descriptions and the roles that God has laid down. Man is to provide and that is possible whether he is laid-back, hard-driving, outgoing, reclusive, or a combination. Women are to submit regardless of their temperament. It may be easier if they are more laid-back by temperament, but if they are not, they are still not exempt from their job descriptions. Temperaments are not to be used as an excuse for shirking one's responsibilities.

A key in marriage is to understand that your spouse has a certain temperament that has certain strengths and weaknesses. The stronger the strengths, the stronger the corresponding weaknesses.

Before looking at Greg and Norma again, let's define what temperament is and contrast it with character and personality. Tim LaHaye writes:

> Temperament is the combination of inborn traits that subconsciously affects man's behavior. These traits are arranged genetically on the basis of nationality, race, sex, and other hereditary factors and are passed on by the genes. . . . Character is the real you. The Bible refers to it as the hidden man of the heart. It is the result of your natural temperament modified by childhood training, education and basic beliefs, principles and motivations. . . . Personality is the outward expression of ourselves, which may or may not be the same as our character, depending on how genuine we are. . . . In summary, temperament is the combination of traits we were born with; character is our 'civilized' temperament; and personality is the 'face' we show to others.[2]

There are four basic temperaments. (Refer to chart 3.1.) Each of us is a mixture of temperaments, but we usually have one that is predominant above the rest. It is not important to determine the percentages of the mixture but rather to determine the predominant *basic* temperament you are and understand its strengths and weaknesses. Using chart 3.1, let's analyze Greg and Norma and see whether we can determine the real problem.

Using chart 3.1, it becomes obvious that Norma is choleric and Greg phlegmatic. Is it any wonder that there is conflict when Norma tries to get Greg to strive more for advancement and even take on a job with less structure? He functions best in specialized, repetitive jobs. She, of course, doesn't understand this because her personality is one of initiation. Greg likes the status quo and security of a fixed income. He likes the identification of a group. Part-time sales is about as far from that as a man can get. It is not fixed income and is done independently for the most part.

Norma, on the other hand, likes the opportunity for advancement and can't understand the status quo mentality of Greg. When she starts working, she moves quickly from part-time to full-time.

The challenge is for each man as provider to be content in his vocation. This is usually possible when his temperament meshes with his vocational requirements. Greg and Norma could avoid the conflict they're experiencing if Norma primarily would realize that Greg is most content in his current environment because of

Chart 3.1
Temperament Insights

	CHOLERIC	SANGUINE	PHLEGMATIC	MELANCHOLY
Best situation	Authority, challenges, prestige, freedom, difficult assignments, opportunity for advancement, heavy workload, diversity and innovation.	Social recognition, popularity, people to work with and talk to, freedom of speech, freedom from control and detail, positive work environment, chance to motivate and influence others.	Status quo, securing situation, time to adjust, sincere appreciation, identification with a group, a specialized work pattern, limited territory, secure environment.	Security, no sudden changes, personal attention, little responsibility, exact job descriptions, controlled work environment, status quo, reassurance, team participation.
Key to motivation and encouragement	Challenge	Recognition	Appreciation	Security & protection
How to manage & lead	Works best for a direct, straightforward manager, someone with whom they can "level" and negotiate commitment.	Works best for democratic manager who is as much a friend as a boss and with whom they can associate outside of business.	Works best for a relaxed, amicable manager who takes the time to be interested in him/her as much for himself/herself as for the work. He wants to work for a friend.	Works best for a supportive manager who maintains an "open door" policy and who is always available and willing to discuss key moves. Needs to have exact job description and detailed explanation.

Job structure	Difficult assignments that provide challenge and hold interest—jobs that provide & involve initiative, stress & pressure increase their interest in the task.	Assignments involving interacting with and motivating people. Tasks providing an opportunity to speak and receive recognition is important aspect of the task.	Specialized, repetitive tasks that can be done at own pace. Work that requires traditional procedures.	Work that can be done without making errors & where responsibility can be shared—assignments that require precision & planning.
Working with people	Generally not sensitive & empathetic to others. Sometimes has difficulty communicating with others.	The High "S" is a people person and works well with others, both as a leader & team member. They are generally effective motivators & can generate enthusiasm.	Friendship is important, although they are selective with whom they associate. Whereas the High "S" has many acquaintances, the High "P" has a few intimate friends.	Team participation is important as is shared responsibility because of security rather than a desire to affiliate with others.
They need to learn	1. Empathy is not a weakness. 2. Some controls are necessary. 3. Everyone (even them) has a boss.	1. Time control helps. 2. Deadlines really are urgent. 3. There is such a thing as too much optimism.	1. Reassurance can come from results. 2. There is opportunity in change. 3. Even friends must be disciplined.	1. Even exact job descriptions vary some. 2. Deadlines must be met, in spite of double-checking. 3. Total support is not always available.

Used by permission of Jack Mohler, Jack Mohler and Associates, Box 153, Garwood, N.J. 07027-0153.

his temperament and learn to be content with his current income. Since temperament traits have a lot to do with how we perceive our vocations and what our vocations are, it follows that our temperaments will have a lot to do with the amount of money we earn.

God has equipped each of us with different skills, temperaments, and abilities to do a vast myriad of jobs that need to be done in society. As we will learn in chapter 4, each job will generate a different amount of income.

I have observed that a lot of marriages experience much conflict because the husband is pressured into a potentially higher-paying vocation even though he does not have the temperament for it. The engineer making $40,000 a year who is not very people oriented goes into a sales job because his wife is not content with $40,000 and wants him to make $50,000. He has a tremendous chance of failure, which adds more pressure to the marriage. The key is to be content: Enjoy what you do and live within the income that your vocation generates. Wives, you need to let your husbands do what they're comfortable doing, because that enables them to feel good about themselves. Their self-image is more critical than the amount of income they generate. Their ability to love you is a function of how they feel about themselves.

Obviously, different temperaments affect other areas of money in addition to vocation. When it comes to budgeting, it is not uncommon for one spouse to like numbers and detail, while the other couldn't care less. I have yet to see the consummate salesman who also liked to sit down and deal with details.

To promote harmony in your marriage and to fulfill the roles as God desires, it is important to understand your spouse and act on that understanding. I have found that as I understand Julie's temperament-based strengths and weaknesses it is much easier for me to perceive her actions correctly. I have found that her actions are in most cases the result of the God-given tendencies that flow from her temperament—whether they be strength or weakness—and not a heartfelt motive. (A heartfelt motive shows up, for example, in a situation where the spouse has an "I'm doing this to get 'em" attitude.) Therefore, when Julie questions me about debt, it is not because she doesn't trust me but rather because of her desire to know the details. I do not take it as a personal affront to my decision making or as questioning of my trustworthiness but rather as a need she has because of the way she is.

Many perceived money problems are not money problems but rather problems with understanding the spouse's temperament. This is easily illustrated in the area of living expenses. Many times conflict results in a family over who does the monthly budget and pays the bills. The husband may have a laid-back temperament and not like to deal with numbers and as a result expects the wife to pay all the bills. The wife may feel he is just trying to shirk his responsibility, when in reality his temperament is such that he does not like the detail of the numbers. It is important to make sure you evaluate whether the conflict is really a money conflict or just the result of your spouse's temperament.

THE WAY WE'RE WIRED (MALE/FEMALE DIFFERENCES)

As we saw in chapter 2, God has given husband and wife distinctively unique job descriptions and roles. Not only did He give distinct roles, but He also wired us uniquely to be able to fulfill our roles. He made us with certain abilities and characteristics both physically and emotionally to equip us to do our jobs. He created us male and female—equal in value but uniquely designed. What is unique about our design? I believe if we better understand the uniquenesses it will help us as couples to better deal with much of the conflict in our marriages. "The differences (emotionally, mentally, and physically) are so extreme that without a concentrated effort to understand them, it is nearly impossible to have a happy marriage."[3] We live in a world that is saying to us that if we are equal, we cannot be different. The world is saying that we are alike and has even gone as far as to use the term *unisex.* The world says that the only differences between male and female are socially induced. "When people forget that the opposite sex is opposite, it can result in men actually resenting women for not being men and vice-versa."[4] As Christians, we need to know the truth about our differences and accept them for what they are—the material we need to do our jobs.

I remember a phone call I received from a friend of mine. He had just been talking with his girlfriend and was extremely frustrated that he could not get her to see things the way he did. His question to me was, "Why doesn't she get on top of it? Why doesn't she think like I do?" I couldn't help but laugh as I told him that that was quite an impossibility. She could not think "like he did" because she was not like him—never was and never will be.

I believe that we would agree that men and women are obviously different physically, mentally, and psychologically. It is probably not as obvious how much these differences affect the roles (job descriptions) God has given us. Charts 3.2A and 3.2B summarize some of those differences for your review. I have highlighted the differences that are directly related to the unique roles.

Not only are we different physically, mentally, and psychologically, but we are different emotionally. It is in the emotional realm that much of the conflict over money occurs. These emotional differences must be clearly understood to maximize marital harmony.

Before looking at each of the different emotional characteristics let me say that we all have some of each of the characteristics. It may be that you have more or less of the characteristics as a result of the background you have, what society has told you, and so forth. My contention, however, is that as male or female, you will tend toward the characteristics listed as more unique to you.

1. The Way They Show Love

Men, for the most part, show love by what they do. Women, on the other hand, interpret love by affection. James Dobson comments, "Love is linked to self-esteem in women. For a man, romantic experiences with his wife are warm and enjoyable and memorable—but not necessary. For a woman they are her lifeblood. Her confidence, her sexual response and her zest for living are often directly related to those tender moments when she feels deeply loved and appreciated by her man. That is why flowers and candy and cards are more meaningful to her than to him. This is why she is continually trying to pull him out of the television set or the newspaper, and not vice-versa."[5]

This difference is important to understand as it relates to work and money. One of the reasons many men are driven to work, even to the exclusion of their families, is that to them it

CHART 3.2A
MEN AND WOMEN ARE PHYSICALLY DIFFERENT

1. Men and women differ in every cell of their bodies. This difference in the chromosome combination is the basic cause of development into maleness or femaleness as the case may be. (Men have XY chromosome and women, XX.)
2. Women have greater constitutional vitality. Normally, they outlive men by three or four years, in the U.S.
3. The sexes differ in their basal metabolism—that of women being normally lower than that of men.
4. They differ in skeletal structure, woman having a shorter head, broader face, chin less protruding, shorter legs, and longer trunk. The first finger of a woman's hand is usually longer than the third; with men the reverse is true. Boys' teeth last longer than do those of girls.
5. Woman has a larger stomach, kidneys, liver, and appendix; smaller lungs.
6. In functions, woman has several very important ones totally lacking in man—menstruation, pregnancy, lactation. All of these influence behavior and feelings. She has more different hormones than does man. The same gland behaves differently in the two sexes—thus woman's thyroid is larger and more active; it enlarges during pregnancy but also during menstruation; it makes her more prone to goiter, provides resistance to cold, is associated with the smooth skin, relatively hairless body, and thin layer of subcutaneous fat which are important elements in the concept of personal beauty. It also contributes to emotional instability—she laughs and cries more easily.
7. Woman's blood contains more water (20% fewer red cells). Since these supply oxygen to the body cells, she tires more easily, is more prone to faint. Her constitutional viability is therefore strictly a long-range matter. When the working day in British factories, under wartime conditions, was increased from 10 to 12 hours, accidents of women increased 150%; of men not at all. **[Man was made to provide—not the woman.]**
8. In brute strength, men are 50% above women.
9. Woman's heart beats more rapidly (80, vs. 72 for men); blood pressure (10 points lower than man) varies from minute to minute; but she has much less tendency to high blood pressure—at least until after the menopause.
10. Her vital capacity or breathing power is lower in the 7:10 ratio.
11. She stands high temperature better than does man; metabolism slows down less.

From the article: "*Are Women Really Different?*" Dr. Paul Popenoe, *Family Life*, February 1971.

CHART 3.2B
MEN AND WOMEN ARE DIFFERENT MENTALLY AND PSYCHOLOGICALLY

1. "Verbal and spatial abilities in boys tend to be 'packaged' into different hemispheres: the right hemisphere for non-verbal tasks, the left for verbal tasks. But in girls, non-verbal and verbal skills are likely to be found on both sides of the brain." This affects their actions and reactions.
2. "From shortly after birth, females are more sensitive to certain types of sounds, particularly to a mother's voice," but also to loud noises.
3. Girls have "more skin sensitivity, particularly in the fingertips, and are more proficient at fine motor performance."
4. Girls are more attentive to social contexts—faces, speech patterns, subtle vocal cues.
5. Girls speak sooner, have larger vocabularies, rarely demonstrate speech defects, exceed boys in language abilities, learn foreign languages more easily.
6. Boys show early visual superiority.
7. Boys have better total body coordination but are poorer at detailed hand activity; e.g., stringing beads.
8. Boys have different "attentional mechanisms" and react as quickly to inanimate objects as to a person.
9. Boys are more curious about exploring their environment. **[A result of their God-given drive to subdue.]**
10. Boys are better at manipulating three-dimensional space. They can mentally rotate or fold an object better. **[More logical.]**
11. Of eleven subtests for psychological measurements in "the most widely used general intelligence test, only two (digit span and picture arrangement) reveal similar mean scans for males and females. There are six differences so consistent that the standard battery of this intelligence test now contains a masculinity-femininity index to offset sex-related proficiencies and deficiencies."
12. Girls who are "assertive and active" and can control events have greater intellectual development, while these factors are not as significant in male intellectual development.
13. More boys are hyperactive ("more than 90 percent of hyperactives are male.")
14. Because the male brain is "primarily visual" and learns by manipulating its environment, listening instruction of boys in early elementary grades is more stressful for them. Girls therefore tend to exceed them.
15. Girls do less well on scholarship tests that are more geared for male performance at higher grades.
16. In women the left hemisphere of the brain is better developed. Therefore:

    —She has better verbal and communication skills **[necessary for nurturing]**

    —She is more sensitive and context oriented

CHART 3.2B *(Continued)*

—She is two times more susceptible to phobias and is more prone to depression because she has less control from the right hemisphere of the brain

17. In a man, the right hemisphere of the brain is better developed. Therefore:
    —He is better at visual, spatial, mathematic, and abstract manipulations
    —He is a tinkerer and explorer **[goes with his job of provision]**
    —He is more sex-oriented and tends to establish "turf"
    —He commits almost all violent crime, and more men are sex deviants and psychopaths because they have less control from the left hemisphere of the brain
18. Women have greater individual mood fluctuation. One in four women are seriously affected in pre-menstruation. Also at this time, women are inclined toward more illness, more tension, and show more inclination to crime.
19. There are more males at both ends of the intellectual spectrum—more retardates as well as more geniuses.

Data gathered by Dr. Richard Restak, neurologist at Georgetown University School of Medicine.

is in working that they show love for their wife and children. As they work hard to provide they feel they are showing their love for their family. Although the husband is responsible to provide, he needs to realize that his wife interprets love by the affection he shows, by his communication, and by time spent with her. Much conflict occurs in marriage if a man allows work to get out of balance and incorrectly assumes that it is okay because it shows he loves his wife.

One of the best ways for a man to show love for his wife is to tell her he loves her. To tell her about his day. To talk to her about his job, the money he makes, and his plans for the use of the money. Not only will money problems be avoided but he will also be communicating love for his wife because he cares enough to talk to her and listen to her.

2. Identity Placement

The wife tends to put her identity in her husband, whereas the husband tends to put his identity in his job. His job gives him status and worth. He tends to focus on it and get his identity from it because of his provision drive. The wife derives status and worth from who her husband is and how he treats her.

The different focus of each spouse can obviously lead to conflict. Since the man's identity is tied up in his job position and what he can accomplish vocationally, it is easy for him to spend an inordinate amount of time working. When he does this, he tends to destroy his relationship with his wife. Her identity is in him, and he is never home. She begins to resent his work. Contrary to what he thinks, even though he makes more and more money, it does not help his relationship with his wife. More money isn't the answer because her identity is not in the money but rather in him. She just wants him to be home some and to be a part of his life.

Needless to say, this difference must be understood by both husband and wife to promote harmony in the marriage. In chapter 4 we will see how this difference manifests itself in the work arena.

3. Tolerance for Risk

This is a big one. Since man is responsible to provide, he tends to have a greater tolerance of risk and rejection. He has to be more comfortable taking risks because it is risky to go out into the marketplace and provide. It is risky to subdue and conquer his environment and protect his territory. There are constant challenges for him to face and conquer as he provides. Someone else may take his job. If so, he must get up from the rejection and go on. He must have the emotional makeup to handle those challenges. He is equipped to do so.

The wife, on the other hand, has the responsibility to nurture. With that responsibility comes the desire to be secure. It is difficult to nurture and raise a family without the security of a home. The home is her territory. It is there that her interests lie. This is why it is much more difficult for a woman to move out of the home than for the husband. To him it is "just a move." To her it is leaving a place of security, a place where she has put down roots. If you want to check the validity of this difference, husbands, tell your wives tomorrow that you are moving across town to take another job. See how quick she is to drag her feet.

How is this difference manifested in the financial realm? If the husband wants to start a new vocation with uncertain income and leave a vocation with a fixed income, who usually drags their feet? Who is more willing to take the risk of an aggressive investment—husband or wife? Who tends to want to make sure the budget is working and that there is enough money to meet all the unexpected emergencies? Who tends to be most uncomfortable with the use of debt? We will look at each of these specific money areas in later chapters and see how the differences manifest themselves, what conflicts can arise, and how to overcome the conflicts.

One other thing about this difference: With the risk-taking bent comes a less worried viewpoint. With the security orientation comes a more worried viewpoint. A man typically doesn't worry too much about events. A woman sees them in a more personal, attached way. She tends to be more subjective and feeling oriented.

This difference in tendency to worry is seen very clearly when the husband loses his job. Who tends to worry the most about it? The wife. It bothers her that he doesn't seem to be that worried. He's not worried, because he knows he'll get another job and provide for his family. The same thing happens if an investment goes bad. The husband's response is typically, "That's the way it goes. It is part of the game." The wife, on the other hand, will tend to worry about all the things they can't do because of the money that was lost.

4. Sensitivity Level

Men tend to be more insensitive and women more sensitive. This is a result of the man being more thing-centered and idea-centered. He is more concerned about projects and abstract principles and getting the job done than he is about how he gets the job done or perhaps even the feelings of the people doing the job. His need to provide causes him to be this way. He leans toward justice and strictness. The wife, on the other hand, is more people-centered and concerned about the process of getting things done. She is more tuned into the human side of things and tends to be more merciful and lenient.

This difference can manifest itself in many different ways financially. Let's say you make an investment in a rental house and are having trouble getting the tenants to pay the rent. The husband will tend to want to "lower the boom" and threaten them and force them to pay. The wife, on the other hand, will probably be looking for all the reasons the tenants can't pay and trying to convince the husband not to be so hard on them.

Another case could involve the budget. Typically, the husband is less sensitive to being delinquent on some of the monthly bills than the wife would be. To him it is no big deal if they need to wait a couple more days. The wife tends to always want to be current. Charitable giving is another area where the wife's sensitivity can cause her to be more inclined to give to a need than the husband. The reason is that typically the requests for money play on the emotions of the individual. The wife, being more sensitive to the need, will tend to pick up on the request to a greater degree than the husband.

This leads me to another difference. It is quite obvious that men are much slower to show emotion than are women. To a large degree, this is a function of their sensitivity levels. This is why women may cry over the checkbook if they can't get it to balance or if there is not enough money to pay the bills. The man may be upset, but he won't show it. As a matter of fact, he comes across as indifferent. This can compound the problem. She can't understand why he seems oblivious to it, and that frustrates her even more.

Since money is such a potentially emotional area of a couple's life, it is important that they have a plan to handle it. The plan needs to be designed to reduce emotional strain—primarily on the wife, since she is more emotional. The man needs to remember that even though money is no big deal to him emotionally, it is a very emotional area to his wife. His understanding of this difference can be exhibited by communicating with his wife and showing sensitivity to her when she is being emotional about some area of the finances. Men, when she gets upset, she does not need your words of wisdom like "Why don't you straighten up?" or "Why don't you understand this?" She needs you to listen (not talk) and be sensitive to her. Since this is not natural for you, it will require that you walk close to God and call upon His Holy Spirit.

5. Ego needs

Since men have the responsibility to provide, and since they take risks to do so, they need to be encouraged. Their greatest ego need is to have a continued vote of confidence, and to be esteemed and admired. They need to be built up. One of the reasons men work extra long hours is because they get their ego needs met at work because their wives do not build them up and encourage them at home. Wives, tell him that he is doing a good job. Tell him that you are proud of him. Failure to do so may result in extra long work hours or it could result in fewer work hours. The husband could become slothful because he feels unappreciated and takes a "who cares" attitude. A woman who strokes her husband's ego will never have a failure for a husband. He will be a success in whatever he does.

A wife who does not encourage her husband in his role, or who is constantly confronting him because he does not make enough money, may drive him to make risky investments, or take on excessive debt, or change jobs unwisely to try to succeed in her eyes and gain approval and admiration he needs.

The woman, on the other hand, typically needs to be supported and promoted in her role. She needs to feel important and needed. Since she tends to be more loving, more emotional, more subjective, and more dependent, she is subject to more loneliness. This loneliness enhances her need for a close interpersonal relationship and heart-to-heart communication. She needs to know that her husband values her input and that she is important to him. This is why getting your wife's input on an investment is so critical. Not only does her intuitive ability give you good counsel, but she feels important since you asked her. This is why we as men must make it our aim to communicate with our wives.

In addition to being supported, women need to be encouraged in their God-given role as help-meet. Child rearing is such a long-term job (they won't know how they did until the children are in their twenties) that they need to be encouraged to hang in there. I believe that some women, though not desiring to leave their children, go back into the workplace to get some positive support and encouragement because they are not getting it from their husbands. Men, if we want to leave a godly posterity, we need to encourage our wives in their roles or not be surprised when they go back into the workplace and put the children in daycare. A better understanding of their need for encouragement on our part can help this problem.

6. Long-Term versus Short-Term Thinking

Because of the provision responsibility it is not uncommon that men tend to have a longer time horizon than women. They tend to see the big picture and look down the road. This is why men are generally more concerned about retirement than women. This is one of the reasons men tend to handle a long-term investment that is not readily converted to cash, such as real estate, easier than women. If it takes ten to fifteen years to get money out of the investment, most women usually aren't too interested. The woman, on the other hand, tends to focus on the here and now. This perspective is necessary for her, of course, because she has the responsibility of nurturing. She has to deal with the short-term needs of the children and her husband. While he is thinking retirement and education, she is thinking groceries and shoes for the kids.

It is obvious how this difference can be at the root of many money conflicts. It is also obvious how we need each other. The short term and the long term are both important in a couple's financial life. The short-term needs must be met, but always with an eye to the future. Harmony is enhanced in the marriage as both husband and wife realize that their perspective is needed and that as they communicate the best financial decisions can be made.

7. Bottom Line versus Detail Minded

Men tend to focus on the essence of the matter. They tend to get to the heart of the situation without showing a lot of concern over how they get there. Women, on the other hand, tend to focus on the details of a situation. This is why the husband may not be concerned about how the investment came about, whereas the wife wants to know all the details.

8. Logical versus Intuitive

All couples who have been married any time at all know this difference exists, though it is likely most of them can't explain it. The male tends to like facts. He analyzes everything in order and step by step to come to a conclusion. Meanwhile, the wife in many cases comes to the conclusion without really knowing how she reached her conclusion. She seems to just "sense" the situation. This difference is most obvious in the area of investments, as we will see.

It is important to realize that the way this difference is manifested can cause much frustration. The husband can spend hours analyzing, sorting, and calculating, only to have his wife give a definitive, curt response in a matter of seconds and not give the matter another thought. His normal response is one of bewilderment. "How can she say that? She doesn't have the facts." The natural tendency then is to discount what she has said. This, of course, will reduce her feeling of importance and value, causing strain on the relationship.

The wife, on the other hand, may have a hard time understanding why her husband has to go through all the calculations and thinking he goes through to come to a decision. She can get to the conclusion with one fell swoop. The key is to know this difference exists and allow each spouse to exercise his or her bent (logic or intuition). Each should be given equal credibility in making decisions. We'll see how this works in chapter 11 on investments.

In summary, we have seen that conflict can be influenced by different backgrounds, different temperaments, and/or an unclear understanding of our basic male/female differences. As we'll see in the remainder of this book, one, two or all three of these areas may be causing conflict over money in your marriage. It is my hope that your understanding of these areas will be the first step in helping you overcome the conflicts that money can cause in your marriage.

GAME PLAN

To help you better understand your spouse, I would highly recommend that you take one of the following temperament tests. Once you have taken the test, chart 3.3 is a good worksheet to promote communication about your respective strengths and weaknesses. This may take some time, but your marriage is worth it and your posterity depends on it.

Personal Profile System, 1977, John G. Geier, Ph.D., Performax Systems Intl., Inc.

The Taylor-Johnson personality test (Psychological Publications, Inc., 5300 Hollywood Blvd., Los Angeles, Calif. 90027).

CHART 3.3

	I APPRECIATE YOUR STRENGTHS OF:	I CAN HELP YOU BECOME MORE EFFECTIVE AND SATISFIED IN YOUR ROLE BY:	THE FOLLOWING THINGS HAVE THE POTENTIAL TO CREATE CONFLICT:
EXAMPLE: Husband to Wife	• Concentrating on the task. • Being a good listener. • Being the calming influence in our home.	• Not changing direction so often without discussing it with you. • By providing a more stable, predictable environment. • Helping you organize complex tasks. • Helping you verbalize. • Listening to your ideas.	• Your need for "status quo" and resistance to any tendency to challenge it. • My tendency to make quick decisions involving both of us without discussing it with you to consider what is best. • Your not verbalizing thoughts.
Husband to Wife			
Wife to Husband			

Part 2

Specific Problems and Solutions Related to Money and Marriage

In Part 2 I will look at *specific* truths about money and how it affects your marriage. I will look at the truth about work, income, debt, living expenses, giving, insurance, and investments. The problems that can occur in marriage as a result of each area will be identified and solutions discussed.

To better understand the flow of the next few chapters and how they interrelate, it is important to have a capsule view of how money flows through your situation. An overview of financial planning appears in the diagram used on the opening pages of chapters 4–12. This diagram was developed by Ron Blue of Ronald Blue & Co., Atlanta, Georgia, and is used by permission. You'll note the following facts about money:

1. *Income* is generated from one's work (vocation). It could also come from gifts, borrowing, and return on investment. However, the majority of a person's income is a result of his or her labor (work).
2. The income is *dispersed in five different areas* as follows:

   A. *Living expenses.* This includes groceries, clothes, vacation, rent, utilities, and so on.

B. *Debt.* This is repayment of any principal owed, such as credit cards, school loans, money owed to parents, home mortgage, and auto loans. In Part 2 of this book I have assumed that debt payments are a part of living expenses.

C. *Taxes.* These include federal and state income taxes as well as social security tax (FICA).

D. *Giving.* This is money given to charity, primarily, but could also include money given to others (family and friends).

E. *Cash Flow Margin.* This is savings, which could also be referred to as margin. In the next few chapters we will use the terms *savings* and *margin* interchangeably when referring to this use of money.

Simply put, your income goes to live, give, pay taxes, and pay debt; what is left over is saved for investments. It can be summarized this way:

Income	________
Less	
Taxes	________
Debt	________
Living expenses	________
Giving	________
Cash flow margin	________

Chapter 4

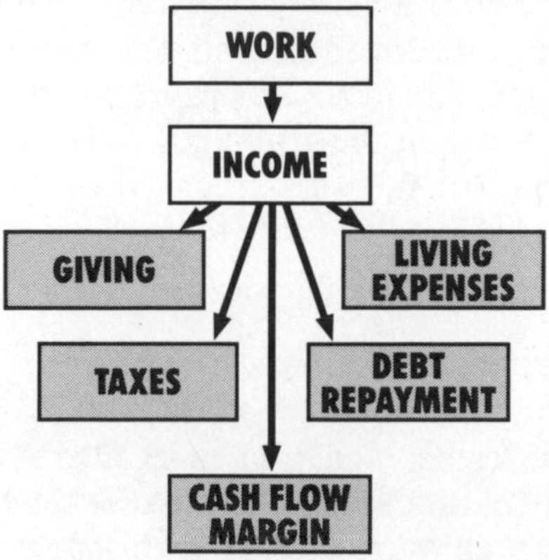

Work: Blessing or Curse?

Much conflict in marriage is the result of incorrect thinking about work. Conflict can result when the husband works too much or not enough (chapter 5), and also when the mother works vocationally outside of the home (chapter 6). Why does a husband work too much or not at all? What causes a mother to go to work outside of the home? In many cases all three of these responses result from a poor understanding of work. It is important that you as husband and wife understand work from God's perspective in order to view your *income* correctly.

WORK DEFINED

Work is defined as the physical and mental energy exerted and directed to some end or purpose. For our discussion we will define work to mean *vocational employment for the purpose of generating income to provide for the family.*

Since work is tied to provision and provision is primarily the man's responsibility, my remarks throughout this chapter are directed specifically to the man. These principles, however, also apply to women who must work to provide for their families.

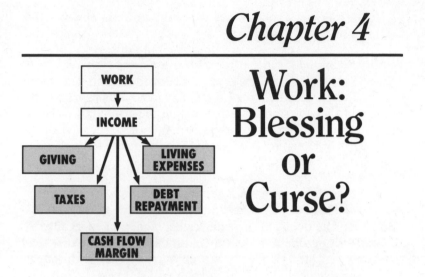

The following basic tenets will help us focus our thoughts on this discussion of work.

1. Man has a God-given drive to provide, and as a result, he works
"Now no shrub of the field was yet in the earth, and no plant of the field had yet sprouted, for the Lord God had not sent rain upon the earth; and there was no man to cultivate the ground. . . . Then the Lord God took the man and put him into the garden of Eden to cultivate it and keep it" (Gen. 2:5, 15). The desire to work flows from man's drive to provide.

2. As a result of his work man generates income for the purpose of meeting the needs of his family
"But if anyone does not provide for his own, and especially for those of his household, he has denied the faith, and is worse than an unbeliever" (1 Tim. 5:8). "For even when we were with you, we used to give you this order: if anyone will not work, neither let him eat" (2 Thess. 3:10).

Let's look now at some truths about why we work, how we keep work in balance, how we find our vocation, and why we might change the form of our work (change jobs).

WHY DO WE WORK?

There are several reasons why we work. First, man works because *work is good.* It is valued by God. We see in Genesis 1 that what God did in the creation of the world was good—very good. We also see as we read Gen. 2:5, 15 that work is good because we are in partnership with God regarding our work. God planted the garden, and man cultivated it. We work because we have the incredible privilege of co-laboring with God. Ps. 8:6 reveals this co-laboring when it says "Thou dost make him to rule over the works of Thy hands; Thou hast put all things under his feet." God allows us to assist Him in the management of creation. We work, then, because of the great dignity God affords us as His co-laborers. Work is a gift from God (Eccles. 5:18–19).

Many feel that work is a result of the curse. It is not a result of the curse. God cursed the ground as a result of the Fall, but not the actual task of working itself. Work has indeed become harder to accomplish as a result of the Fall, but it still remains a good and proper activity. Although Ecclesiastes teaches that all labor is "vanity," or useless, it is still to be undertaken and even enjoyed. The frustration we experience as we toil is balanced by the joy of accomplishment and provision our work produces.

The second reason we work is because *Scripture commands us to work.* We find in 2 Thess. 3:10 that if a man does not work, he is not to eat. If a man does not work and is slothful, he runs the risk of failing to provide for his family and being a bad testimony not only to his family but to the world. He also runs the risk of seeing the marriage roles reversed as his wife takes on the provision responsibility that is really his. With the role reversal comes the potential for disharmony in the marriage. (Disharmony results any time someone or something is not fulfilling the function for which it was created.) In this scenario the man is not being diligent to fulfill the command to work and provide for his family.

The third reason we work is because the *process of working is a significant means of fulfillment for a man.* A man is fulfilled when he works because that is what God has created him to do. The God-given drive to provide carries with it the drive and desire to work.

In my consulting role, I have the opportunity to work with many individuals who have "arrived" financially. In many cases they have millions of dollars because of selling a business they have worked in for twenty to thirty years. They are in a position where they do not have to work in an income-generating vocation ever again. Many of these men are extremely frustrated. You would think they would be fulfilled, but they are not. They cannot receive satisfaction and fulfillment by just investing their money. They may for a couple of years, but after a while they want to do something productive. They are usually quite miserable until they find something that they can work in again and be gainfully employed. I have had many of them comment to me, "Russ, I have got to get back to work. This doing nothing is just driving me crazy. I can only play so much golf, and I'm tired of playing golf." This is why retirement to a life of leisure is dangerous. It removes the individual from the opportunity of fulfillment that the PROCESS of working provides.

The fourth reason why we work is that it *gives us an environment for living the Christian life, sharing our faith in Christ, and growing with other believers.* Christianity should not be just a segment in one's life; it should overflow into every aspect of life, especially in our work. That is our ultimate purpose as believers. The marketplace gives us a unique and challenging opportunity to fulfill our God-given responsibility of being salt and light. We do not work only to make money, but to share Christ, to grow as believers and to be obedient.

The fifth reason we work is that our work is an *avenue through which God enables us to generate income to meet the provision needs of our family.* It is very easy to conclude incorrectly that our abilities or intellects enable us to provide for our families. Scripture, however, makes it clear that work is simply the vehicle of our provision—God is the source. (Prov. 10:22; Deut. 8:16–18).

Though income is a result of our work (the product, if you would), it should not be our pursuit. If we focus on the product (income) rather than the process of working, we can experience frustration and lack of fulfillment. All that we produce will be burned up (2 Pet. 3:10). Solomon realized the futility of focusing on the product of his labor. In Eccles. 5:15 he said, "he [man] will take nothing from the fruit of his labor that he can carry in his hand." If we pursue money, it takes wings like an eagle and flies away (Prov. 23:3–4). Though money has utilitarian value (we can use it to buy things we need to meet our physical needs), it has no long-term, intrinsic value because it will not last. It is vain to focus on it.

Another reason we can be frustrated if we focus on income is that we will constantly be evaluating our worth and success on the basis of what we earn in comparison to others. As we discussed in chapter 1, such a comparison is futile because the income we earn is in God's hands and has nothing to do with whether or not we are successful.

If we pursue income as the sole purpose of our working, our lives will be marked by that focus. We will work longer hours, forgetting that working more hours does not guarantee more income. We will be competitive, anxious, unsatisfied, self-centered wealth seekers, always measuring what we do by the product of our work. The key truth about work is summed up as follows: *It is your responsibility to work hard and excellently (Col. 3:23) at what God has called and equipped you to do, realizing that the income you generate is determined by Him and is His responsibility. God is more concerned about the process of your working than He is about the product of your work.* Tremendous freedom can result in your life if you will grasp this awesome principle. If you ever find yourself thinking that your income is not *fair,* or that it doesn't seem right that you earn what you earn and another person earns much more, then it is likely that you do not have the correct perspective on work (why you do it and its relationship to your income). Regard those thoughts as a warning indicator to spend time with God learning to think correctly about your income and perception of work. If you don't, your work could get out of balance and cause stress on your marriage.

THE BALANCE OF WORKING

So far we have said that God has equipped different men to fulfill different vocational jobs. Man is responsible to work hard and excellently at his job, and the income is in God's hands. In the "working hard and excellently" comment is implied *balance.* It stands to reason that if our income is in God's hands, He will meet our needs without our overworking and getting out of balance. We see this verified in Ps. 127:2. "It is vain for you to rise up early, to retire late, to eat the bread of painful labors; for He gives to His beloved even in his sleep." Prov. 10:22 says, "It is the blessing of the Lord that makes rich, and He adds no sorrow to it."

As Charles Spurgeon once said, "All men must work, but no man should work beyond his physical and intellectual ability, nor beyond the hours which nature allots. No net result of good to the individual nor the race comes of any artificial prolonging of the day at either end. Work while it is day. When night comes, rest."[1]

What is our allotted time? If your marriage relationship is important and your children (posterity) are important, then it is critical that you build time in your day to spend with your wife and children. This implies that you control your work hours and not overwork. *Overwork is defined as any situation where a man is spending hours on his vocation to the exclusion of other priority areas of his life.* He is out of balance. To avoid overwork or imbalance in your life you must not only understand the source of your income (God) but also set priorities for the use of your time. If you do not prioritize your life time-wise, you will prioritize it after income. You will work more and more in the pursuit of more income. (The "game plan" at the end of this chapter will help you determine whether you have balance.)

Though you could generate more income by working more hours, holding down two jobs, and so on, you need to realize there will be a cost. It is wiser to heed Prov. 10:22 and seek the blessing of the Lord, which makes one rich without bringing sorrow. If you live within the income the Lord allows you to earn with a balanced work schedule, you will not have the sorrow that can come from getting out of balance and trying to earn more income. "But those who want to get rich fall into temptation and a snare and many foolish and harmful desires which plunge men into ruin and destruction" (1 Tim. 6:9). This ruin and destruction could be in the form of a rocky marriage, undisciplined kids, bad business deals, and so on. You need to trust God to generate the income you need as you work hard and not take the income generation into your own hands. If you remain confident that God will meet your income needs, then you will experience freedom in your work, realizing that it is your part to do what you can do in your allotted time and trust God to do what you cannot do.

The key to balancing work and family is to realize the source of your income and have a long-term perspective. This long-term perspective enables you to see that retirement will never really be an option if you are to be fulfilled. As a result, you realize that you have your entire lifetime to accumulate, and consequently you will be more inclined to have balance early on in your career. You will not want to work the twelve-to-fifteen hour days to the exclusion of your family in order to "arrive" or "retire."

This perspective also enables you to realize that the very thing you are working for (money) will be passed on to your children. As a result, you will be more inclined to keep balance in your life so you have time to train your children. If you do not spend time training them and being a role model for them, then it is very difficult for them to learn the truths you want them to learn, especially about money. It is a travesty to see someone who has worked his entire life and amassed a fortune only to make comments like, "Russ, I really can't leave this to my children because they can't handle it." You must spend TIME with your children to train them. This is why the development of a godly posterity is so critical. They will grow up just like you. Don't get to the end of your life and say, as Solomon did, that it was vanity because you focused on money instead of your posterity (Eccles. 2:20–22).

To find out whether your perspective of work is long term, and whether you have balance, ask yourself these questions: Can I leave the work at the office? Can I relax? Can I sleep? Am I anxious? Is my self-image tied directly to my job? Do I measure how I am doing by comparing myself to the other guy?

Your answers to these questions will help you understand your view of work and its focus. If you can sleep, relax, enjoy what you are doing, and have a good self-image apart from your job, then you probably have a proper understanding of why you work and who is the ultimate source of your income. If you find yourself able to spend time with your family, enjoy vacations, and really know your children, then you probably have good balance related to your work.

DETERMINING YOUR VOCATION

Throughout this chapter I have stated that you should do what God has called you to do. To determine your job calling you should consider the following factors: Are you equipped for it? Is the vocation worthwhile? Do you enjoy it?

God does not call us to a vocation we are not *equipped* for. Therefore, in evaluating your vocational calling, look at the God-given resources that you have (your design, temperament, experience, background, and training), look at your options and opportunities, look at your feelings, desires, and motivation, and choose a job. You need to match up your abilities as closely as possible with the job.

Any job you do should be evaluated as to whether or not it is *worthwhile.* Any job is worthwhile if it makes a contribution to people. Whether you are a grocer, an electrician, a teacher, a doctor—whatever—practically everything a person could do vocationally is worthwhile to society. The way you make a contribution to people through your vocation is to focus on them as you are in the process of working. In other words, be sensitive to the needs around you in the marketplace. The way to do this is to focus not on your income but rather on the way you work.

Whatever you do you should *enjoy.* In Ecclesiastes Solomon makes it very clear that we are to enjoy our labor. Remember that it is a gift of God (Eccles. 3:13). "Nothing is better than that man should be happy in his activities, for that is his lot" (Eccles. 3:22).

This does not imply that work is easy or that it will always be enjoyable. We are told in Gen. 3:19 that work will be hard. What it does mean is that for the most part you should enjoy and like what you do. Typically, this is most easily accomplished as you match up your gifts, temperament, and abilities with your vocation.

CHANGING VOCATIONS

If you are working hard and excellently at the vocation God has equipped you for and if you have your work in proper perspective, is there ever a time you would change jobs? Yes, there is. Motivation is the key. Your motivation should not simply be "to make more money." If someone changes only to make more income, he will forever be frustrated because income is not the source of fulfillment, job satisfaction, or contentment. The person who seeks more income typically goes from job to job and is unfulfilled.

Job changes should come from a desire and a need to better fulfill our life purpose. This presupposes, of course, that each of us is already fulfilling his God-given purpose in his current vocation. The key is to be involved in God's purpose where you are; then, if He wants you to change jobs to better fulfill that purpose, He will open the way. Income considerations should be secondary.

CONCLUSION

In this chapter we have focused on two crucial issues which go together—work and income. Here is a summary of the key points we've discussed from the biblical perspective.

God has called and equipped man to work as a means of providing for his family. Work is good, and in order for man to be fulfilled he will work his entire lifetime. Man is to work excellently at his vocation with the realization, however, that the income generated is ultimately in God's hands. Since the income and assets man accumulates from his work will be left to those who come after him, he must train his posterity. Since this training takes time, man will need to make sure early on that his life is ordered by *time priorities,* not income priorities, and that he has balance in his life. In the process of his working, man should focus on people rather than on his income, which is in God's hands. Man should view his work as an environment to reach his world for Christ. Job changes should occur not simply to make more money but to allow man to better fulfill his purpose.

Evaluate your own purposes in working, your work habits, your life priorities, and your short- and long-term goals. Not only can you revolutionize your present life and have harmony in your marriage relationship by bringing your thoughts of work and income in line with God's Word, but you will impact your eternity in heaven through the development of a godly posterity. That makes it all the more worth the time and effort.

GAME PLAN

To begin to order your life after time priorities rather than income priorities, make a list of all the areas in your life that are important to you—family, children, work, exercise, Bible study, and so on. Add to this list all the things you have to do daily, like eat, sleep, get dressed, etc. Now go through the list and put down how much time you would like to spend in each area. It should become obvious that you must have balance in your work hours in order for you to have time to focus on the other areas you feel are important.

	Russ	You
Sleep	56	
Eat	7	
Bible study	8 (includes study & I Group)	
Time with children	7	
Dressing/showering	3 ½	
Exercise	3 ½	
Quiet time	3 ½	
Unaccounted for time	16	

(Domestic jobs, yardwork, etc. The five and ten minutes here and there between other things.)

	Russ	You
Work	50	
Time with Julie	10	
Leisure	3 ½	

This list may also reveal to you some changes you may need to make in your life. One obvious area that may need some adjustment is time spent watching TV. In doing this exercise, I found that I had very little time to watch TV if I was going to do an excellent job at work and spend time with my boys and Julie. If you make the same discovery, the following thoughts from Life Ministries in Seattle, Washington, may be the motivation you need to do something about it.

The 23rd Channel

> The T.V. set is my shepherd, My spiritual growth shall want. It maketh me to sit down and do nothing for His name's sake, because it requireth all my spare time. It keepeth me from doing my duty as a Christian, because it presenteth so many good shows that I must see.
>
> It restoreth my knowledge of the things of the world, and keepeth me from the study of God's Word. It leadeth me in the paths of failing to attend the evening worship services, and doing nothing in the Kingdom of God.
>
> Yea, though I live to be a hundred, I shall keep on viewing my T.V. as long as it will work, for it is my closest companion. Its sounds and its picture, they comfort me.
>
> It presenteth entertainment before me, and keepeth me from doing important things with my family. It fills my head with ideas which differ from those set forth in the Word of God.
>
> Surely, no good thing will come of my life, because my T.V. offereth me no good time to do the will of God; Thus I will dwell in spiritual poverty all the days of my life.[2]

Chapter 5

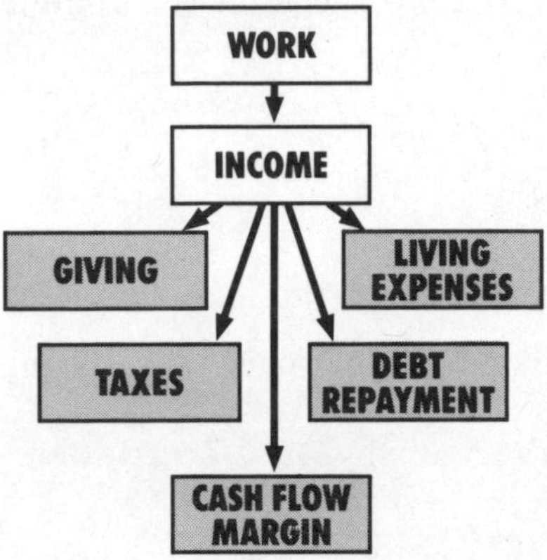

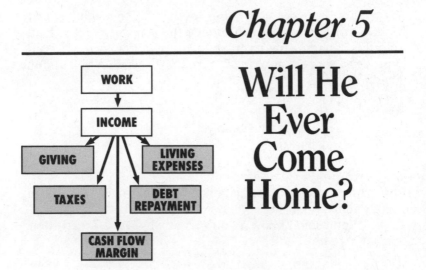

Will He Ever Come Home?

6:00 A.M.

"Honey, is that you?" asked Sally groggily.

"Yes, I've got to be at the office early for a meeting," mumbled Bob.

"Will you be late again tonight?" asked Sally.

"I don't know yet," muttered Bob as he stumbled toward the shower. "I shouldn't be. It all depends on how the day goes. You know."

"That is what you always say. I thought this new job wouldn't take as much of your time," groused Sally. "The kids hardly ever see you. You leave before they get up, and most of the time you get home after they have gone to bed."

"That is not true!" exclaimed Bob. "They do too see me."

"When?" questioned Sally.

"On the weekends I spend a lot of time with them."

"How about last weekend? You worked half a day and then played golf with a client."

"Oh yeah, but that was an exception," countered Bob.

"There seem to be a lot of exceptions lately," continued Sally.

"I don't know why my hours bother you so much. I need to work hard to make enough money to keep this place afloat," retorted Bob, growing more agitated by the moment. "I really wish you'd support my career. You know I do it for you and the children."

8:00 P.M.

"Mommy, is Daddy home yet?"

"Not yet, darling."

"Why not?"

"He's working late at the office."

"Mommy, why does Daddy always work late? I like having Daddy at home."

"I know son. I know. I don't know why. . . . I really don't know."

One area that can cause much conflict in a marriage is a situation where the husband never seems to be home because he is working all the time. We want to look now at why a husband may work too many hours. We will also look at a wife's response to his overworking and the potential consequences of that choice.

REASONS FOR A MAN TO OVERWORK

The first reason a man may overwork is his *God-given drive to provide.* Every man who is conscientious to this provision drive will be inclined to work and work hard, perhaps even to the detriment of time with his family. Thus, a man's provision drive taken to an extreme can become a negative rather than a positive. A man can spend so much time providing that he doesn't spend time with those he is providing for. He accumulates prosperity (world's definition) to the exclusion of his posterity.

Granted, there are some situations where men are slothful and are not properly exercising this drive, but it has been my observation that in most cases a man will tend to work too much rather than too little.

The man's provision drive often causes him to pursue financial independence as quickly as he can. The desire to be financially independent is not the problem but rather the time frame. I have consulted with many men who have developed an idea that if they are not millionaires by the time they are forty, they are failures. They forget that work is normative and that they will do it their entire lifetime. This incorrect time horizon can lead to some wrong decisions regarding family and other priorities.

The key is balance. The husband needs to realize that if he does not pay special attention to the needs of his wife (primarily time related—spending time with her), then all his pursuits and long-term endeavors, however noble, will be hollow.

The second reason a man may be overworking is that his *needs are not met at home.* Two of man's greatest needs are to be admired (to have his ego stroked) and to have domestic support.

I am always most encouraged when Julie tells me how much she appreciates what I do vocationally. I love it when she tells me that I am the best. It makes me very pleased when she tells me that I am the greatest provider in the world and that she is continually amazed at what I know about finances and how well I do my job. Wow! What do you think her comments do for me? They give me great confidence and fulfillment. I know I am successful in her eyes, and that is all that really matters. I would do anything for her. When my day is done, I want to be with her. I don't want to spend too much time at work because it will take away from time with Julie. This brings me to the second need.

Men want "peace at home." They have a tremendous need to be esteemed, to be honored and respected as the head. A wife who is quick to meet her husband's needs will have a man who wants to come home. He will not need to stay at the office to get his needs met. I remember when Julie was working as a Certified Nurse Anesthetist (CRNA) right after we were married. Everything went well initially, but as her time at work gradually increased and her time at home doing domestic functions got shorter, the situation began to frustrate me. My needs were not being met as well at home. Although she quit working, I could easily see how a man might look to his vocation to build him up if he is not being built up at home.

Wives, are you meeting your husbands' needs? If you are employed outside the home, are you tuned in to your husband and meeting his needs? A friend of mine summed it up when he commented, "I can handle anything as long as I know she is behind me and supporting me in what I do."

The third reason a man may be working long hours is that he has a *misplaced focus.* He is focused on generating more income as a measure of his success. Although the biblical definition of success has nothing to do with income or accumulation, most men find this a hard definition to come to grips with and weave into the fabric of their experience. The world has bombarded us for so long with the philosophy that the "man with the most toys at the end of his life wins" that it is very difficult not to focus on income and what it can buy. It is easy for a man to reason that long work hours are a small price to pay for the prestige and power that money appears to be able to bring him. The only problem is that the power and prestige are really a mirage. When he gets them, he realizes what he really wanted was a meaningful purpose, a good self-image, and to love and be loved. He probably gave that up in the pursuit of money.

The best investment is usually not the flashiest. Your posterity fits that description. "Like the fledgling company, a child seems so small, nondescript, and easy to handle with minimum concern. . . . but big returns never happen in the future unless sizable investments are made in the present. . . . Is there a price to be paid? Unquestionably! And it is paid right up front, at the beginning of the child's life; the returns come much later."[1] Many are unwilling to pay that price. Men, how many investments can you make that will pay off in eternity? Don't let this once-in-a-lifetime opportunity slip through your fingers.

Fourth, a man works long hours in pursuit of *position.* He is climbing the ladder in pursuit of a position in his company or profession because he wants to "be somebody" among his peers. Notice I said "a" position. Therein lies the fallacy of this pursuit. Position is defined as a person's standing in relation to another person. It implies that one has arrived. It means he is looking horizontally at how he is doing in comparison with others around him. As a Christian I am not to compare. I am to look vertically and focus only on God and do the very best I can in an excellent manner (Col. 3:23). God will then exalt me. I am in a process; I can never arrive.

What does this mean? It means that for Christians, position is not an option because we never arrive in this lifetime. Since I am in an ongoing process, any position I may be in at a given point in time has been determined by God, but it will be changing as I continue on in the process. How unsettling to work long hours to arrive at a position that at best is only temporary! I need to seek God, work hard, and relax in the process. This is how I achieve balance in my life.

A fifth reason a man may overwork is because work is *exciting and enjoyable* to him. As I indicated earlier, a man should do what he enjoys. I find it hard to believe, however, that a man who understands what is eternally significant would enjoy his work so much that he would overwork to the potential detriment of his family and other priority areas. Still, a man could get so caught up in the excitement of what he does that he would overwork.

The final reason, probably one of the most common reasons that a man may overwork, is that his *wife has driven him to it.* I remember several years ago some friends invited us over for dinner. The husband asked me what I thought about a new job he was about to be offered. The new job would involve more money, but would also involve a minimum of three nights away from home each week. I commented to him that he should think through his goals regarding family, as well as his income, and carefully weigh the pros and cons before making the decision. I encouraged him to think through the issues *before* he was actually offered the job. If he did not decide ahead of time, the income could be so attractive that he would take the job, overlooking some of its negative aspects since they would be outweighed by the money. Money has a way of clouding our thinking regarding the really important issues.

Sure enough, about six months later we heard from his wife. She was very frustrated because her husband never seemed to be home and was always traveling. She was concerned that the children were growing up without their father.

As we discussed the situation, Julie reminded me of some comments the wife had made to her prior to her husband's taking the job. She had indicated to Julie that she was not happy with the carpet in their house and that she was "sick and tired" of driving the car they had. She didn't know how she could ever entertain until they did a lot of remodeling on the house. She did not understand why her husband wouldn't give her the resources to do the things she wanted to do around the house.

It was very clear to Julie and me that one of the reasons that her husband had been motivated to take the job was her subtle yet incessant demands for more. He felt the only way he could get his wife what she wanted was to work more. That started a cycle that could only lead to much frustration because not only did he have trouble making more money, he began to spend less and less time with his wife.

If we do not allow the Lord to provide the income we need within the time allotted, there can be want and sorrow with the attempt at the extra income. In many cases there is a lost spouse or children. The key is not to make more income but to learn to be content with the income a person makes.

WIFE'S RESPONSE TO HUSBAND'S OVERWORKING

There are many responses that a wife could have to the long hours that her husband puts in. We will discuss three common (though inappropriate) responses followed by suggested solutions. The first response is typically one of being *unfulfilled.* A wife is fulfilled when she has conversation, affection, honesty, and openness with her husband. If he is working long hours, and "burning the candle at both ends," it is very difficult for him to have the time necessary to communicate with his wife. Dr. Willard F. Harley, who has more than twenty years of experience as a marriage counselor, recommends to his couples that they spend at least fifteen hours a week together, excluding sleeping and eating. If a husband is working long hours, like Bob in our case study, it would be difficult for him to find fifteen hours a week to spend just with his wife in different activities such as recreation and communication. Is it any wonder that many times men who are finding their fulfillment at the office will find their wives seeking fulfillment in the children, church social activities, or a job?

The very thing the wife wants—time with her husband—she often doesn't get because she is not content with his income. By wanting more she subtly puts him under pressure to work more to try to make more. She ends up getting what she doesn't *really* want (money) while losing what she finds in the long run she really wants (him). Wrong thinking about money brings discontent that can have devastating consequences on a marriage.

A second response the wife may have will be *feeling inferior or second class.* A woman is usually very relationship centered and puts her identity in her man. She loves to create beauty and be a companion to the one she loves. However, if he is never home and never takes time to comment on all she does, it is very difficult for her to feel that she is worthwhile in fulfilling her role. She concludes that there is "no use" trying to please her husband because work is obviously more important to her husband than she is.

I remember early on in the financial planning business working some very long hours (twelve to fourteen hours a day). Julie began to demonstrate frustration and communicated to me that she felt unimportant because of the hours I was working. (Women spell love t-i-m-e.) Although I was not verbally telling her that she was less important to me than my work, my actions were saying it. Since that time I have realized that it is important not to allow my work to take precedence over my wife. This is not to say there will not be some long days. There will be; a man needs to have the freedom to work hard and put in long days to meet the need of his employer. Long days should, however, not become the norm to the exclusion of the family.

The key is to be sensitive to my wife. Through both long and short days I stay tuned in to Julie and focus on her need to be at the forefront of my thinking. Over the years I have communicated this in different ways. One day I went home for lunch (a thirty-minute drive) and took her some flowers. My showing up made a statement to her that even though I spent a lot of hours at work she was still first. I also send cards to her when I travel on extended business trips. I mail them so she'll get one each day I'm gone. Men, since we can so easily put our identity in our jobs, we must be quick and creative in communicating to our wives that "out of sight" does not mean "out of mind." This goes a long way in promoting harmony in the marriage.

The final way that the wife may respond is to begin to *nag* her husband to be at home. We see in Scripture that a nagging, contentious wife is like a dripping faucet (Prov. 27:15). Though most women do not want to imitate a faucet, that is the way many respond to the long hours their husbands work. Needless to say, nagging and harmony are not synonymous. The backlash of this response, of course, can be for the husband to work more and more so that he does not have to listen to the nagging. When this happens, time with her husband becomes less and less attainable.

A nagging wife can also drive her husband to change jobs and perhaps go into a vocation for which he is not suited. This can lead to frustration for both spouses.

WHAT ABOUT THE SLOTHFUL HUSBAND?

What about the husband who is guilty of the opposite of overwork —slothfulness? Since the man was created by God with the drive to provide, a man who does not work is unfulfilled and his self-image is affected. As his self-image wanes so does his ability to love his wife the way God intended. As his love wanes it becomes next to impossible to maintain the level of harmony in the marriage that God desires.

As a result of his slothfulness, the wife begins to take over the provision responsibility. As she does this the roles begin to be reversed, and it becomes difficult to model the correct roles that God intended. Since they are not functioning the way God intended, marital harmony is affected. In the next chapter we will look at what the wife's response should be to a slothful husband. Husbands, you know what your response should be—work in order to provide. God says so!

SOLUTIONS TO THE CONFLICT

What are the answers to the dilemma of the husband working too many hours?

1. Husband and wife need to have a very clear understanding of work and income (review chapter 4). Both husband and wife must understand that their income level is a function of their vocation and is not necessarily dependent on working a greater number of hours. As Spurgeon said, "No net good results from the artificial prolonging of the day at either end." The harmony in your marriage will be enhanced as this truth is worked out in your individual situation.

2. It is critical for the wife to understand the drive her husband has to provide. She must be careful not to tear it down by nagging at him; rather, she should encourage him in his role. If a man feels that his wife is content with his income, he will not be as inclined to overwork. It will be easier for him to settle into an "allotted time."

3. It is important to view overworking correctly. Overworking does not occur in one day or week but is a prolonged state of

working exceedingly long hours to the exclusion of other endeavors. It is important to realize that you will go through cycles where you may be overworking in the short term. For example, if you're starting a new job, it may require a lot of additional time. If you change positions in your company, it may require additional time. If you take a second job for a short time period for a specific purpose, it may take more time.

The key is that over any extended period of time (six months to a year) you should be able to observe a movement toward balance in your life. Too often men extend the period over their entire working lifetime. They keep telling their wives that it will be better next year—that they will balance out and not work such long hours. The wife needs to be prepared for some late nights, but these should not become the habit and the norm.

4. If the husband continues to exhibit a pattern of overworking, the wife needs to talk with him and make sure she has not said or done something that could be driving him to try to generate more income to please her and meet her needs.

In conclusion, it is important for men to work hard to provide for their families, but be careful not to neglect them. You should strive at all costs to keep balance in your life between work and family. If leaving a godly posterity is your goal, then you need to have time to do other things in your life in addition to work. It is absolutely critical that you develop priorities that enable you to develop your posterity while you are working. Your children need you now, not "next year," and they need *you,* not a substitute. Tim Hansel explains:

> The home is the single most important influence on my family. I can delegate a lot of my responsibilities at work but I cannot delegate my hopes for my family. The primary values, attitudes, skills, and competencies that my children will grow up with will be learned (or not learned) in my home.
>
> Time is the very crucible of fathering. The most profound way I let my family know I love them is by giving them time.
>
> A father is a man who is honest enough to realize that his *responsibilities* must determine his priorities.[2]

A harmonious marriage is the only way to leave a godly posterity, and a harmonious marriage is only possible through the investment of quantities of *TIME.* Time spent consistently over months and years. To do this, work must be kept in balance. May God give you wisdom as you strive for this balance. "But if any of you lacks wisdom, let him ask of God, who gives to all men generously and without reproach, and it will be given to him" (James 1:5).

GAME PLAN

A Challenge to Husbands

Men, we have the God-given responsibility to transmit a spiritual heritage (our posterity) to the next generation. We may or may not leave a monetary estate. In the final evaluation the monetary estate is not the important thing. It cannot and will not last. Our children and other people we touch will last. They are the only investment we can make that will go to heaven. Are you working long hours for the wrong goal? Do you work at training your children and discipling others as zealously as you work to make money?

Hard work is good if kept in focus. Out of focus it goes terribly awry in accomplishing eternally significant goals. Psalm 127 declares that it is vain to rise up early and go to bed late. Meditate on this psalm and see how recognition of God's providential care can keep your work, your rest, and your family in proper perspective. Note your reflections in the space below.

Chapter 6

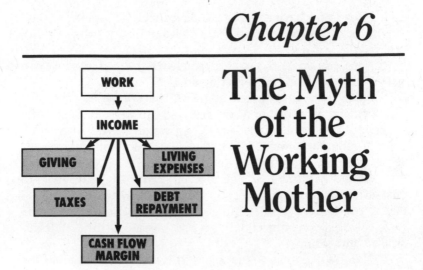

The Myth of the Working Mother

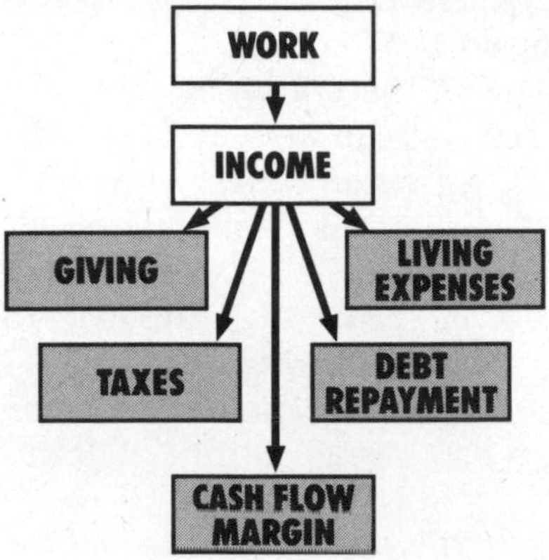

6:00 A.M.

"Good morning. It is 6:00 A.M. in the Windy City, and it is going to be a beautiful day with temperatures expected to reach . . ."

"Oh no, time to get up already?" muttered Sally as she rolled over.

"Yep," mumbled Bob almost inaudibly. "Time to get out there for another day."

"Are you going to take the children by the daycare today or do you want me to?" asked Sally.

"I don't care. Didn't you say last night that your boss wanted you to be there early?" inquired Bob.

"Yeah, he did want me to come in a little early, so if you don't mind dropping the kids off, that would really help out," said Sally.

6:45 A.M.

"Kids, hurry up and eat your breakfast. We've got to get going," shouted Bob as he gulped down another cup of coffee.

"Dad, do I have to go to the daycare center again?" asked Bobby as he played with his cereal. "I don't want to go. I don't feel well."

"Yes, you do, Son. Now hurry up with your cereal so we can get you upstairs and finish getting dressed."

"Mom, why do I have to go there?" questioned Bobby.

"Bobby, it is so your Mom and Dad can work and make the money that we need for the family," answered Sally.

"I still don't want to go there," stated Bobby matter-of-factly as he got up from the table.

About that time Laura chimed in, "Mom, do I have to go to that 'after school' place until you get off work again?"

"Yes, Laura. You need to go there until Mommy can come pick you up," exclaimed Sally as she hurried up the stairs to brush Laura's hair.

"I don't like to go to that place. It is so boring and all of the other kids pick on me, Mom."

"Quit complaining, Laura, and hurry up and finish getting dressed. We've got to leave immediately," shouted Sally as she grabbed her coat.

Why is it that half the mothers with children under one year of age go off to work? Why are there ten million preschool children in daycare centers? Why are there three million "latchkey" kids—children that go off to school with a key on a chain around their neck and let themselves in when they get home because no one else is there to let them in? Why will 66 percent of mothers with children under age five be employed by 1992?[1]

I recently watched a television special on latchkey kids. It saddened me as they shared the story of an eight-year-old boy who had to lock himself in the house for three hours until his mother got home from work. He not only had to go straight home from school, but he could not turn on the microwave, talk to his friends, or go outside and play. He could not do anything except watch television until his mom returned. I did not find it surprising that the child was reluctant to give his mother a hug and kiss (which she wanted) upon her arrival home.

As many problems as there are with daycare centers (illness, overcrowding, inadequate help, and so on), the greatest tragedy—

of which we have yet to see the total consequences—is that someone else (other than Mom) is nurturing and teaching millions of children their values. We saw earlier that it is the God-given role of the woman to nurture her children. Why do so many mothers abdicate this responsibility and work vocationally outside of the home? There are many reasons. We will look at those reasons and some of the potential consequences in the remainder of this chapter.

REASONS A MOTHER WORKS

The first and most common reason a mother works is the need for income—at least, a perceived need for income. A recent article in the *Atlanta Journal and Constitution* quoted several couples as saying that they *had* to have two incomes to make it. One mother commented, "I can't afford to stop working. It is not supplemental income anymore. I travel 110 miles a day, and I wouldn't do it if I didn't have to. If I didn't work, we wouldn't have clothes. We wouldn't have food."[2]

Though there are always exceptions, it is my strong conviction from observation that only in very rare cases does the married mother *have* to work out of necessity. Although the woman just quoted feels she cannot afford not to work, I wonder whether she really knows what she is contributing to the family unit's net income as a result of her work outside of the home. (Working outside of the home is defined as being gainfully employed in a vocation that takes her away from the home and from fulfilling her God-given job description.) I believe that the necessity for a mother to work in this way will be seen as a myth if her actual contribution to the bottom line of the family's income is correctly calculated and analyzed.

Let's take a close look at how much the wife's gross paycheck is actually contributing to the family unit's net spendable income. Chart 6.1 offers some interesting insights regarding the working mother's paycheck. As you will note, some expenses are fixed while others are variable. Income taxes are the greatest fixed expense, and I have also assumed the tithe to be fixed.

The income taxes are made up of the federal, state, and one that many forget—social security. The state income tax bracket will be anywhere from 0 to 15 percent depending upon what state you live in. The social security tax is 7.51 percent of the first

CHART 6.1
MOTHERS, WHAT'S YOUR PAYCHECK REALLY WORTH?

Salary	$10,000	$20,000	$30,000
Expenses			
Fixed			
Federal income tax[1]	1,500 (15%)	5,600 (28%)	8,400 (28%)
State income tax	600	1,200	1,800
Social Security tax	751	1,502	2,253
Tithe	1,000	2,000	3,000
Daycare credit[2]	(1,440)	(1,200)	(960)
Variable			
Transportation	600	600	600
Meals $2/day	480	480	480
Clothes	400	600	800
Hairdresser	300	400	500
Daycare (Cash flow)[3]	6,240	6,240	6,240
Miscellaneous[4]	600	600	600
Total Expenses	(11,031)	(18,022)	(23,513)
Contribution to Family Income	($1,031)	$1,978	$6,487

[1] 15% bracket if line 37 (taxable income on tax return) is less than $29,750; over $29,750 the bracket is 28%.

[2] Credit equal to 30% of $2,400/child at $10,000 salary level and scaled down to 20% of $2,400/child at $30,000. Limited to 2 children.

[3] 2 children at $65/week.

[4] Convenience foods, forfeited savings on thrift shopping, etc.

$48,000 of income if employed and 13.02 percent if self-employed on the same amount. The federal income tax rates are 15 percent on the first $29,750 of taxable income and 28 percent on every dollar over that up to $71,900. On taxable income dollars between $71,900 and $149,250 the rate is 33 percent.

Given these tax facts, the tax bite on the working mother's income is usually at least 33 percent and more than likely 40–45 percent depending on whether or not she is self-employed. In the two-income family (with both spouses working) the taxable income usually rises above the $29,750 level, which means that every dollar the wife earns is being taxed at the marginal rate of 28 percent for federal plus the applicable state and social security taxes.

In chart 6.1 I have assumed a 28 percent bracket when the salary is over $20,000 for the wife. I have also assumed two children in daycare costing approximately $65 a week each. This cost may vary from place to place and state to state, but it seems to be a realistic—and perhaps even conservative—average. I have also assumed a 10 percent tithe on the wife's additional income.

Given these assumptions, a best-case scenario would see discretionary funds rise at most 50 percent of the second income. This does not include any expenses other than fixed expenses.

The variable expenses listed will vary from family to family and situation to situation. Some families will not use daycare and instead use other family members to avoid that cost. For our illustration, the amounts given for the variable expenses (transportation, meals, clothes, hairdresser, and miscellaneous) are realistic estimates. (Of course, the mother mentioned earlier who drives 110 miles a day will have a significant car expense including gasoline, servicing, and upkeep.) Each family should determine exactly what actual expenses are in each area so as to correctly evaluate the value of the mother's outside work. (In my illustration, it would take $20,000 to break even!)

Many mothers assume that if they did not have the daycare expense, then they would be contributing much more to the family's income, but this is not really the case. In the $10,000/year example, if the mother did not have the daycare expense she would be $4,800 better off which would add a positive $3,769 (the daycare cost of $4,800 less the negative cash flow of $1,031) to the family's income. Although this is better than losing the $1,031, the question is, "Is the $3,769 worth it to allow somebody else to raise my posterity?"

Make sure you have really counted the cost (James 4:13–15) and know exactly what you are contributing to the total income before going to work outside of the home. Also make sure you clearly understand the concept of prosperity versus posterity. Given the fact that fixed expenses alone will in almost all cases take at least half of your income, you may want to rethink your decision. (The worksheet at the end of this chapter will help you figure what you are contributing.)

I feel the second reason many women work is to meet their emotional needs. If the husband is not encouraging his wife in her role as a homemaker and mother, it is very easy for her to desire to go back into the marketplace and work because there she gets positive reinforcement for the things she does. Work is a place where she is appreciated. Since it is so difficult for most men to communicate their appreciation to their wives and encourage them, it is no wonder wives go back to work. It is absolutely critical that we as husbands encourage our wives in their very significant role of homemaker. After all, they play a vital role in the development of a godly posterity. George Gilder points out that "women in the home are not performing some optional role that can be more efficiently fulfilled by the welfare state. Women in the home are not 'wasting' their human resources. The role of the mother is the paramount support of civilized human society. It is essential to the socialization of men and of children. The maternal love and nurture of small children is an asset that can be replaced, if at all, only at vastly greater cost. Such attention is crucial to raising children into healthy productive citizens."[3] In other words, "the hand that rocks the cradle rules the world."

A third reason a wife may go back to work after children come is because of the slothfulness of the husband. The mother in the *Atlanta Journal* article may really have had to drive 110 miles to work because her husband was not doing his job. In some cases the husband is lazy and is not fulfilling his God-given responsibility of "providing for the family" (1 Tim. 5:8). He may be slothful because the wife is not encouraging him in his role. It could be a chicken-and-egg dilemma. Who didn't encourage who to get the whole cycle started? Although there is no easy answer, it has been my observation that if the wife is content to live within the income the husband provides and is committed to him, he will be motivated to provide what is needed. There will then be no need to risk the role reversal that can occur if the wife goes back to work. As always, there are exceptions, but we are seeking harmony and God's best as it relates to the design of our marriages. The man is the provider and the woman the help-meet, nurturer, and companion.

The fourth reason the wife may go back to work is to get some money of her own. If a husband is very tight on his control of the cash and does not include his wife in the spending decisions and allow her to have some cash and be a part of the budget system, it is very easy for her to want to go to work to get some money of her own to do her own thing. It is important for the harmony of the marriage for any cash-flow system to include both husband and wife to avoid this motivation.

The fifth reason the wife may want to go to work is that she may have some materialistic expectations about lifestyle. She may have grown up feeling that she would live in a certain type of house and have a certain type of car and wear certain clothes. If the income generated by the husband is not enough to provide these things (though the amount provided meets their *needs*), she may not be content and may feel that she needs to go to work to have some of those things she "deserves." In most cases, however, she is not better off working from a straight dollar-and-cents perspective. She may *feel* she is better off, but in reality she is not. As a matter of fact, if she feels that way and spends accordingly, she can compound the problem.

Finally, a woman may work because society has told her that she could not possibly be fulfilled as "only" a homemaker. Society makes her feel "second class" if she does not work outside the home. Everywhere she turns she is bombarded with the world's concept of working (vocationally outside of the home) and told that she should reach her potential and be somebody. She went to college and she can't just throw all that training down the drain, can she? After all, she is more talented than many of the men she knows. Why shouldn't she work in the marketplace? Hasn't the homemaker of yesteryear been replaced by the new "career" woman? Isn't the concept of superwoman valid? Can't a woman do it all—wife, mother, career? For many years now, secular humanists and feminists have told us that a woman could do it all. But can she? Should she?

The issue, as we discussed briefly in chapter 2, is a difficult one at best. The woman's primary role is that of homemaker and mother. But what exactly does that mean? Is she confined to the home? What should she do with all that talent that she has? What should she do after she has fulfilled her primary responsibilities of companion, nurturer, and helpmate? What can she do after the children are grown up or at least in school? I feel we find some guidelines that may help in Prov. 31:10–31.

> An excellent wife, who can find? For her worth is far above jewels. The heart of her husband trusts in her, and he will have no lack of gain. She does him good and not evil all the days of her life. She looks for wool and flax, and works with her hands in delight. She is like merchant ships; she brings her food from afar. She rises also while it is still night, and gives food to her household, and portions to her maidens. She considers a field and buys it; from her earnings she plants a vineyard. She girds herself with strength, and makes her arms strong. She senses that her gain is good; her lamp does not go out at night. She stretches out her hands to the distaff, and her hands grasp the spindle. She extends her hand to the poor; and she stretches out her hands to the needy. She is not afraid of the snow for her household, for all her household are clothed with scarlet. She makes coverings for herself; her clothing is fine linen and purple. Her husband is known in the gates, when he sits among the elders of the land. She makes linen garments and sells *them,* and supplies belts to the tradesmen. Strength and dignity are her clothing, and she smiles at the future. She opens her mouth in wisdom, and the teaching of kindness is on her tongue. She looks well to the ways of her household, and does not eat the bread of idleness. Her children rise up and bless her; her husband *also,* and he praises her, *saying:* "Many daughters have done nobly, but you excel them all." Charm is deceitful and beauty is vain, *but* a woman who fears the LORD, she shall be praised. Give her the product of her hands, and let her works praise her in the gates.
>
> Prov. 31:10–31

It is obvious that the woman described in Proverbs 31 is very talented and gifted. We find a portrait of a woman, the wife of a man of rank, who is also a wise, careful, and godly matron in her domestic responsibilities within the home. She also has the ability to perform "marketplace vocational" functions (she considers a field and buys it and plants a vineyard: v. 16). The interesting insight, however, is that *she does not go into the marketplace to the exclusion of her home.* All the functions she performs are done in the context of her "primary responsibility"—the home. Scripture is clear in other places as well that the woman fulfills her role primarily by being in the home. Ps. 128:3 says, "Your wife shall be like a fruitful vine, within your house." When God inquired of

Abraham in Gen. 18:9, "Where is Sarah thy wife?" Abraham responded, "Behold, in the tent." Where else would she have been? That was the *best* place to fulfill her God-given role. The key guideline is that a woman should only be involved in activities (vocational or volunteer) outside the home if she is fulfilling her God-given role within the home—nuturing, companion, etc. How does a mother do that in today's society?

Some might argue that in Bible times society was agrarian, and as a result it was easier for the woman to be in the home and fulfill her role at the same time that she was involved vocationally. Her vocation consisted of helping with the farm work. Others might suggest that labor-saving devices at home have given today's mother much more time, and, therefore, it is unrealistic to expect her to stay in the home. Although the shift from an agrarian society to a highly automated, industrialized, urban society may make the implementation of the guidelines more difficult, the issue is still the same. *"Can a mother fulfill her God-given role excellently, the way God intended, and be involved outside the home either in volunteer work or vocationally?"*

I know of many women who are doing an excellent job of fulfilling their God-given job descriptions and who still have time to be involved in other activities. Many are involved in volunteer work, neighborhood outreaches, discipling other women, political awareness activities, and other nonpaying jobs. Others are involved in jobs that either save them money or make them money and still allow schedule flexibility so they can be home when they need to be.

There is one job that a mother can do that saves money and allows her to utilize the same education and skills she would normally take to the marketplace: home schooling. Home schooling your children (Deut. 6:6–7; Ps. 78:1–4; Prov. 6:20; Eph. 6:4) can provide a high-quality education for little cash outlay, not to mention strengthening family relationships. If you are interested in home schooling, I would recommend the work done by Raymond and Dorothy Moore, *Better Late Than Early—Homestyle Teaching* and *Home Grown Kids,* and Mary Pride, *The Big Book of Home Learning.*

A mother can also be involved vocationally and remain at home through home-based employment. An increasing number of corporations are utilizing home workers with computers for data entry, telemarketing, claims processing, and word processing. Home-based workers also include accountants, architects, stock brokers, computer programmers, and consultants.

Although there are many areas in which a woman can be involved, research shows that a woman with children cannot be wholeheartedly devoted to her career. A survey by Mark Clements Research, Inc., found that 84 percent of mothers employed full or part time agreed that they would rather be at home with their children.[4]

George Gilder notes, "Margaret Mead found that women are most contented not when they are granted 'influence, power, and wealth,' but when 'the female role of wife and mother is exalted.'"[5]

Whether you have young children, school-age children, or grown children, and whether you are employed in a paying vocation or involved in other activities, you need to have a clear understanding of the magnitude of the role and an appreciation for the awesome responsibility you have in the development of your posterity. Some mothers spend so much time playing tennis, going to luncheons, playing bridge, and being on committees that they are effectively not fulfilling their role even though they are not vocationally employed outside the home. Not only do you have tremendous input into the development and growth of your children, but you are responsible to meet the needs of your husband. Can you work outside of the home and do that? Only you can answer that question. If you do not fulfill your job-description, who will? Many serious consequences can result if you don't fulfill it. Let's look at some of those consequences now.

POTENTIAL CONSEQUENCES OF A WORKING MOTHER

There are several potentially devastating consequences to the harmony of the marriage if a mother works vocationally outside of the home. First, she may begin to usurp her husband's authority and position of leadership in the family. Regardless of the reason for her working, the wife who works can cause tremendous resentment and stress in her husband. As she conforms to the desires of her employer it is easy for her to become more and more independent of her husband. As she becomes more independent it is easy for her not to give the honor and respect to her husband that he so desperately needs. She can cause a subtle yet definite shift toward role reversal.

The more ambitious she is in her "outside of home" pursuits, the more stress she can put on the marriage. "*American Couples,* a work financed by the National Science Foundation and rated by the *New York Times* as the 'largest and most comprehensive study ever undertaken on the subject of couples' concluded that 'most men are not happy when their wives earn more than they do. When roles are reversed, with men doing the housework and women providing the income, couples become dreadfully unhappy. Women were found to be happier and relationships more stable when the male partners were ambitious and successful, but the husbands surveyed often resented ambitious wives.'"[6]

I think the greatest challenge facing couples in America today is the challenge to establish families in the biblical model—to get the roles right and model them for the next generation. We need families in which the men are men and provide, and in which the women are women and nurture and provide domestic support. If we think correctly about money, as we are learning in this book, we will find that this is still possible. We will find that the comment that "we *have* to have two incomes" is really not true. It is a matter of values and priorities. It is a matter of deciding whether we want God's best for our marriages or are content to settle for second best. If we do not model the correct roles, if we allow the roles to be reversed, we will reap the consequences in the next generation. We will have children growing up and marrying without having a clue about how a marriage is to look, and the moorings of the family will be loosened even more. (We see this happening now with an ever-increasing divorce rate.)

The obvious comeback by some wives is to say, "What if my husband isn't working hard?" I have two responses. First, make sure your attitude is correct and that you are encouraging him in his role and communicating that you are willing to live within his income. Secondly, instead of taking things into your own hands, give him the opportunity to provide. Remember that within each man is the God-given drive to provide. It *is* there. Wives, you can promote it or destroy it. The choice is yours.

Regarding the consequences of role reversal, consider the example of Sweden, highlighted in George Gilder's fine work, *Men and Marriage*. Sweden, over the past twenty-three years, has slowly destroyed the essential supports of the traditional nuclear family. Feminist pressure led to universal daycare and family-planning programs along with paternity leaves for fathers. Tax laws were changed to favor two-income households and penalize maternal care of preschool children. Families were penalized if children were not put into daycare. "The male role as principal provider was effectively abolished."[7]

The result in Sweden? "The marriage rate fell to the lowest level ever recorded in world demographic data." Forty percent of all births were illegitimate. The abortion rate soared. The economy foundered. Despite heavy taxes, the government deficit increased alarmingly.[8]

Gilder warns that "the United States is enacting many of the policies that brought sexual suicide to Sweden." Even though we can observe what has happened in Sweden, we do not seem to be learning. Clearly, "profound and irretrievable damage [is] inflicted by a policy of driving mothers of small children out of the home and into the work force."[9] The effect is the same whether they are driven out by government intervention or by their own choices based on inaccurate data and ignorance of biblical truths.

A second consequence is that a wife can fail to fulfill vital home functions and meet the needs of her husband. A recent *Atlanta Journal* article regarding stress on the American family stated, "Roger understands that his wife Betty works to help pay the children's college costs, but he still bristles when her job keeps her late and she's not at home to welcome him when he arrives."[10] Men need to have their needs met, and the best way for a mother and wife to do that is be "in the home" (Psalm 128). If a mother gives her time, energy, and talent to a job outside of the home it is very difficult for her to do her job in the home excellently. This is true, if for no other reason, because of lack of time.

Not only does your husband have needs that your being home can meet, but your children have needs as well. Most of their needs are unscheduled. The teachable moments can occur anytime. That is why children do not need just "quality time"; they need you "all of the time." If mom is not there she will miss the important times.

This "quality time" bit is a lie that has been propagated to excuse many who are neglecting their children and spouses.

It is difficult to be alert at home after a tough day at work because of the additional set of pressures and tensions, both physical and emotional, that the marketplace can produce. Also, it is easy to transfer these pressures to the spouse and children. This is not the way to promote harmony.

Third, and potentially most devastating, is the permanent impact on the children. More and more studies are showing how important it is to have a mother at home, especially with young children, for bonding and long-term security and stability in their character, not to mention the inculcation of values. Dr. Willard Gaylin, psychiatrist and president of Hastings Center, a New York research center that studies ethical issues in medicine and the social sciences, has deep misgivings about substitute child care. He believes children, especially infants, need a lot of nurturing. Although the mother is not the only one who can give the nurturing, she is the best one. He goes on to explain that in the first year, human contact is essential for the survival of the species. If a child is not taken care of psychologically as well as physiologically, its capacity for love, capacity for tenderness, affection, morality, and conscience can be destroyed by the way it is treated in those first few years.[11]

Robert Coles, noted research psychiatrist and Harvard Medical School professor, agrees. He says that because family life is such a low priority, lagging way behind self-indulgence and material gain, many children are experiencing an emotional deficit that is approaching tragic proportions. He is especially critical of the highly competitive middle-income families. In the suburbs, there are children with their own kind of deprivation and disadvantage, where parents offer fancy homes and every kind of gadget, six-figure incomes, and a trust fund—but no trust.

Coles goes on to say, "A child's trust must be accumulated over the years, by constantly nurturing and attending to his emotional needs. Not 15 minutes of 'quality time'—but hours and hours and days and days of it."[12] All in all, kids need someone who is crazy about them and communicates that to them.

Nothing could be more mistaken than the belief that a woman must work outside the home to contribute to the good of society.

Gilder notes that ". . . full-time work by mothers of small children comes at a serious twofold cost: first, the loss of the immeasurable social benefit of the mother's loving care for her child; second, the frequent loss of the husband's full-time concentration on his career. The yield of the mother's job to the economy or the man's help in the home only rarely can offset these costs of her employment. The society will pay the costs one way or another; not only through tremendous outlays for day care but also through economic declines, population loss, juvenile delinquency, crime, mental illness, alcoholism, addiction, and divorce."[13]

Who can estimate the worth of a godly mother? Dr. Leila Denmark, an eighty-eight-year-old Atlanta pediatrician, made this statement: "The hardest job on this earth, and the most important, is mothering. It's twenty-four hours for twenty-one years. When you take the baby out of the cradle and put it in a nursery (daycare), you've wrecked the nation. You can't tell them you love them and drop them off and drive off each day. One . . . patient who was going back to work so they could buy a new house said, 'Please check my baby for the nursery (daycare).' I said, 'Do you mean to tell me you're selling that baby for a house? Twenty years from now that house will be no good and your baby will be gone.'"[14]

Moms, do you really want your posterity to be raised by somebody else while you are off pursuing more money? May the facts at the conclusion of this chapter challenge your thinking in this area.

SUMMARY

In conclusion, it is critical for you as a couple to understand God's roles for you as husband and wife. You may be in a more nontraditional situation in your marriage (both working out of the home), but my challenge to you is that you prayerfully ask God to give you wisdom as you study His Word and study His principles to determine what His design for your marriage should be.

Before leaving this chapter, let's summarize our thoughts on income that we have discussed in the prior three chapters:

> God has wired in every man a drive to provide. To fulfill this drive, men work in the marketplace. They work in a vocation that meshes well with their strengths and temperament. The

vocation generates "x" amount of income. The family should live within that income. (We'll see how to do that in the next three chapters.) If the husband works longer hours to *try* to generate more income, or if the wife goes to work out of discontent or in an attempt to increase family income, there are many potentially devastating consequences that are usually not weighed properly. The key is for each spouse to encourage the other in their God-given roles for maximization of harmony in the marriage.

GAME PLAN

Challenge to Wives and Mothers

First, you should complete the worksheet at the conclusion of this chapter to determine how much you actually make by being involved vocationally in the marketplace. Second, prayerfully consider the following facts as you contemplate your decision about whether or not to work outside of the home. (These facts were taken from *Daycare: Hard Realities—Tough Choices,* a document created as the result of an extensive review of daycare literature, its supporting research, and a conference of international authorities on daycare and child development held February 1988 in Philadelphia.[15] Items (8) and (10), however, were taken from articles in the *Atlanta Journal and Constitution.*)

1. Money cannot buy well-adjusted kids. Make the kids a priority.
2. The emotional relationship (bond) established between the infant and mother, and among the infant, mother, and father, is the basis for the formation of personality, and for those qualities essentially human—the capacity to love and the exercise of conscience.
3. The child's primary task in its early psychological development is to attach to the mother and through her to the father and the group beyond.
4. The care of the child under three is *care of the developing personality,* not of the formed child-person. Trauma, conflict, and deprivation introduced during this period affect the ultimate fate of the personality in most profound and radical

ways. Personality disorder can be corrected or rectified only with the greatest expenditure of time, effort, love, and financial resources.

5. One of the central tasks of the earliest period of development is the creation of a stable inner world of values, morals, and ideals that reflects a healthy, caring experience of love in the context of a loving family.

6. Daycare research (specifically that which was organized and cited by Jay Belsky, psychologist on faculty of Penn State University) has begun to show a consistent pattern of problematic outcomes for infants who have been placed in nonmaternal and nonparental care before the first birthday and who have received twenty or more hours of daycare a week.

7. A child who has known shifting or unstable partnerships in the formative period of personality may have permanent impairment in his capacity to love, to learn, to judge, and to abide by the laws of human community. In effect, he has been deprived of his humanity.

8. A study released by University of Texas-Dallas researchers Deborah Lowe Vandell and Mary Anne Corasaniti reveals that children placed in nonmaternal care at an early age are less cooperative, less popular, and less confident than their peers. The study also noted that these children have poorer study skills and make lower grades.[16]

9. The mother is the primary love figure for the infant, and as such cannot be substituted for without introducing the risk of substantial disturbance.

10. Traditionally the family has been the source of support for the child. Look at what happens as this support crumbles:

    Suicide rate is up dramatically.

    The number of high-school dropouts is increasing.

> Drug and alcohol abuse by children is increasing, and the average age of the first use is dropping to eleven and twelve.[17]

The mother/child relationship is crucial. Research dramatizes the need to restore prestige to the role of motherhood and to help mothers to stay at home.

CHART 6.2

The following worksheet will help you determine how much the wife is netting from her gross paycheck if she's working or how much she would net if she went to work.

Line 37 on tax return (Taxable Income) _____ minus wife's salary _____ (2) equal _____ (1).

Wife's Salary (2)		_____	_____
Less:			
Fixed expenses			
Federal income tax 28,000 – 1 = _____*(3) × 15% =	_____		
Plus (2) – (3) × 28% if (3) is not greater than (2)	_____		
SIT = State tax rate × (2)	_____		
Social Security Tax = 7.52 × (2) if employed	_____		
or 13.02 × (2) if self employed	_____		
Tithe	_____		
Daycare credit †	_____		
Subtotal		_____	
Variable Expenses			
Transportation	_____		
Meals	_____		
Clothes	_____		
Hairdresser	_____		
Daycare	_____		
Misc.	_____		
Subtotal		_____	
Contribution to Family Income — Totals			=====

*If (3) is zero or less, use zero.

†Daycare Credit Formula: Credit equal to 30% of $2400 per child at $10,000 salary level and scaled down to 20% of $2400 per child at $30,000. Limited to 2 children.

Chapter 7

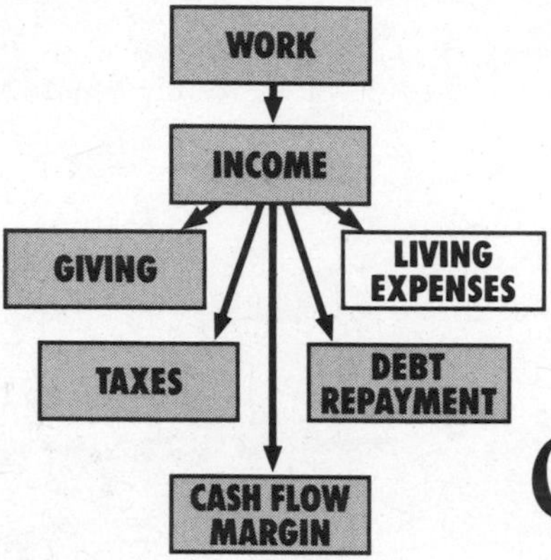

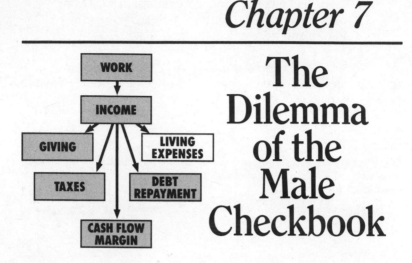

The Dilemma of the Male Checkbook

July 28, 1979. That date is a very special day in my life. It was on that day that Julie and I were married. Like most couples we went into marriage with our own expectations, our own unique bents, and our own individual way of doing things. We were both a little older than many newlyweds (I was twenty-six and Julie twenty-four) and therefore had each had a chance to be in the workplace and earn some money before being married. We each had a chance to handle money before marriage and with that came the expectations of how we would handle it in our marriage. As we drove away on our honeymoon on that wonderful Saturday night neither of us realized that how we handled our money *together* was something we should talk about or that we would have to talk about it soon.

I remember that shortly after returning from our honeymoon Julie and I had our first discussion about money. It started when I got ready to balance the checking account and looked at Julie's checkbook ledger. It seems that she had written in most of the transactions, but there were a few missing—you know, just check numbers with no dollar amounts out beside them. I asked her about it, and she commented that she had never really worried about it because she always knew there was enough in the account. That was okay while she was single, but now there were two of us using the account and I really felt we needed to have more control. After all, I had set up a nice budget with amounts in all the appropriate categories, and we needed to stay within the budget. All I had expected her to do was keep track of what she spent, and I would keep the running balance in my checkbook.

After getting the account balanced that month, I decided it would be wise if I kept closer tabs on what she was spending. Over the next few months I would ask Julie almost every day what she spent, so I could keep the balance correct. Although my motive was pure, little did I realize that every time I asked her what she spent I was driving a little wedge into our relationship. Why was that? What had happened? Why had we succumbed to the dilemma of the male checkbook?

This dilemma occurs when *the husband controls all of the finances with little or no input from the wife.* It is one of two extremes that can happen regarding the control of living expenses, that is, budgeting. We'll look at the other extreme in the next chapter. Both extremes create anxiety and frustration in the relationship, and both are a function of how the husband responds. His response to the family budgeting process is critical to family harmony. Let's look at the reasons why he might exert excessive control over the family finances with little involvement and input from the wife.

Reasons for the Dilemma

First, the dilemma could be caused because the husband knows how tight the budget is and wants to keep close reins on the funds so as not to blow the budget. The husband responds by always asking his wife how much she has spent. "Honey, did you write any checks today?" "What did you write them for?" "How much cash do you have?" "Did you use much cash today?"

This was what had happened to me. We had just moved from Kansas City to Atlanta so I could start in a new business. Because our income had been reduced, money was tight on a month-to-month basis. I also knew that it would cost more to buy a house in Atlanta than in Kansas City. Therefore, it was paramount that we stay within the strict budget that I had set up to save additional funds for a down payment. I wanted to keep a close watch on the funds to make sure we didn't go over. Thus, I asked Julie what she spent so I could make sure on almost a daily basis that we were not overspending. (My mistake—one most husbands make—was that I neglected to tell Julie why we were on the strict budget.)

In this scenario the husband will not only start to ask questions but will also find it very easy to become agitated if any of the money is spent in a way that he doesn't feel is necessary. If the purchases are necessary, he will tend to question the amount. More than likely, it will always seem to him that the wife has spent too much. Usually, as he becomes more and more frustrated, he will resort to stricter control, which results in going to the use of only *one* checkbook. If there is only one checkbook, he reasons, he has total control and she cannot mess up the budget. He keeps the checkbook and doles out cash. In doing this he has reduced the possibility of overspending by reducing her freedom. He has reduced her flexibility and increased her frustration.

The conflict this type of arrangement can cause in a marriage is obvious. The man, with his tendency toward bottom-line thinking, neglects to communicate the details of the budget. He feels she really doesn't need to know. His wife, however, wants to know the details and his thoughts to be motivated to stay on the budget and be his partner.

The second reason the husband could have for taking total control of the finances with no input from the wife is that she has done something with the finances that makes him uneasy and causes him to want to have closer control. She may have spent money without his knowledge in a way that upsets him. She may have spent money that caused an overdraft. Whatever has happened, it has caused him to become more possessive of the funds, to keep very detailed records, and to give her no freedom.

The third reason the husband may have for using financial restraints is his desire to keep his wife dependent on him. If he controls all of the money and determines when it is spent, then he feels she will always need him and be dependent on him. A man wants to have someone or something dependent on him. He will provide, lead, and protect that someone or something. If the wife does not submit to him, follow his lead, and build him up as the provider and protector, then he may use money to try to get her to respond in the way that he needs.

What are the wife's responses to the dilemma? Let's look at them now.

WIFE'S RESPONSE TO THE DILEMMA

The wife's first response is typically one of *apathy.* She really doesn't care. Money has become an area in her life that she would just as soon didn't exist. It is always negative. All she ever hears is, "Why did you spent that?" "Why do you need more money for that? Isn't what I gave you enough?" "I can't believe you can't make it on what I give you." She feels as if she is fighting an uphill battle. After all, she has had no input into the development of the budget. She doesn't know why she is supposed to spend what she spends. All she knows is that she has to keep reporting in to "him." She tries to give him input about different budget amounts, but he really isn't interested. He just wants her to stay within what he gives her, with no questions asked. So why should she care? The husband doesn't understand why she doesn't get on with the program. He wonders why she isn't excited about the budget. Since she doesn't seem to care he gets more frustrated and exerts more control. And the vicious cycle continues.

After a while the wife's second response is likely to surface. She begins to *spend frivolously.* This could be motivated by revenge, apathy, or lack of goals. Whichever may be the case, she will not take responsibility for her spending. Since she doesn't feel a part of the process and he won't talk to her about it, overspending is a good way to get his attention. She thinks that if she is always short on money he may listen to her and explain what is going on with the budget. This may get his attention if he is tuned in to her. More often than not, however, it just adds fuel to the fire. He begins to distrust her with the money. As his trust level falls he restricts her freedom even more, and the frustration and anxiety level in the marriage rises higher.

Much devastation can occur in the relationship when the "trust component" is questioned. As we said earlier, 80 percent of all divorces are a result of money problems. I am afraid that one of the reasons this is true is that money is a vehicle where trust can be questioned. Trust is defined as the assured reliance on the character, ability, strength, and truth of someone. We place confidence in those we trust. Too often, when money is the issue each spouse does not place confidence in the other. If the wife does anything with the money that causes the husband to doubt her judgment or to begin not to trust her, this doubt may carry over to other areas. "If I can't trust her with money, can I trust her with the kids?" "What about other men?" "Why is she doing this to me? Doesn't she know how hard I work for this money?" "Doesn't she respect me for all that I do to earn this money?"

This is also true about the men. If a man does not exhibit trustworthy behavior related to the finances, his wife could begin to distrust his decision making in other areas. "If I can't trust him with the money decisions, can I trust him with leading us as a family?" "If he's not making good decisions with the money, how is he doing at work?" It is so easy for mistrust to rear its ugly head in the financial area if mutual discussion and communication have not taken place regarding the budget. There needs to be a mutual commitment to the budgeting process.

If there is mutual commitment in the development of the budget amounts and agreement on who is responsible for what, then each spouse can be trusted by the other to make wise decisions in his or her area of responsibility. For example, Julie is responsible for a set allocation for groceries. We do not need to discuss whether she buys prime rib or ground chuck. I trust her to make those decisions in her area of responsibility. She also has a miscellaneous allocation. I trust her use of that money. If she wants to spend the entire amount at one time, that is her decision. If you start out not trusting your spouse (far too many marriages begin this way) or expecting that person to make bad decisions, your attitude will not promote the harmony and trust you want.

A marriage can only exist and flourish in an environment of mutual respect and trust. Each spouse must irrevocably and without a hint of doubt trust the other. Each spouse must think the best of the other. In the great love chapter in 1 Corinthians 13 we read in verse 7, "Love bears up under anything and everything that comes, is ever ready to believe the best of every person, its hopes are fadeless under all circumstances and it endures everything [without weakening]" (Amplified).

Another response the wife may have to the control the husband has over the finances is to begin to *hide money.* She figures that the only way she will ever have anything she wants is to try to squirrel some away. She doesn't dare ask her husband for any. She has tried that in the past, and it only upsets him. Of course, when she starts to hide money, she also has to become dishonest. When she tells him she is out of money and needs more, that is really not the case. She has begun to lie to him to get more money to do some things she wants. We just talked about trust, and there is no surer way to destroy trust than lying. And just think. This has all started because of *money!*

At times the wife will want to have some extra money to be able to buy the husband gifts. If she must ask for money from him specifically to buy something for him, that takes some of the fun out of it. I mention this here to indicate that there are some legitimate reasons a wife may want some money squirreled away. Don't make your wife lie to you to get extra money to buy something for you. You need to develop a budget system that will allow her to have some discretionary funds—funds that she can spend however she wants. We'll look at this type of system in chapter 9.

As the husband's control continues the wife may respond by wanting to go out and get a job (or keep a job she already has) so she can have her "own" money. Since she cannot have a say in "their" money, she will go back to work and get some of her own. There is no greater pressure than this issue of "his" and "her" money. There is no greater way to disrupt harmony and promote disunity in a marriage than to have "his" and "her" money. When a man and a woman marry, they become one. This is true about their finances as well.

It has not been uncommon for me to sit down with a couple and have them say that they have two separate accounts. When I ask them why, there is a long pause. Usually the answer is something to the effect that it makes it easier that way. What they mean to say is that having separate accounts is their way of avoiding the communication that should and must take place for maximum harmony in the marriage. I have never seen separate accounts solve any budget problems. As a matter of fact, it usually compounds the bookkeeping problems and contributes to overspending. There are some reasons to have separate accounts (to separate business from personal accounts, for instance, or to separate investment from personal accounts), but to avoid communication with your spouse is not one of them. Separate *checkbooks* on the same account are allowed for personal use—separate *accounts* are not.

Another negative aspect of having separate accounts is that it promotes a lack of trust. Working from the same account can promote trust and harmony. In today's culture it is not uncommon for a couple planning marriage to negotiate and sign a prenuptial agreement. This agreement says in effect "just in case things don't work out I want to make sure I keep all of my assets." Wow! What a way to start a marriage! Each party is saying up front "I don't really trust you. I really don't want you to have a part of what is mine. Let's just keep things separate." With that kind of a start there will most certainly be problems.

Men, any budget system you use should give your wife a feeling of contribution and freedom. She should feel that if she stays within the budget she is contributing to the family's positive financial position. She should be a part of the process and development of the system. You should build in some discretionary funds for her so she does not feel that she needs to go earn her "own" money. After all, as a couple, it is "your" money. There is no "his" or "hers" about it. It is "ours."

As the husband continues to control the money the wife may even become afraid to ask him for money. She would rather keep quiet than bring the subject up and create conflict. So communication in the marriage, instead of being enhanced, is being destroyed. The word *money* becomes taboo. It is not to be spoken; therefore, finances are never discussed.

Instead of a harmonious, united marriage we have a situation where the wife is apathetic and potentially deceitful. She wants her own job because she is afraid to ask her husband for money. The husband is oblivious to what she is thinking and feels that he must keep control of the finances. Husband and wife mistrust each other.

What steps can be taken to overcome the barrier of the male checkbook? Let's look at those steps now.

SOLVING THE DILEMMA

The first thing a husband must do to solve the dilemma of the male checkbook is to include the wife in the process of developing the budget amounts. Instead of being the husband's budget that the wife must fit into, the result of joint planning is truly "their" budget. They each feel an element of responsibility to make sure the budget is carried out. The goal of making the budget work is held by both parties. Instead of working against each other they are part of the same team.

Each year Julie and I sit down at the end of the year and discuss our budget. We review the year and make allocation decisions for the upcoming year. I share with her the overall financial plan for the upcoming year. This includes explaining what my income is likely to be and what the taxes will be on that income. I then get her input on budget issues, such as what she feels we should give to charity. I listen very carefully to her views on the budget amounts because she is in a far better position than I am to know what are realistic amounts for groceries, children's clothes, and the like.

I have observed that if the wife is involved in the process of determining the budget amounts, not only do you get more accurate amounts (who knows better what should be allocated to groceries—you or your wife?), but you have much greater motivation on the part of the wife to make the system work. In our situation one of the reasons Julie was frustrated was that she did not know why we were on a budget. Once I explained to her that we needed to be on a strict budget to save up additional funds because buying a house in Atlanta would be more expensive than in Kansas City, she was more than happy to do her part to the make the system work.

The second critical step in solving the problem is to have a plan of spending that includes an allocation system involving both spouses. An allocation system ensures that both spouses are part of the process and feel that they are contributing.

Without an allocation system managing your money would be like playing doubles tennis with only one partner having a racket. Can you imagine how helpless the partner with no racket must feel? That is how the wife feels (or the husband) if they do not have a part to play in making the budget (the plan) work. An allocation system that assigns responsibility for the budget is a must, we feel, for harmony in the marriage. (A detailed system is described in chapter 9.)

Another reason it is important to involve the wife in handling the finances is for *training*. In my business it is not uncommon to run across widows whose husbands had handled all the money, and they had not been involved at all. In many cases, they do not have a clue as to where the wills are, what insurance is in force, and (in some cases) even how many bank accounts they have. Part of our responsibility as men is to train our wives and involve them in the process so they will be aware of what is going on financially when something happens to us. (A very important thing is to establish some good relationships with people you trust that your wife can turn to at your death. I have found that this is one of the reasons many of our clients have established a relationship with my firm. By already having a relationship established with us, the husband has given the wife a place to turn for counsel when something happens to him.) Although I balance the checkbook, I periodically have Julie do it so she knows what is going on. It helps her know what bills we have, how much they are, and so forth. We also go over our wills, insurance, and investments.

As part of the training, the wife should have a checkbook, debit card, credit card, and cash just as the husband does. She should not be relegated to just being on the dole for cash. She should have all the same cash-flow resources as the husband.

As a continued solution to this dilemma the husband should evaluate his motive. Why does he want to handle the finances this way? Why does he want to have so much control? Has his wife done something in the past that has contributed to his desire for control? Does he perhaps have a particular reason not to trust her? It is the husband's responsibility to deal with these questions and talk with his wife about them. He is the head of the relationship, and he needs to make sure that money is not allowed to become a source of disunity in the marriage. After talking with her he may find that she didn't even know she had done anything to lose his confidence. And even if she did she will more than likely want to make it work out. Both should strive to make Ps. 34:3 a verse for their relationship. "O magnify the Lord with me, and let us exalt His name *together!*"

Lastly, the wife should make sure that she is respecting and honoring her husband. If the husband does not feel that he is in control or respected and honored, he may use money and the strict control of the budget to gain the position he needs. Eph. 5:33 says, "and let the wife see to it that she respect her husband." The wife must search her heart and make sure she is doing nothing that may drive her husband to clutch control. Even if her husband is not doing what she wants, she still needs to honor him.

The dilemma of the male checkbook can be devastating if allowed to go uncurtailed. May you be motivated to communicate and to implement a system that will not allow this to occur.

GAME PLAN

Sit down as husband and wife and talk through what should be allocated to each category on the following living expense summary sheet on pages 100–101. Then assign responsibility for each category to husband or wife. In chapter 9 we will see how to use this allocation sheet.

FAMILY BUDGET
YEAR: ______

		Paid Monthly	Paid Annually	Total Annual Amount
Housing:				
Mortgage/rent		$______	______	______
Insurance		______	______	______
Property taxes		______	______	______
Electricity]		______	______	______
Heating]		______	______	______
Water]		______	______	______
Sanitation		______	______	______
Telephone		______	______	______
Cleaning		______	______	______
Repairs and maintenance]		______	______	______
Supplies]	**Annual**	______	______	______
Improvements]		______	______	______
Furnishings		______	______	______
Total housing		______	______	______
Food		______	______	______
Clothing **(Annual)**		______	______	______
Transportation: (not paid by corp. if applicable)				
Insurance		______	______	______
Gas and oil		______	______	______
Maintenance and repairs **(Annual)**		______	______	______
Parking		______	______	______
Other		______	______	______
Total transportation		______	______	______
Entertainment and Recreation:				
Eating out]		______	______	______
Babysitters]		______	______	______
Magazines and newspapers]		______	______	______
Vacation **(Annual)**		______	______	______
Clubs and activities		______	______	______
Total entertainment and recreation		______	______	______

Medical Expenses:			
Insurance	____	____	____
Doctors	____	____	____
Dentists	____	____	____
Drugs	____	____	____
Other	____	____	____
Total medical **(Annual)**	____	____	____
Insurance:			
Life	____	____	____
Disability	____	____	____
Total insurance	____	____	____
Children:			
School lunches	____	____	____
Allowances	____	____	____
Tuition (grade & high school)	____	____	____
Tuition (college)	____	____	____
Lessons	____	____	____
Other	____	____	____
Other	____	____	____
Total children	____	____	____
Gifts:			
Christmas	____	____	____
Birthdays	____	____	____
Anniversary	____	____	____
Other	____	____	____
Total gifts **(Annual)**	____	____	____
Miscellaneous:			
Toiletries	____	____	____
Husband lunches and miscellaneous	____	____	____
Wife miscellaneous	____	____	____
Dry cleaning	____	____	____
Animals (license, food, veterinarian)	____	____	____
Beauty and barber	____	____	____
____________	____	____	____
____________	____	____	____
Total miscellaneous	____	____	____
Total living expenses	$____	$____	$____

Chapter 8

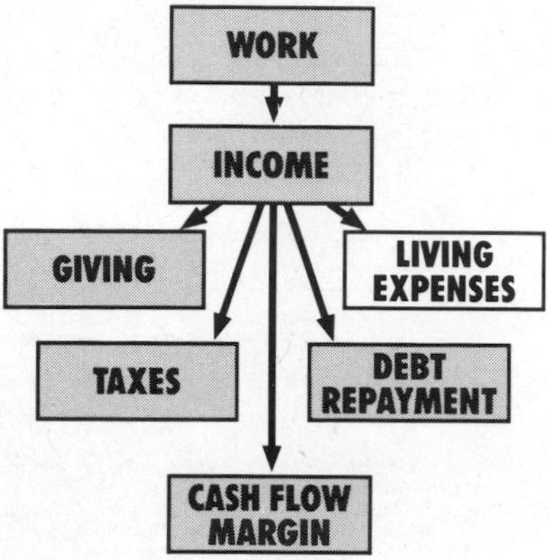

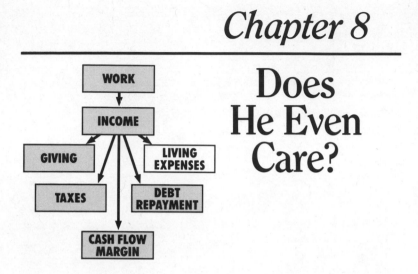

Does He Even Care?

It was almost six o'clock as Bob started home from work that Friday afternoon. He knew dinner was at 6:30, but he felt he still had time to stop by the automatic teller machine and get some cash for the weekend. He figured another $50 might come in handy—you just never knew what might come up. As he inserted his card into the machine he decided he might as well get $100 while he was there. After all, he had been wanting to buy Sally a gift. With the cash in his wallet he hurried toward home. It was 6:43. He knew he was late but he just had to have the cash for the weekend.

Sally had just glanced at the clock and had decided to go ahead and let the children eat, when Bob walked in. "I didn't know if you were going to make it," Sally said as she pulled the dinner from the oven. "Where have you been? I know you left the office almost an hour ago."

"I stopped by the ATM to get some cash for the weekend."

"You what!" exclaimed Sally in utter disbelief. "Don't you know that we are close to being overdrawn right now? How much did you get?"

"I only got $100," Bob muttered as he sat down to eat.

"That does it!" Sally cried through the tears. "I'm through trying to keep the books straight in this house. No matter what I do, you always seem to blow it. What's the use?"

In the last chapter we saw a situation where the husband exercises total control over the flow of money. More prevalent, perhaps, is Bob and Sally's situation. The husband is aloof and removed from the day-to-day spending decisions. He really doesn't know what is going on, nor does he seem to care. He compounds the problem by using the credit card excessively and the automatic teller machine (ATM) card for cash.

I'll never forget the night Julie and I were asked to meet with a young couple that, by their own admission, were "having trouble in their marriage due to their finances." As we listened to them the first thing that became obvious was that he was not involved at all in the process. As a matter of fact, the extent of his involvement in the budget process was to use his ATM card to get cash "whenever he needed it." It was up to her to try to keep the checkbook balanced. This had caused her to become resentful and angry at him. She knew the budget was tight, but when she tried to talk to him and get his input he wasn't interested. He also wasn't interested in asking her before he got his cash advances. As a result, she would find out about them when she got overdraft notices from the bank or was trying to balance the checkbook.

Why does this happen? Why would a husband not seem to care? Why would he leave the budgeting all up to the wife?

Reasons the Problem Occurs

The first reason the husband may abdicate his responsibility to give the family direction in the budget area is that he separates his personal financial responsibilities from his work responsibilities. He figures he is working hard for long hours to make the money and that is enough. Once he deposits it in the account, it is no longer his responsibility. He spends enough time dealing with money at work. She can worry about it once he gets it home. He has plenty to think about without being bothered with small issues like what amounts should be spent on gifts, groceries, and the like. She can do whatever she wants, as long as she doesn't overspend.

The second reason the husband may have for refusing to be involved in the budgeting process is that it may make him feel like a failure. If cash flow is tight and barely enough to cover living expenses and as a couple they are always living month to month, then each time he has to deal with making a priority decision about what bills to pay and not pay he is reminded of his income level. This may frustrate him and make him feel as though he is not providing enough. As a result, he withdraws from the situation and becomes uninvolved in the process. He lets her make the priority decisions on what to do—what bills to pay first and so on.

Along with the feeling of failure comes the desire to have "no accountability." It's as if he feels that if he is free from having to think about or deal with the budget, then he can escape from the reality of the responsibility. I have observed that this feeling of no accountability usually manifests itself in the misuse of credit cards and cash cards. I have met with more than one couple where the husband was continually getting cash at the ATM machine (like Bob above) or charging items and letting the wife worry about how to make the checkbook balance.

As a matter of fact, in all of the financial plans I have done, it is the exception when the wife is the one to "blow the budget." In most cases if there is a living-expense problem, it is the use of the credit card and excessive cash by the husband. This stands to reason because usually the wife wants security. She is typically secure if she knows they are spending within their means, and she, in most cases, won't spend more than is being made.

The third reason the husband may be removed from the budgeting process is that his temperament is such that he really doesn't like dealing with numbers. He transfers the number responsibility to the wife by having her pay the bills and balance the checkbook.

As I have worked with couples in the financial area I have found that the entrepreneurial, gregarious, outgoing man usually finds it difficult to want to be involved in the numbers. He naturally tends to be much more relational and less detailed. This makes it easier for him to transfer the number responsibility to his wife. This, of course, can result in much anxiety and frustration in the marriage relationship, especially if the wife does not like numbers or have the aptitude for them. As we will see later, it really doesn't matter who handles the day-to-day budgeting (although assigned accountability is best). What does matter is that the husband is shouldering the burden of responsibility for the living expenses regardless of who pays the bills. His temperament is not an excuse for abdicating his responsibility. He should take responsibility for the final decisions and not make his wife feel the responsibility.

Wife's Response to the Problem

If the husband is not involved at all in the budgeting process, the wife's first response is usually one of *anger, frustration,* and *fear.* She is angry at him for putting her in a position that in many cases is quite uncomfortable. She doesn't like to try to decide which bills to pay when. She doesn't like to deal with the creditors who call or to receive the overdraft notices from the bank, especially when the overdraft is caused by her husband's uncontrolled spending. Men, it is embarrassing to our wives to "cover" for us, and we need to be careful not to put them in that situation.

Paying bills can make the wife more acutely aware of how much money it takes to meet the family budget needs. In many cases, this awareness can threaten her security orientation, resulting in her worrying more and more. Money becomes her focus, and she becomes nervous. Her frustration mounts every time there is an overdraft or a bill that can't be paid. She questions whether there really is enough money. She begins to wonder if her husband is caring for her adequately.

Contrary to what you may think, the wife is not only frustrated if funds are tight but also if there are unlimited funds and the husband still has no input. With an unlimited budget she is insecure because there are no boundaries. She doesn't know what he is thinking. If she spends too much, will he become angry and frustrated with her? No input or communication from the husband gives her insecurity no matter how much money there is.

I was recently in a meeting where the client made an income well into six figures. His living expenses were in excess of $10,000 a month. The first thing the wife said to me in the meeting was "I just want to know what I am responsible for. I can live within any boundary but I just need to know what the boundary is. What the expectation is. I don't like not knowing . . . I don't like the nebulousness of it all."

Why do you think she felt this way? There is no freedom when there is no control. As with our children, there is insecurity when there is not a boundary. Most wives don't really care what the budget amount is; they just want to know what the boundaries are. They don't want to pick the boundaries by themselves. They want to have input, but they want the husband involved too. They are more secure if they know they are within some boundaries that he is comfortable with.

A second response of the wife is to become independent. Since she has the responsibility for handling the finances she begins to make more and more decisions without consulting him. Two things happen. First, they communicate less and less and tend to drift more and more apart and into their separate interests. He does not want to be bothered and likes to be left alone. She quits talking to him because he never gives any input anyway. Money can be either a tremendous promoter of communication or a destroyer of communication. In this case it gradually becomes a destroyer.

Second, she begins to lose respect for her husband. She loses respect for him because he is not giving her the leadership and direction she desires in the financial area. As her respect for him dwindles she finds it easier to belittle him and tear him down. She does not build him up and give him the encouragement he needs.

Isn't it awesome what a temporal nonessential functional medium of exchange (money) can do to a marriage? And it is so subtle. Money, which is no big deal, has become a huge deal as it relates to the marriage. What, then, are solutions to this problem of the husband's apathy? Let's look at them now.

SOLUTION TO THE PROBLEM

The first part of the solution is for the husband to understand his provision role. 1 Tim. 5:8 says, "But if anyone does not provide for his own, and especially for those of his household, he has denied the faith, and is worse than an unbeliever." This provision is not only "bringing home the bacon" but also having input into how the "bacon" is used.

Men, whether we make much or little, we still are the ones accountable before God as to how the funds are used. Even if your wife has an aptitude for numbers and likes to handle them, you are still responsible for the overall direction and input regarding your family's finances. Our wives are our help-meets in the process, but they are not the ones God will ask "How did you do with what I entrusted to you?" He will ask us men. (If you do not think this is your responsibility, men, reflect on God's questioning in the Garden of Eden. God came to the couple but "called for the man" [Gen. 3:9]. Adam and not Eve was responsible for the family unit, and as a result God asked Adam how they—not just Adam but both of them—did regarding the directions He had given them.) Men, we will be asked. How will you answer for your responsibility for the money entrusted to you?

The second part of the solution is to determine who will keep the books. Who will have the overall responsibility for balancing the checkbook and paying the bills? The husband may delegate all or part of the bookkeeping to his wife. She may like working with numbers and have desires and abilities in this area. He may be too busy to give it appropriate care. If he delegates the monthly books to his wife, he needs to make sure that he retains responsibility for priority decisions, especially when funds get tight. He also needs to be sure that he only delegates as much of this responsibility as his wife feels comfortable handling or desires to handle. If there are certain bills she does not desire to pay or that cause her anxiety, then the husband should take over the responsibility for paying those. Personally, Julie and I feel that assigned accountability is the best method for paying monthly bills. We also feel it is best if I balance the checkbook monthly because it maintains my focus and constantly sharpens my awareness of my responsibility before the Lord.

A third part of the solution is for men to realize that a money surplus does not negate the need for guidelines and communication. Even with plenty of cash, a husband's uninvolvement will cause his wife much frustration because of her need for guidelines and boundaries. Taking time to talk things through will ensure that husband and wife are on the same wavelength and in agreement on what the boundaries are. This will enhance their ability to be good stewards of what God has entrusted to them.

The final part of the solution is for the wife to build up her husband. One of the reasons for his lack of interest, as we saw, is that he feels he is a failure and not making enough money. As his wife, you need to make him feel good about what he makes. Let him know you are committed to live within his income and that you are on his team. You want him to know that you are content with the income level and that you need his leadership in the budgeting process.

In the next chapter we will look at a budgeting process that has worked for Julie and me and reduced this potentially volatile area of budgeting to an area of harmony. But first may I encourage you to put this book down for a minute and make a commitment to your spouse and to God that you will no longer allow budgeting money to be a problem in your marriage. Develop a system that will work for you to promote harmony and a unified trust in your marriage. Make a commitment to better fulfill the roles that God has assigned to you of "headship" and "help-meet." Money is temporal, while your marriage has eternal significance through your posterity. Don't allow money to damage your marriage.

GAME PLAN

In the following space write in your own words what Phil. 2:2–4 means to you as it relates to your finances. Then before the Lord consider making the commitment to promote harmony in your marriage.

> Make my joy complete by being of the same mind, maintaining the same love, united in spirit, intent on one purpose. Do nothing from selfishness or empty conceit, but with humility of mind let each of you regard one another as more important than himself; do not merely look out for your own personal interests, but also for the interests of others.
>
> Phil. 2:2–4

"Dear Lord. Today I commit before You to walk closely with You and trust You to make me sensitive to communicate with my spouse in this important area of budgeting. I realize that apart from You I can do nothing; therefore, I ask that You will fill me with Your power and enable me to put my spouse's interests before mine. May I recognize and understand my spouse's needs and be committed to promoting harmony in our relationship. Thank You, Lord, for Your patience with me. In Jesus' name."

____

____

Harmony: The just adaptation of parts to each other; things intended to form a connected whole; concord; concord or agreement on facts, views, sentiments, manners, interests, and the like; peace.

Chapter 9

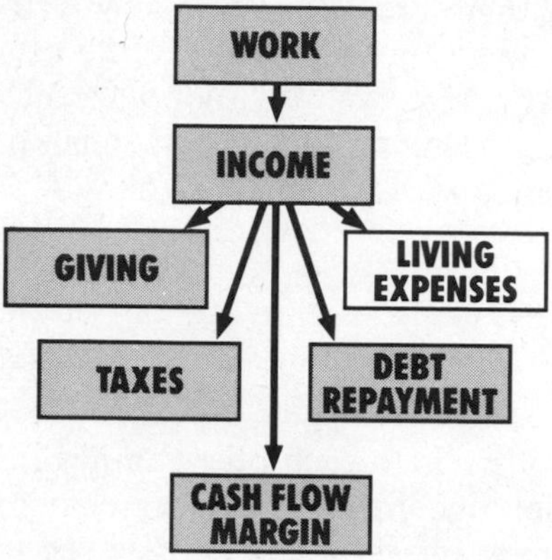

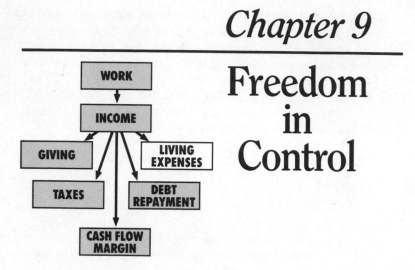

Freedom in Control

Since living expenses are typically the largest of the five outflows of money and the most discretionary and volatile, it is important to look carefully at them. Some system of control is the solution to most of the problems that occur in the living-expense area.

WHY HAVE A SYSTEM?

THE SQUEEZE HURTS

What is the squeeze? It is the financial pressure that plagues so many couples in America today. It is the "too much month left at the end of the money" syndrome. It is the never-ending pressure of living from paycheck to paycheck. It is the frustration of always seeming to have more options available for the money than money available. It is never having any cash.

Many would say that if they just had more income the squeeze would not be a problem. That is not true. Though the problem is perhaps more acute at the middle income level, being squeezed at any level is the norm. The reason for this is twofold: First, a lack of perspective regarding lifestyle causes us to want what we cannot afford; second, lack of a control system to tell us what we can afford leaves us with no trustworthy boundaries and guidelines. Without control couples will almost without exception spend more than they make regardless of their income level. If we spend more than we make, we will always be squeezed.

The key to financial contentment, peace, and harmony is to spend less than you make. This was made very clear to me by one of my professional clients who sent me a small placard stating "Happiness is a Positive Cash Flow." The note he enclosed revealed how much freedom he now enjoyed in his finances as a result of a control system that gave him a positive cash flow. This chapter will help you develop a control system so you can experience the happiness brought on by a positive cash flow and avoid the squeeze.

LOSS OF PERSPECTIVE LEADS TO THE SQUEEZE

Before looking at the problems caused by lack of control, let's examine the pressure brought upon us in this whole area of living expenses by loss of perspective. You might begin by asking several people, "What do you think of when you hear the word lifestyle?" If they are honest and like most people, they will mention houses, cars, and other expensive items. We have defined lifestyle to mean our level of materialism and how we look to others. Since we have lost perspective and failed to define lifestyle in biblical terms (i.e., lifestyle as a condition of the heart and of character rather than materialism), we have brought tremendous pressures on ourselves financially. The pressure comes from demanding a certain lifestyle to keep up with our friends that requires things that cost a lot of money, many times more than we can earn.

If this is not the case, then why does it seem so hard to make it today on two incomes (64 percent of working husbands have a wife that works too) when a few decades ago our parents made it on significantly less and typically on only one income? Why does the wife work outside the home because she feels she "has to," as we saw in chapter 6? Are today's dollars really worth that much less than they were twenty years ago? Has inflation been that devastating?

No. The problem is not inflation. In today's dollars the average breadwinner of today earns 30 percent more than his counterpart did in 1960. The families in the decades before the 1960s lived more simply. They were working class or at best fledgling middle class and were content with modest amenities. The problem lies in the fact that today couples feel that they deserve and want to be upper middle class (that class that came upon the American scene with John and Jacqueline Kennedy in the early 1960s). The middle class does not want to be the middle class.

They feel that the four-bedroom house with two cars in the garage and all the amenities one could imagine are a "need" they have. There is no way they could get along without it, is there? They do not want to live simply and live within their income. This faulty perspective on lifestyle has caused many mothers to work outside the home and many fathers to neglect their "posterity" to pursue "prosperity." This faulty perspective frequently causes a couple to be squeezed financially.

THE SQUEEZE IS A RESULT OF LACK OF CONTROL

Let's look now at what can happen to couples who do not control their living expenses. First, without control one's income need will always go up. In other words, we always tend to spend a little bit more than we earn. In chart 9.1 you will see the amount of money families can spend based on certain income levels. This chart was developed by starting with the income, calculating the taxes on that income given the assumptions noted, and then backing into the amount left to live on. If we elevate living expenses $5,211 ($34,440 – $29,229), our income need goes up $10,000 (from $40,000 to $50,000). Although taxes went up almost $4,000 (from $6,771 to $10,560), they are not the reason for the dramatic increase in income needed. The increase is primarily because of the increased living expenses, which are paid for with after-tax dollars.

Many people feel that taxes are the problem ("I would have more money to live on if my taxes weren't so high"). For example, if I make $50,000 my taxes will be $10,560 and I really can't do anything about that unless I spend less than $34,440. If I spend the entire $34,440 and pay my taxes, there is nothing left over from my $50,000 to invest or plan with; therefore, I cannot reduce my taxes. *Taxes are never the problem, but only a symptom of a living expense or debt problem or both.*

CHART 9.1
THE COST OF LIVING

Income needed for a family of four living in Georgia:

If you desire to spend $______ on living expenses . . .	$15,218	$22,287	$29,229	$34,440	$40,952	$49,816
And you want to give 10% to the Lord's work . . .	2,000	3,000	4,000	5,000	6,000	7,000
You will have to pay taxes of: Federal	780	1,710	2,767	5,456	7,444	10,580
FICA	1,502	2,253	3,004	3,604	3,604	3,604
State	500	750	1,000	1,500	2,000	3,500
TOTAL	$2,690	$4,713	$6,771	$10,560	$13,048	$17,684
And therefore your salary must equal . . .	$20,000	$30,000	$40,000	$50,000	$60,000	$75,000
Assumptions:						
(1) Assumed home payment/mo	$400	$550	$700	$800	$900	$1,000
(2) Total deductions include:						
Home interest	4,500	6,300	8,000	9,200	10,350	11,500
Contribution	2,000	3,000	4,000	5,000	6,000	7,000
Real estate tax and state tax	1,000	1,500	1,750	2,500	3,250	4,400

(3) Employed, not self-employed (assumed 1989 FICA rate of 7.51% on $48,000 base).

(4) Tax Reform Act of 1986 assumed for tax calculations.

The most universal problem contributing to the squeeze in which most American couples find themselves is the inability to get control of their finances early on in their marriages. They elevate their lifestyles beyond what their incomes will support and as a result take on debt. They are not committed to live within their income and develop a system to ensure that they do. Once they have overspent and gone into debt, let's see what happens.

If their income goes up $10,000, from $20,000 to $30,000, you would think they would have some breathing room. They don't, however, and find themselves still strapped. Why? Their discretionary income (living expense amount) has gone up $7,069 (the difference between $22,287 and $15,218) while their income has gone up $10,000. The problem is that they have been overspending a thousand a year for four to five years and now owe $4,000 to $5,000 in debt plus interest. So, instead of being able to enjoy the $10,000 increase in income, they are still strapped. And so it goes. The lack of control early on sentences them to a strapped lifestyle in the future. They must pay back the amounts overspent earlier with after-tax dollars. A vicious cycle traps those who are not committed to living within their income every step of the way during their lifetime. The choice is control for a lifetime or "trapped" for a lifetime.

Julie and I have some friends who bear this out vividly. They have been married twenty years and are still strapped financially, or, to hear the wife tell it, "behind the eight ball." They are there because never once in twenty years have they been content to live within the income they were making each year. They always were stretching and as a result to this day are strapped with no freedom. To stop the cycle will take some drastic steps, like selling the house and moving into a less expensive house or taking the kids out of private school. If they do that, in a couple years they'll have financial freedom. If not, the cycle will continue.

Referring to the chart, you will notice that the house payment is a large part of the living-expense outflow. It is usually true that this will be the biggest expense a couple will have in their budget. This is usually the area that will tend to push a couple to spend more than they make. You have undoubtedly had the real estate agent tell you, "Go ahead and stretch; it is a little high for you now, but you will get a raise and you'll be glad you did." But what if you do not get the raise? What if we do not have inflation?

In the area of housing it is so difficult to wait to have what we can afford. We want to look like mom and dad or "keep up with the Joneses." We want to look good. The house, if it causes you to spend more than you make, will eventually be a source of frustration and a squeeze to you. I have seen innumerable couples with tremendous stress in their marriages because they stretched to get their "dream house." The dream has turned into a nightmare. The husband works long hours; the wife puts the children in daycare so she can work long hours too—all for the mortgage. They are not even there to enjoy the house. What about their children? The children couldn't care less. All they want is mom and dad around to love them. Stop and think about it. Do you really think your five year old (or fourteen year old for that matter) really cares how big the house is?

Chart 9.2 may be a source of encouragement to you. This chart illustrates the cost of renting versus buying. Contrary to what one may think, renting is not always a bad situation. Let's

CHART 9.2
HOUSING
Illustration: Buying vs. Renting

	Rent	Buy #1	Buy #2	Buy #3	
Cost of Home:	-0-	$65,000	$86,000	$110,000	____
Expenses:					
Mortgage payment	-0-	6,000	8,400	11,000	____
Rent payment	6,000	-0-	-0-	-0-	____
Utilities	600	1,200	1,500	1,800	____
Taxes	-0-	800	900	1,000	____
Insurance	350	500	600	700	____
Repairs/maintenance	-0-	400	500	600	____
Closing costs	0	1,000	1,250	1,500	____
Tax savings	-0-	(1,905)	(2,752)	(3,465)	____
Total annual outflow	($6,950)	($7,995)	($10,398)	($13,135)	____
Gain:					
Appreciation	-0-	$6,500	$8,600	$11,000	____
Interest income (net of tax)	$536	-0-	-0-	-0-	-0-
Effect on net worth	(6,414)	(1,495)	(1,793)	(2,135)	
Effect on net worth with 7% commission on sale		(6,500)	(8,420)	(10,605)	

Assumptions:
Facts: $10,000 down; 10.5% interest on 30-year mortgage; 33% tax bracket (28% Fed and 5% state).
Appreciation is calculated at 10% of sales price.
Interest income is calculated at 8%.
Assume 7% realtor fee if sold.

look at the facts. If you rent, your cash outlay is $6,950 and you keep your $10,000 of cash that you had for a down payment. You will earn $800 in interest on the $10,000 and after paying taxes on the earnings have income of $536. Therefore, the total cost to you if you rent is $6,414.

If you take the $10,000 and make a down payment on a house, you see that your cash outlay is greater on an annual basis—anywhere from $7,995 to $13,135. This takes into account the deductibility of the real estate taxes and the interest on the mortgage. (This is the line noted "tax savings.") On a straight annual cash-flow comparison it is less expensive to rent than buy. The positive side of buying, of course, is the potential appreciation on the house. If we assume 10 percent appreciation, we see that the effect on your overall situation is improved if the house can be sold with no real estate commission. However, if the house is sold after one year with a 7 percent real estate commission, you would have still been better off renting ($6,414 compared to $6,500 to $10,605).

This analysis points out an interesting fact to consider when trying to decide between buying and renting. In most cases, *you are better off to buy only if you can live in a house for at least two years.* This assumes a sale through a realtor and no special appreciation factors such as buying below market, foreclosure, or above inflation appreciation. *The higher the initial cost of the house, the longer you must live in it to make it cost-effective over renting.* (The annual cost of house #3 is more than double the cost of renting on an annual basis—$6,414 versus $13,135.) If the appreciation of the house is less than the 10 percent assumed, it would be necessary to live in the home longer to make it pay from a net worth standpoint over renting. Of course, the opposite is also true. If we have runaway inflation and the house appreciates more than 10 percent, it will become less costly than renting.

Therefore, in considering whether to buy a house you should take into account your occupation and your lifestyle needs and goals. From a strictly financial viewpoint, as our analysis has shown, you will be better off renting rather than buying if your vocation is one that requires relocation every two to three years. If you are uncertain about when vocational changes may occur or if they are likely to occur more infrequently than every two or three years, then buying will make more financial sense to you than renting.

Vocational and financial considerations aside, there may be other reasons for buying as opposed to renting. Even if you may live in a home for only a short time, the responsibilities and satisfaction that can come from owning rather than renting may override your potential financial costs. You may find that your desire to do domestic home duties—such as mowing the yard, decorating, and so on—is only met through home ownership, and you are willing to incur additional costs.

The key to this decision is your evaluating the purchase of a home with a proper perspective on the real cost, both financially and as they relate to your lifestyle and marital harmony, all the while realizing that the underlying need is to live within your income. Stretching budgets may make sense to the world, but my observation is that the potential risk to the marriage is not worth it. If you buy when you cannot afford to buy (i.e., you stretch beyond your income and deplete all emergency funds), then the home, rather than becoming a place of security and a place to exercise your domestic talents, becomes a burden. If marital harmony is what you want, do not allow a house to disrupt it. Buying a home may be the American dream, but use wisdom in deciding whether it is best for you at your current station in life.

The second largest outgo that can cause a couple to overspend is the purchase of an automobile. Julie and I bought two new automobiles this year. We were able to do that because we drove our existing ones for eleven years and saved for the new ones. In going back and analyzing it, we determined that the impact on our budget during those eleven years was $91.58 a month. In other words, we had to save that much each month to be able to buy the new automobiles. What was our alternative? Our alternative was to have a car payment of $250 to $400 a month. See the difference? Our living expenses were $158.42 to $308.54 less per month by saving to buy versus buying now and paying later—using debt. You may say that you could deduct the interest on the car. Under the new tax law you cannot deduct it. Even if you could, you would still be out of pocket more than the amount you had to save.

My challenge in this area is for you to drive an older car and save the $250 to $400 a month for two to three years. In three years at $250 a month you would have $9,000 saved up to buy a new vehicle. You could pay cash and then start the process all over again. It will always be cheaper to save and pay cash than to finance.

In addition to the two major expenses mentioned—house and car—a couple must also control the use of the credit card. They must plan to spend rather than responding on the spur of the moment. We'll look at how to do this a little later in this chapter.

A final problem that contributes to the squeeze is the problem of assuming that more income is the answer. Once a couple concludes this, they typically send the wife back to work. As we saw in chapter 6, it is a myth that the working mother contributes much to the bottom-line income of the family. At most a working mother can contribute only 50 percent of her gross pay to the family budget. Most people do not believe this, however, and then they compound the problem by spending the gross income of the wife. If the gross income is spent, then when it comes time to pay taxes they must borrow, and the debt cycle starts all over again. At best a couple should only spend the net of the wife's income (gross income less taxes and additional expenses).

Living expenses are in most cases the largest outflow any of us will have. If they are not controlled, we will always be squeezed and have no freedom in our finances.

As I have worked with couples at all income levels I have observed that those who control expenses typically experience less stress related to finances than those who ignore the control factor and are driven to try to make more income. There is freedom in control. Let's look at why this is so.

CONTROL BRINGS FREEDOM

A control system allows you *to achieve freedom in your finances.* You are free because you have guidelines and boundaries that—when adhered to—will help you to live within your income. A system also helps you not to succumb to the lure and pressures of the world found in 1 John 2:15–16; namely, the lust of the flesh and the lust of the eyes. You are able to resist the temptations to overspend because you know what you have to spend and where you are on the spending plan.

Being committed to having a system of control and to living within your income is not easy in today's society. Peer pressure is severe. Commitment to a control system may mean that you live in a smaller house or drive an older car than your peers, but in the long run you will be better off. If you are content with where God has put you and will resist trying to look good, you will have less potential for conflict and more harmony in your marriage. I am convinced that while many couples appear to have financial freedom (a large house, nice cars, dream vacations, etc.), they really have no freedom at all. Their appearance is a mirage. These families can afford the monthly payments behind everything they own and do (usually with two incomes and no emergencies or problems), but if anything out of the ordinary happens (increased expenses or decreased income) that causes an aberration in cash flow, they are in trouble. That is not freedom.

Budgeting, which used to be an area of constant discussion, has become a non-issue in our marriage. Julie and I have agreed on the boundaries and the guidelines for our living expenses, and the system ensures that we stay within them. We know the rewards of adherence—not only new cars, as mentioned, but goals met and harmony achieved. We have been freed up to spend time cultivating our marriage rather than arguing about every little spending amount. Control has indeed given us freedom.

CONTROL PROMOTES HARMONY

A system of control also *promotes harmony and teamwork* within the marriage. As Julie and I develop our system and agree on the amounts in the various living-expense categorics we must communicate positively. Since we have different backgrounds and different temperaments, communication is critical to ensure that we are on the same side of the net, playing together rather than against each other. Money will either be a source of communication enhancement in your marriage or a source of conflict. The choice is yours. We have concluded that our marriage is important and that money is a tool. We use the tool to promote what is important—the marriage.

Having a control system also promotes a positive attitude within the family. It removes a lot of the potential financial stress that can occur if one is overspending. As the heart of the home, if the wife feels that everything is under control, that attitude generally permeates the entire family. If she is secure and knows that the financial end of things is taken care of and in order, everything is okay on the home front. However, if she senses that everything is out of control, her subsequent anxiety will tend to permeate the family atmosphere.

BARRIERS TO HAVING A SYSTEM

The first barrier to the development of a system is a poor understanding of why one is needed. Hopefully, the thoughts just shared will be ample evidence (a) that a system is crucial to ensure that the family lives within the husband's income and (b) that living within his income is important for the attainment of harmony and unity in the marriage.

The second barrier is not taking time to set up the system and sticking with it to work out the kinks. Once Julie and I decided to develop a "plan of spending," it took us the better part of two years to refine it and adapt it to its current state.

The reason it takes so long to make the system work is that it takes time to adjust the budget amounts to realistic amounts. It also takes time to adapt your spending habits to fit the system. We really didn't know what we were spending on various items like gifts, clothes, etc., so it took a while to come up with dollar amounts that were realistic and workable within our income level. I remember when we started I told Julie to put down $150 a month for groceries. Well, needless to say, within a couple of months we had determined a more realistic amount. Over time you will refine other items such as household supplies, auto repair, vacations, and medical expenses. You will also learn how to assign responsibilities.

It is my observation that a couple will only be motivated to discipline themselves to make a system work if they are really convinced it will make a difference. *A system of control is essential to promote harmony in your marriage.* It is essential because it promotes communication and encourages both husband and wife to fit into their God-given roles. If you are not disciplined, then you really don't have a discipline problem. You have a problem being convinced that your marriage is worth it.

The third barrier to a system is developing a system that is too complicated. Most people I know that try to go on a budget attempt to keep track of every dime they spend. If they buy a soft drink, they had better not forget to write it down or the entire system fails. Although writing everything down to get an idea of realistic amounts for the budget categories is a good idea initially, over time it becomes an unrealistic goal. As we know, a goal that is unattainable or unrealistic usually goes by the wayside and is not pursued at all. Therefore, we need to have realistic goals that work in a practical way. It is impractical to assume that we would *always* write everything down.

Some systems are not only too complicated, they are impractical because they do not make use of the cash-flow tools that are a part of our society. For instance, it is practical and convenient to use checks, debit cards, cash, and credit cards in our society. A system should utilize several of these tools. I have found that it is easier to use a credit card when buying an item by mail order or through a catalog than it is to use a check. The reason for this is that it is quicker and in some cases less of a hassle to get a refund or exchange with the credit card than with cash or a check. Therefore, if a system is to work long-term, it needs to utilize the tools of our society.

The fourth and last barrier to the system may be the husband's feeling of failure. Any system may be an all-too-constant reminder of his income level. I remember a friend of mine who was continually being urged by his wife to get together with me to set up a budget system. For over two years he dragged his feet and did not want to meet with me. Finally, he relented, and they are now on a system that is working for them and contributing to harmony in their marriage. I am confident that he, like many men, felt that money was an area that he should know about and shouldn't need help in. He also was probably a little uncomfortable with his income level as a reflection on his success, and he really didn't want anyone else to know what it was. It seems to be universal that men are hesitant to ask for help in the financial area.

A wife can do much to counteract such feelings of failure by encouraging her husband and letting him know that she is content with his income. This attitude will go a long way in motivating him to be willing to develop a system of control. Budgeting probably doesn't come naturally to him. By design he is not as detailed and also doesn't need the security a system can bring. He can live on the ragged edge. A wife's encouragement, however, will help a lot to overcome this barrier.

GENERAL COMPONENTS OF A SYSTEM

Regardless of the specifics of the system you finally settle on, there are four absolutely necessary essentials. Your system may have more bells and whistles than this, but at a minimum it must have these components:

1. *An allocation must be made into all possible budget categories.* If you will refer to the living-expense sheet you completed at the end of chapter 7, you will notice that there are both monthly expenses and nonmonthly (quarterly, semi-annual, and annual—we'll refer to all nonmonthly expenses as "annual" from this point on in our discussion). You must put an amount in every category in which expenditures may occur during the year. The normal response at this point is to say, "but I don't know what auto repair will be." Granted, you don't, but you must allocate something. If you do not, you will not know whether your budgeted living expenses fit within your income. The allocation into a category like this also gives you an idea of what could be spent for auto repair without blowing the budget. I have also found that allocation by category makes it possible for you to see what God does in your situation during the year. Without a base amount to work against you can't pinpoint what happened during the year. Several years ago Julie and I had some major medical expenses that caused us to go over our allocated amounts. But when we got to the end of the year, we realized that we had not had any major car repair. The surplus left in that category offset the excess in the medical category. Without the allocations we might have missed seeing what God had done for us.

2. *The responsibility for each category must be assigned to either the husband or the wife.* This is called "assigned responsibility." It defines who is responsible for each of the individual items within the budget. Even though the husband has the overall responsibility to make sure there is enough income and to make any priority allocations of cash if a squeeze occurs, it is practical to assign each item to the spouse who is most likely to be dealing with that expense. For example, it is easier for Julie to get the groceries than for me. It is also more prudent for her to handle medical expenses and children's costs. On the other hand, we both need an allocation for gasoline and for cash. As indicated earlier, all items could be assigned to one spouse or the other. However, at a bare

minimum each spouse will need an allocation for cash. The key thing is that the assignment makes sense from a practical operations standpoint and from a temperament standpoint.

3. The total living expense amount should fit into your overall financial situation. To do this, *you subtract projected taxes and giving based on your projected income to come up with an amount that is the maximum amount available for living expenses.* (See chart 9.3.) (I have assumed for the sake of our diagram and discussion that debt is a part of the living expenses.) You are free to allocate to living expenses as much as is available. What is not allocated will be savings. Because unexpected emergencies are part of life, living expenses should not be set at the maximum figure. There should be an amount left over for savings as a cushion.

This exercise of determining taxes and giving to come up with a maximum living expense amount is critical. You cannot just skip this step. No system will work if you put what you want into living expenses with no thought for taxes and giving. This, however, is what most couples do. They spend first and worry about taxes and giving later. In order to determine your taxes you may need to consult your accountant or pick up some of the financial planning helps that are available. *Master Your Money,* by Ron Blue, is an excellent book on how to set up a financial plan. Andrew Tobias' software package, "Managing Your Money," is an excellent system to project taxes and will even assist you in your cash-flow control.

4. *Your system should use the cash-flow control tools available,* choosing those which are appropriate for your own method of operation. If you want to pay cash for everything and don't mind having a lot of cash lying around, use cash. (The envelope system —depositing cash in envelopes the first of each month for the

CHART 9.3

	Income	______
Step 1:	Taxes	(______)
Step 2:	Giving	(______)
Step 3:	Maximum amount left for living expenses and debt payments.	______

various budget categories—may still work for some people. My experience is, however, that practically speaking an all-cash system is difficult to make work in today's society.) If you like to use a credit card for major purchases of clothes, gasoline, and gifts, then build that into your system. As I share the system that has worked for Julie and me I will give you some guidelines on the use of the various tools. It is never the tool that causes the problem but rather the misuse of the tool. Credit cards are not the cause of overspending. Lack of a plan and control is the cause.

A SYSTEM THAT WORKS!

So how do Julie and I do it? The first thing I do is sit down before the end of the year and project my income. Based on my projected income and given such deductions as home mortgage interest, charitable giving, and real estate taxes, I calculate my taxes. Once my taxes are projected, I make sure my employer withholds enough so I won't owe any taxes or be getting a large refund.

My next step is to sit down with Julie. Together we go over allocations for the various categories. I find out if she needs to have more for groceries or clothes. I get her input on what should be in the children's allocation. I also review the year just concluding and see if there are any budget categories that have increased. For instance, since I have some term insurance, it goes up a little bit each year, so I need to add more to that category. Also my property taxes have gone up, and so has my auto insurance since I bought different cars. All of these things are factored into the budget. Julie and I also discuss whether there are any categories that should be assigned differently. Should she take over paying the utilities to free me up? Do I need a large miscellaneous allocation for lunches? The assignments are reviewed and agreed upon.

After coming up with the allocated amounts and the assignment adjustments, I make sure the amounts allocated are within the amount I have available for living expenses.

Chart 9.4 is a sample budget sheet reflecting the implementation of these steps. This budget is built on a projected income of $40,000. Referring to the living expense line in chart 9.1 again, you will see that the maximum available to spend at that income level is $29,229. This budget shows that living expenses will be $27,480. This is acceptable and leaves a margin (savings) for emergency of $1,749 or approximately $150 a month.

CHART 9.4
FAMILY BUDGET
YEAR: ______

	Paid Monthly	Paid Annually	Total Annual Amount
Housing:			
Mortgage/rent	$ 700		8,400
Insurance	40		480
Property taxes	60		720
Electricity			
Heating	200		2,400
Water			
Sanitation			
Telephone			
Cleaning			
Repairs and maintenance			
Supplies **Annual**			1,000
Improvements			
Furnishings			
Total housing			13,000
Food	400		4,800
Clothing (**Annual**)			1,000
Transportation: (not paid by corp. if applicable)			
Insurance	50		600
Gas and oil	100		1,200
Maintenance and repairs (**Annual**)			1,000
Parking			
Other			
Total transportation			2,800
Entertainment and Recreation:			
Eating out			
Babysitters	50		600
Magazines and newspapers			
Vacation (**Annual**)			1,000
Clubs and activities			
Total entertainment and recreation			1,600

CHART 9.4 *(Continued)*

Medical Expenses:			
Insurance			
Doctors			
Dentists			1,000
Drugs			
Other			
Total medical (**Annual**)			1,000
Insurance:			
Life	40		480
Disability			
Total insurance			480
Children:			
School lunches			
Allowances			
Tuition (grade & high school)			
Tuition (college)	50		600
Lessons			
Other			
Other			
Total children			600
Gifts:			
Christmas			
Birthdays			
Anniversary			
Other			
Total gifts (**Annual**)			1,000
Miscellaneous:			
Toiletries			
Husband lunches and miscellaneous			
Wife miscellaneous	100		1,200
Dry cleaning			
Animals (license, food, veterinarian)			
Beauty and barber			
________________			
________________			
Total miscellaneous			1,200
Total living expenses	$	$	$

Once the allocations and assignments are complete and fit within the overall plan, it is time to implement the budget. The system that we have found to work utilizes four check*books* on *one account.* Notice the distinction. We are dealing with one account and four checkbooks, not four different accounts. This distinction is critical because we do not want "his" and "her" money. Husbands and wives should have checkbooks on the same joint account in order to promote harmony. Charts 9.5 and 9.6 illustrate what happens.

I deposit all income into the "deposit checkbook." Julie has a living-expense checkbook and so do I. From the deposit checkbook I will transfer (debit) to both of the living-expense checkbooks the amount allocated for the assigned categories. In this case it is $1,240 a month to me and $550 a month to Julie. An obvious question is, "What if you do not have the full monthly amount to allocate all at once?" The obvious answer is to allocate what you can. If you get paid weekly, make weekly allocations. If you get paid twice a month, allocate twice a month. Let me say, however, that this system works best (as does any system) if you have a savings amount in the deposit checkbook to start the year with. If you have $2,000 to $3,000 in the account on January 1, you can make all of the transfers on the first of each month rather than paycheck by paycheck. (In our illustration I use a savings amount of $3,000.)

It is next to impossible to make any system work if you do not first accumulate a small amount of savings to "prime the pump." No system will work on a paycheck-to-paycheck basis because there are too many emergencies that can mess things up. Recognizing this should be the greatest motivation to spend less than you make and accumulate some savings. Once you have savings you can make any system work. I have not seen anyone get out from under the squeeze of living paycheck to paycheck without first having a savings amount.

This becomes obvious when I determine my bimonthly income. If I am having my taxes withheld, my take-home pay on a bimonthly basis is $1,384.54. Referring to chart 9.6, you will see that this amount is deposited into the "deposit checkbook." With that amount by itself (with no savings) I cannot deposit in the living expense books the total amounts for the month. However, if I have the savings of $2,000 ($1,000 is allocated to the "annual

CHART 9.5

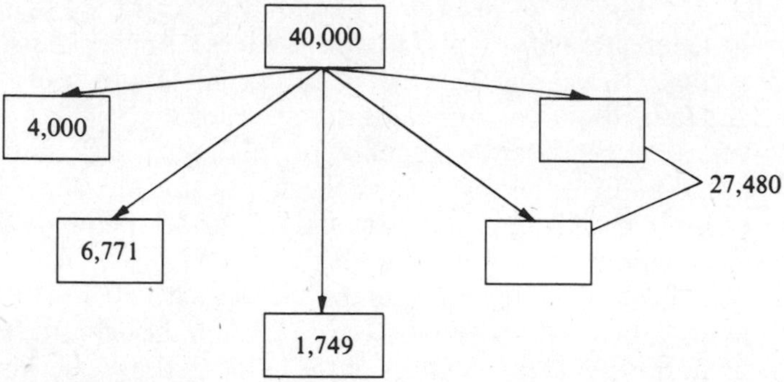
40,000
4,000
6,771
1,749
27,480

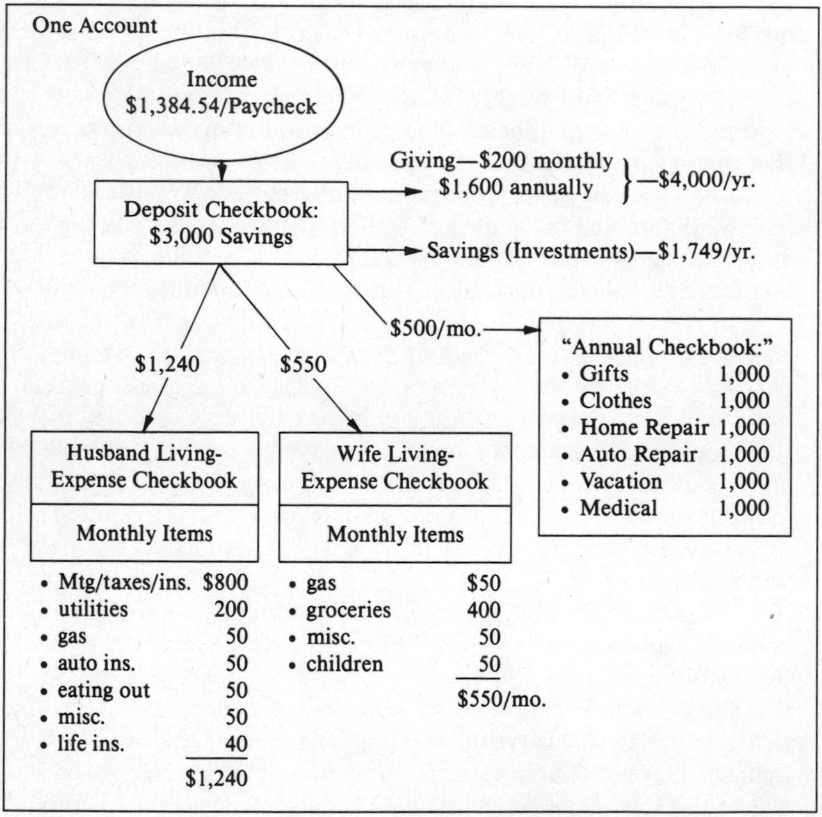
One Account
Income
$1,384.54/Paycheck
Deposit Checkbook:
$3,000 Savings
Giving—$200 monthly
$1,600 annually
—$4,000/yr.
Savings (Investments)—$1,749/yr.
$500/mo.
"Annual Checkbook:"
• Gifts 1,000
• Clothes 1,000
• Home Repair 1,000
• Auto Repair 1,000
• Vacation 1,000
• Medical 1,000
$1,240
$550
Husband Living-Expense Checkbook
Monthly Items
• Mtg/taxes/ins. $800
• utilities 200
• gas 50
• auto ins. 50
• eating out 50
• misc. 50
• life ins. 40
$1,240
Wife Living-Expense Checkbook
Monthly Items
• gas $50
• groceries 400
• misc. 50
• children 50
$550/mo.

Chart 9.6

Deposit Ledger

#	Date	Description of Transaction	Payment	Deposit	Balance
					3000.00
	12/31	transfer to annual	1000.00		2000.00
	1/1	deposit		1384.54	3384.54
	1/1	transfer to husband	1240.00		2144.54
	1/1	" " wife	550.00		1594.54
	1/1	" " annual	500.00		1094.54
	1/15	deposit		1384.54	2479.08

Annual Expense Ledger

#	Date	Description of Transaction	Payment	Deposit	Balance
	12/31	transfer from deposit		1000.00	1000.00
	1/1	transfer from deposit		500.00	1500.00
3011	1/5	Marshalls - sale clothes	300.00		1200.00
3012	1/15	Tom's Auto Repair	300.00		900.00
3013	1/28	Dr. Kaal	200.00		700.00

Annual Subledger—on separate sheet of paper or kept in this book

gifts	1000.00	
clothes	~~1000.00~~	700.00
home repai	1000.00	
auto "	~~1000.00~~	700.00
vacation	1000.00	
medical	~~1000.00~~	800.00

Husband—Living Expenses

#	Date	Description of Transaction	Payment	Deposit	Balance
	1/1	transfer from deposit		1240.00	1240.00
1011	1/3	XYZ mortgage Co.	800.00		540.00
Card	1/10	Big Day Restaurant	15.00		525.00

Wife—Living Expenses

#	Date	Description of Transaction	Payment	Deposit	Balance
	1/1	transfer from deposit		550.00	550.00
2011	1/5	Kroger Supermarket	110.00		440.00
Card	1/7	Shell Oil - gas	12.00		428.00

checkbook," as I'll explain later) in my account, then with the deposit at the first of the month I have $3,384.54. I can then make my transfers to the other accounts. The check I receive in the middle of the month will add back to my deposit checkbook so that I will always have the $2,000 as a base at the end of any month. The $2,000 is not being spent but simply is being used to allow me to make my allocations to the other checkbooks the first of each month.

I have found that monthly allocation is a tremendous way to free a couple from the focus on money during the month. Basically, Julie and I do not need to discuss money during the month. We do not have tension around the middle of the month trying to decide what bills to pay and which ones to hold for the mid-month paycheck. Harmony is enhanced when the system allows for freedom to spend whenever one wants to anytime during the month and not have to go through the mid-month squeeze.

Being able to allocate on a monthly basis is also more practical. If, for example, I could only allocate $1,000 of my $1,240 at the first of the month then I am going to be strapped after I make the mortgage payment of $800. I may not be able to pay the utility bills and still have cash in my pocket. I am under tension to juggle until the 15th when the next paycheck comes in. *A savings amount is critical for the smooth operation of the system and the promotion of harmony.*

Once the allocations have been made to the living expense checkbooks, Julie and I are free to spend the total amount down to zero by the end of the month. Because there is a balance in the deposit checkbook, we do not have to worry about overdrafts and service charges when we go to zero in our living-expense books. This is another reason to have a cushion. It allows you to avoid service charges and per-check charges levied on your account when you drop below a certain amount. The total *account* has a positive balance even though your living-expense check*book* may have a zero balance.

Two other factors concerning the monthly allocations need to be understood. First of all, you can get cash for any or all of the items in your assigned list. I could get $150 cash and use it for gas, miscellaneous, and eating out. I do not need to keep track of where all the cash goes as long as I know that I cannot go back to the checkbook and get more once my living expense book shows zero. If I'm out of cash by the middle of the month, then the next month I may want to keep track so I know where the money is going and so I won't run out so quickly. The control factor, however, is my checkbook, not the writing down of where I spend every dime. I'm working against a standard that does not change.

This is a key distinction. When I ask most people if they are on a budget, they say, "Yes, I write down what I spend at the end of the month." That doesn't do it. A spending plan must be measured against a standard. If it is not, then there is no way to know whether you are on your budget or not. (Businesses do this monthly through the use of profit and loss statements.) It is not too much for an individual to do it too.

One of the reasons to allocate to a separate checkbook and spend to zero is the psychology of seeing a smaller balance in the checkbook. If I were using one book and I saw a $2,000+ balance, it would be easier to spend more. If I only see $1,240 (or, in Julie's case, $550), there is a built-in check that controls spending.

On the monthly items *credit cards should never be used!* What you are after is control, and to know how you are doing against a predetermined allocation. Since credit cards get paid a month later, they make it difficult to stay current. I know you may feel that you can go ahead and debit your account, but that makes balancing at the end of the month difficult and confusing at best. Occasionally I am challenged on this point by those who point out that I am giving up the interest I could earn on my money by not paying it until the next month when the credit card bill comes in. In other words, if I charge $500 during the month and don't have to pay it until the next month, I earn interest on my money in the meantime. This is called the "float" and is a valid concept. However, it is my contention that the small amount earned is no offset for the amount saved by being on a system that ensures monthly control and prevents overspending.

Julie and I have found that using a *debit card* for our monthly items gives us the same freedom and flexibility as a credit card but allows us to stay current. The debit card looks just like a credit card and can be used in the same way. The only difference is that items purchased with it come right out of your account (are debited) as it is used—just like a check. You get no bill the next month. See chart 9.6 to see how to note this in your ledger. You simply note your bank card, depending on what your debit card is, and subtract as you would a check. (To get a debit card you need to check with your bank. Many banks have them, though not all. Also most money market funds, such as Merrill Lynch, Dean Witter, and Paine Webber, have them on their various cash management accounts.)

Now that we have looked at the monthly categories, what about the nonmonthly categories ("annual" checkbook)? These are the categories that as a matter of course are not monthly and may be quarterly, annually, or as needed. You will note that I have listed gifts, clothes, home repair, auto maintenance and repair, vacation, and medical in this way. In our sample budget we have allocated $1,000 to each category for the year for a total of $6,000. This means that on a monthly basis we must allocate $500 to the "annual" checkbook to be used for these items.

The budget system will not work if I do not have some dollars in savings to prime the annual checkbook. In other words, I need to make an allocation to this checkbook while my monthly deposits are allowed to accumulate; the system will obviously not work without an amount to put in the account to get it started. Let me illustrate. If my annual allocation is $6,000, or $500 a month, and I put $500 in the annual checkbook in January, what happens if my wife finds a good sale and spends $300 on clothes and the car breaks down to the tune of $300 and we have medical expenses of $200? I have to spend $800 that month, and that puts us $300 behind. I have not, however, blown my budget because the amounts spent are all within the allocated annual amounts. I do, however, have pressure because of the timing. This is why I need to allocate some amount to the annual checkbook to start the year. I cannot just wait for the monthly amounts to accumulate. Emergencies don't always come up when I happen to have my monthly allocation current.

The absolute ideal is to have enough in savings to fund the entire $6,000 in the annual checkbook on January 1. This way, you can spend against the allocated amounts whenever you want to throughout the year. Emergencies do not become a source of frustration because the money is always there. (This is another reason to have an emergency fund.) You still put $500 a month in the account and by the end of the year you still have the $6,000 you started with. Most of us do not have enough extra liquidity lying around to fund the entire year. Therefore, we should do what we can. If we have a savings amount at all, we should allocate at least $1,000 of it to the annual checkbook on January 1. This will allow flexibility with the annual budget items and be a source of tremendous freedom in the face of emergencies. (In chart 9.6 you will note that I allocated $1,000 of the $3,000 to the annual checkbook at the beginning of the year.)

I keep track of my annual expenses against actual budget on a separate subledger in the checkbook (see chart 9.6). You could use a separate sheet of paper to note the annual categories and subsequent reductions in the accounts. Whenever you write a check out of the annual checkbook, simply go to your subledger or sheet of paper and note the reduction in the amount left in the category. For instance, you will note in chart 9.6 that when a check was written for clothes at Marshalls a notation was made in the clothes allocation. This means there is $700 left in this category for the rest of the year. The auto has $700 left and the medical $800. If I see that one category is going to go way over, I need to cut back in another category. Remember, the key is not to overspend in total. One category can be over as long as another is under the allocated amount. This kind of allocation gives tremendous freedom to both spouses to take advantage of sales and respond to unpredictable circumstances without feeling strapped on a month-to-month allocation. Yet they are still staying within the budget.

One last consideration regarding the annual expenses: It is okay to use a *credit card* for these items. For example, I could charge clothes, gifts, and a vacation. When I get the credit card statement, I pay it from the annual checkbook and deduct from the respective categories the amount of the bill that applies to them. Referring to chart 9.7, you will note that I charged several items for a total of $429.32. Referring to chart 9.8, you will note that I wrote one check for that amount to my bank card. Then I reduced each respective category by the appropriate amount as determined from the statement. In this example, vacation was $307 of the

CHART 9.7

BANK CARD BILL

DATE	DESCRIPTION OF TRANSACTION	AMOUNT
9/17	MARRIOTT vacation	44.00
9/26	MUSES clothes	52.00
9/30	DELTA vacation	263.00
10/04	PAYMENT RECEIVED THANK YOU	507.40 C
10/09	MAURI IMPORTS gifts	50.32
10/15	BAILEY, BANKS & BIDDLE gifts	20.00

Prev. Bal.	Purchases	Fin. Chg.	Paymt.	New Bal.	Min. Paymt.
0.00	936.72		507.40	429.32	53.00

	Account Number	Stmt. Date	Due Date
	0000 0000 0000 0000	11/12/88	12/10/88

CHART 9.8

Annual Expense Ledger

#	Date	Description of Transaction	Payment	Deposit	Balance
					700.00
3014	2/5	Bankcard	429.32		270.68

I write the bank card check and then make the debit from the appropriate account in my annual subledger as noted below.

Annual Subledger

gifts	~~1000.00~~	929.68	
clothes	~~1000.00~~	~~700.00~~	645.00
home repair	1000.00		
auto "	~~1000.00~~	700.00	
vacation	~~1000.00~~	693.00	
medical	~~1000.00~~	800.00	

total, clothes were $52, and gifts were $70.32. This system allows us to use the credit card and still make sure we are within our allocated amounts.

You will notice I did not include giving in either the annual or living-expense checkbooks. It does not matter where you put it. I personally allocate some of it to my monthly living-expense book for giving on a monthly basis, and the rest either stays in the deposit book or goes to the annual book to be given as needs arise. If I allocate $200 a month to my living-expense book, then during the year $1,600 will accumulate in the deposit book or annual book ($133 a month). That is available to be given as needs arise. If I allocate to my monthly book, I will need to transfer $1,440 instead of $1,240 each month. Also, I will need to increase the transfer to the annual book by $133.

Using our illustration, if our living expenses are controlled both in the annual categories and the monthly categories, at the end of the year the balance in the "deposit checkbook" will have increased from $2,000 to $3,749 and I will still have $1,000 in my annual checkbook. The increase comes from the savings amount of $1,749 accumulated during the year. All the other checkbooks will be at zero and ready for new allocations to begin the new year.

You may need to adapt or modify this system to your own situation. The main thing is that you develop and use a system that works for you.

Is it worth all the effort? It is if you value harmony and unity and oneness in your marriage. It is if you want to reduce conflict over finances in your marriage. It is if you want the freedom that can only come from spending less than you make. Julie and I are convinced that it is!

Questions and Answers

Certain questions crop up frequently as couples begin to apply this system to their unique situations. Very likely some of these questions have already been raised in your mind as you read this chapter.

What if I do not have a savings amount to prime the pump?

You need to do whatever you can to come up with the savings. As I indicated, it is impossible to make *any* system work without a cushion to begin with. It may require selling an asset, working a second job for a brief amount of time, or really sacrificing in some area of your expenses until you've accumulated the amount.

What if you miss your projection at the first of the year and your income is less (or more) than projected?

If during the year you see that your income is going to be less than projected, you need to adjust your living expenses accordingly—unless, of course, your margin (savings) amount is enough to offset the reduction. This is a good reason to have an annual cushion and not spend all that you are making. Remember, though, that a reduction in income is not a dollar-for-dollar reduction. If your income goes down $1.00, the reduction is really only a percentage of that depending on your tax bracket. If you are in a 30 percent bracket, your taxes will go down $.30, so your living expenses will only be reduced by $.70. If your income is more than projected, great! Just remember the previous example and do not spend more than 70 percent of the increase or you will be in trouble with taxes at the end of the year. Also, you may be moved into a higher tax bracket, so you need to make sure you check that with your accountant. Of course, if your income goes up, you can always add that increase to savings or give it. Don't automatically opt for a more opulent lifestyle. If you always increase living expenses as your income goes up, you will never accumulate the savings necessary for long-term financial independence.

How do I balance the account?

You balance the account the way you would any account except that you need to gather up all four checkbooks rather than one to determine the outstanding checks. You add the outstanding balances of all four books together rather than having only one book.

What if I have items deducted from my paycheck such as insurance premiums?

You need to make sure you include that as a living expense, which it is, but then it will not show up on either of the living expense books. The mistake people make is to forget to add this to their living expenses; as a result, they understate the total outgo.

Can I start a system at any time during the year?

Yes. Although it is easiest to start at the beginning of a calendar year, you can start at any time. You need to go through the same process to determine the calendar year amounts. You then can allocate the monthly amounts just as described. On the annual amounts you will deduct what you have already spent to that point in the year and prorate the remaining amounts throughout the rest of the year.

What if I do not have a set salary and am on commission?

No matter how you receive your income you need to go through the same process. It is even more critical for a person who receives his income on commission to have a cushion to weather the down months. I have observed that there is the potential for much more frustration in the marriage where the income is sporadic. One month is feast and the next is famine. This is usually quite stressful to the wife because of her tendency to be security oriented. It may not bother the husband, but he needs to be sensitive to his wife's potential for frustration. One way to reduce your wife's anxiety level if you have a fluctuating income is to increase your cushion and make sure you at least fund the monthly living-expense books consistently on a monthly basis. You will find that this creates a much smoother month-to-month existence on the home front.

What if I am always running out of money in the monthly living-expense book before the end of the month?

There are only two possibilities. Either you do not have a realistic amount allocated and need to increase the amount, or you have a realistic amount and need to break down the monthly books to individual categories to better control the outflow. The way Julie and I found to do this was to subdivide our checkbook ledgers using paper clips (see figure 9.1). This way we knew how we were doing in the children's allotment, groceries, and miscellaneous at any given point during the month and could anticipate and adjust accordingly. You can make the subdivisions as detailed (many different categories) or as broad as you want. We started out with several paper clips, but as we established our spending habits we found that we were able to reduce the number and still stay within the overall monthly allocation.

FIGURE 9.1

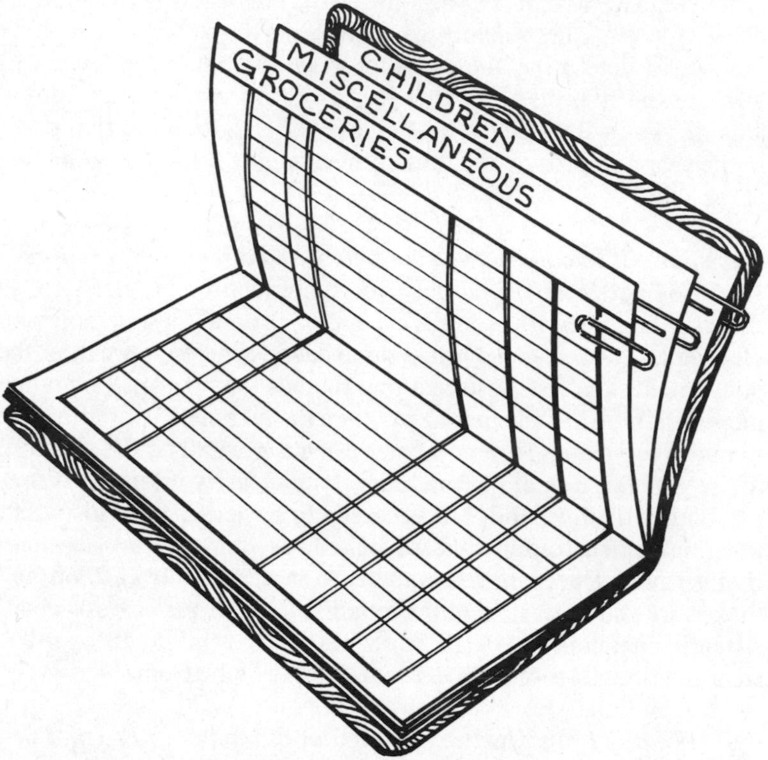

What if I pay for something that is in a category assigned to my spouse?

If Julie buys gas for my car, then I will need to transfer from my checkbook to her checkbook the amount she spent. Since we have one account it is simply a notation in my ledger of the transfer and a notation in hers of the deposit.

What if I overspend one month?

Let's say you got a cash advance on the 25th of the month to put you into a negative balance. You should simply show the negative amount. When you receive your allocation the next month, it will be added to the negative balance. For example, if I am $100 short at the end of the month, when I receive the $1,240 I will have a balance of $1,140 for the next month. Of course, I can't keep borrowing from the next month or I will overspend by the end of the year. But once in a while it is okay to go negative if I know I will gain it back next month. (A good illustration of this is that you may entertain one month and go over in groceries, knowing that the next month you'll catch back up.)

The reason, of course, that you can carry a negative balance in a checkbook is that you're using one account. Just make sure the negative is not in the "deposit account"! If you are negative there, the account is overdrawn and the system is not working!

When can I do something about my taxes?

The answer is quite simple, though not very popular. You cannot reduce your taxes until you have a positive margin. You must spend less than you make. If you do not have a positive accumulation after living, debt payments, giving, and estimated taxes, you do not have money available to make investments that may reduce your taxes. (See chapter 11 for a discussion on investments.)

What are the major budget breakers?

Budget breakers are generally found only among the discretionary budget items. These items are gifts, clothing, vacation, house furnishings, miscellaneous cash, and allowance primarily. It is interesting to note that the nondiscretionary items (fixed expenses) very seldom are the culprit. It is also interesting that most expenses in the budget are fixed. Therefore the key is to control the half dozen or so mentioned that tend to blow it. Julie and I found that if we controlled vacation and gifts, we were okay. (Note: Of course, if your fixed expenses are too high—you've bought a house that is too much for your income or have a car payment you can't handle—then the fixed expenses will also contribute to your budget problems.)

What if my spouse spends money on an "annual" expense?

Since, typically, the credit card is used for those expenses and the credit card bill is paid out of one checkbook, there is usually no problem. If one spouse uses part of his or her monthly amount to pay for something annual, just transfer the amount spent from the annual checkbook to the appropriate living-expense book.

What if I am self-employed? How do I handle my taxes?

You will simply need to set up another category in your "annual" checkbook for "taxes." You should then deposit one-twelfth of the projected tax amount for the year into this category each month so the money will be available for estimated tax payments on the appropriate dates.

Do I have to have one account?

No. As I have said all along, you need to adapt the system to fit you. Julie and I have found that one account makes for more flexibility and less paperwork. You may find that you like to allocate to separate accounts. You may have a relationship with more than one bank and as a result want to have more than one account. You can have as many accounts as you want. Just remember that the more accounts you have, the more "minimum balances" you need to maintain. Also be sure to avoid the problem of "his" and "her" money (discussed in chapter 7).

Is there an amount that is too much for a Christian to use for living expenses?

As with many areas of the Christian life, it would be easier if there were a definitive answer. Then we could say that with a set amount of income a person should only spend X amount to live. There is no such answer. God allows us a large area of freedom in this lifestyle area. He gives us definitive boundaries—spend less than you make, give to the Lord, pay your taxes—but once we do those things, the amount left over is ours to do with as the Lord leads. Maybe we should give more. Maybe we should increase our standard of living. This matter is between you and the Lord. As long as you seek Him in prayer and are tuned into His desires you are free in this area. Accountability in this area will also help make sure you are on track.

Many would like to tell you what is right for your life. "But no matter where you draw the line, it is never an absolute."[1] You may strive for a simpler lifestyle, but how simple is simple? No matter how much you reduce your lifestyle, likely someone in the world has a lower lifestyle. Downward mobility is not necessarily next to godliness. Neither is opulence. No matter how much you strive to elevate your lifestyle, someone in the world likely has a higher lifestyle.

The answer is simply to walk with God daily and ask Him for wisdom. He will freely give it, and you will be free in your decisions regarding lifestyle.

GAME PLAN

It is my encouragement to you that you make a commitment today as husband and wife to develop and utilize a system that works for you. May the following prayer express the desire of your heart.

"Oh, Lord, help me to come to a better understanding of the benefits of control in my life. Control even in the area of finances and budgeting. Help me to be committed for the benefit of my marriage and to fulfill my stewardship responsibility better by having a plan of spending for our finances. Give me the motivation and discipline to make the necessary choices, though some may be hard, to make it work. Thank you, Lord, for giving me insight into how important harmony is in my marriage and how budgeting is essential to maintain that harmony. Give me sensitivity to my spouse as we work together to develop and put into action the system. Amen."

Chapter 10

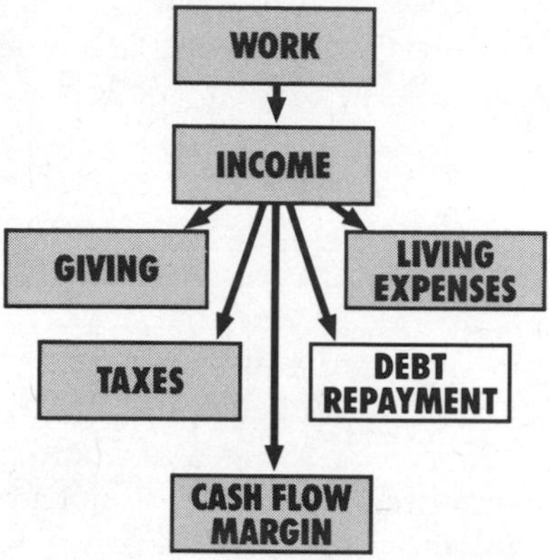

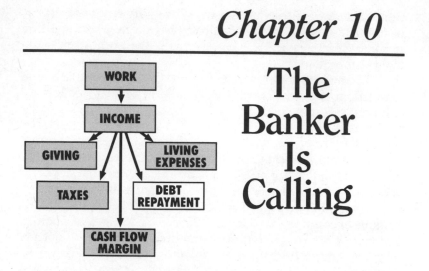

The Banker Is Calling

As the young businessman drove home from the jewelry store shortly before Christmas he was beside himself with excitement. He had been planning all year to buy the diamond necklace for his wife. Although it had been a tough year at his business and he had borrowed most of the money for the diamond necklace, he knew the thrill on her face would be worth it. After all, he thought he had exhibited wise stewardship by getting a home equity loan to keep the interest deductible. The necklace did not add all that much debt to the house, and he was sure he could handle the monthly payments based on his income projections for next year.

Once home, he carefully placed the box under the Christmas tree. He began to watch with anticipation as his wife would look at the box and shake it, wondering what it might be.

Finally the big day arrived. Christmas morning was the time for his wife to open the box. As she opened it and saw the diamond necklace she looked stunned rather than excited. She wanted to be thrilled to please her husband and show her gratitude for the thought that he had put into getting her the necklace. However, no matter how hard she tried to be thrilled, she could not control the anger that welled up inside of her. She knew he had to have taken on more debt to obtain the necklace, and the more she thought about it, the madder she got.

When her husband began to realize that she was not excited as he had hoped, he became frustrated and commented, "Don't you like it?" Through tears his wife responded, "Oh yes, I love it. It's just that I know we don't have the money for something like this. You know how much I don't like debt and especially more debt on the house. Oh honey, I'm sorry. . . ."

This story illustrates many principles about debt as it relates to husband and wife. First of all, let us look at why debt has become such a noteworthy phenomenon and why it exists in the majority of marriages. We will then look at how husbands and wives respond differently to debt. Finally, we will explore solutions to break down barriers that may occur.

Reasons for Debt

The first reason debt exists in most marriages is that borrowing seems like the American thing to do. After all, everybody has debts. It is a way of life.

In preparing a financial plan for a client it is necessary to determine assets and liabilities. I need to know what he owes and what he owns. Numerous times I have asked a client whether he has any debt and he'll say, "No . . . except my home mortgage." We have come so far in our thinking on debt that we don't consider what we owe on a home to be debt!

The concept of OPM (Other People's Money) has been taught in all the business schools for years. After all, if you can use other people's money and with inflation pay it back with cheaper dollars later, why not? You can have more bang for your buck now. This satisfies man's insatiable desire to have more than what he can afford now. The lust of the eyes and the greedy longings of the flesh can be satiated with debt. Therefore, instead of saving for a larger down payment on the house so we take on less debt, we do as we are told by the world: we stretch and take on more debt. After all, we will pay it back with cheaper dollars and will always get a pay raise with our job, won't we?

Debt is such a subtle trap. A couple may be staying close to the budget and only overspending $20 a week, but over the course of a single year this adds up to over $1,000. Over several years that $20 a week adds up to several thousand dollars and creates a significant debt problem. What started out as a very minor overspending problem ends up being a huge debt problem that is next to impossible to overcome.

How does this happen, and why is debt so hard to overcome? Let me illustrate. If I overspend $1,000 a year for ten years, I owe $10,000. Assuming a 10 percent interest rate, if I decide to begin to repay the debt at the end of ten years, I will have to reduce my standard of living $3,000 in my first year of trying to get out of debt. First of all, I have to quit overspending $1,000 and then I need $1,000 to pay the interest on the $10,000 and another $1,000 to begin to pay down the principal. So what seemed to be a minor problem of overspending $1,000 a year ($20 a week) now will cause me to reduce my lifestyle by $3,000 a year. *It is three times as hard to get out of debt as it was to get in.* This is the subtlety of debt.

The reason the debt problem is so hard to overcome is that debt must be paid back with after-tax dollars. This means that if I owe $4,000 and am in the 33 percent tax bracket I must earn $6,000 to have the $4,000 left over to pay the debt. It is hard enough to control living expenses, let alone add the additional problem of having to pay off debt.

The lending institutions and television advertisements today contribute to the lure of debt with such comments as, "With a home equity loan you don't have to wait until 'someday' to travel . . . you can do it now." "Repayment is comfortable with a minimum monthly payment." "You can arrange to pay interest only for five years."

I am always intrigued by the subtlety of the world. There is a particular credit card advertisement that always causes me to smile. They show a young lady just starting out furnishing her entire apartment using the card. The phrase in the commercial is "so worldly, so welcome." She is smiling and has all this nice furniture. There is nice music and all seems to be well. But is it really? There is no mention of paying the debt back that was incurred with the card. The credit card is, after all, debt. The advertisement, however, makes getting into debt seem so innocuous. It all appears to be so pleasant and easy to do without consequences. It is hard to be contented when the world bombards us with an apparently risk-free way to have what we want now. The lie is that you deserve more. It won't hurt. If you don't make enough, it's okay. Go ahead and get it. You can pay it back later. As we saw, however, the "later" is extremely difficult. Debt and overspending always reduce our lifestyle in the future.

To live debt-free requires a radical lifestyle difference. It requires that we be strong enough to withstand the pressures of the world and say "no." Most of us are unwilling to pay the price of being different from the world and as a result succumb in this area of debt.

The second reason for debt in marriage flows from the husband's basic drive to provide. As we observed earlier, God has placed within each man a powerful drive to provide for his family. With this drive comes a greater risk tolerance—greater ability and aptitude for risk taking. Therefore, it is quite easy for the man to assume large debt loads in his pursuit of provision and protection of his family. Debt will never be as big an issue to him as it is to the wife. He sees how he can service the debt and reasons that even in the worst case (bankruptcy) he could start over. The wife sees it quite differently. Debt makes her uneasy.

A friend of mine had been quite successful in using debt in establishing and developing his business. However, one day he realized he needed to establish some personal credit. He went to the bank and took out a $500 loan. Upon arriving home he proudly announced to his wife that he had just taken out a $500 loan and would begin immediately to repay it. Upon hearing this she promptly went into a rage. "How could you do that and risk our future with personal debt?" She began to question him. What was wrong with their finances? Why did they need to have the debt?

This story points out the basic fact that debt is perceived much differently by a woman than a man. Debt is a tremendous threat to the woman's bedrock needs of security and comfort. Since debt is such a threat to her, it is essential for a man to help a woman understand the place of debt, the different types of debt and their potential uses. We will look at this later in this chapter.

Since men typically show love by doing, it is quite natural to desire to buy "things" for their wives. A lot of times we do this to salve our consciences because we know we should spend more time with them. The use of debt to buy these things only compounds the problem. Not only have we gone into debt, we have not dealt with the real issue of spending more time with our wives.

The third reason that debt exists in a marriage is that one of the spouses is discontented. Sometimes it is a husband who is discontented and takes out debt to satisfy his desires. If he does not have a good self-image and a good understanding of the definition of success, he may use debt to look a certain way to impress others. Debt can allow people to look successful by the world's definition when all the while they are barely making it from paycheck to paycheck.

I have observed, however, that many times the wife is the source of the problem. Without knowing it, she can force her husband to take out more debt than he would like because of her comments. I remember a friend who took on a lot more debt because his wife kept making comments like, "I wish I had new curtains"; "I can't entertain until we redecorate"; "It's embarrassing to pick the children up in this old car"; "This apartment is no place for children—we need a house"; "I wish I had new carpet." Although these comments seemed innocuous, they were sending a message to the husband that he was not providing enough. She wanted more, and without knowing it she was jeopardizing her basic security and comfort orientation with her comments.

A woman, however, like her husband, can overspend if she has a poor self-image and is trying to impress others. Also, if she is angry at her husband or is trying to get his attention, as we saw in chapter 8, she may overspend, causing debt to be used.

The fourth reason that debt exists in a marriage is because of the husband's ego. Many men allow their egos to distort their drive to provide. If their focus is not right (if their pride causes them to desire to look better than the Joneses) they can artificially amass (the appearance of) a fortune through the use of debt. Debt can allow them to buy a bigger house or a bigger boat;

with debt, they can establish a larger business than their true income can support. This, of course, is when the problems start. They start when debt is taken on and the income is not sufficient to support it.

Once debt exists in a marriage (and as we have seen, it undoubtedly will), it is important to be aware of the different responses of both the husband and the wife.

HUSBAND'S RESPONSE TO DEBT

First of all, the husband will tend to become a *workaholic.* He knows that he needs to service the debt. He justifies his long hours at work by saying, or at least thinking, "I have to work harder because of the large debt load." Even though, as we have seen, income is not a function of hours worked, it is difficult for the man to get this correct in his thinking. More work hours are always his first response to debt. Of course, the husband's response is not what the wife normally wants. She wants him to be home more. And thus the conflict starts. Maybe her discontented comments about all the things she wanted that she didn't have weren't so innocuous after all.

Second, the husband stops telling his wife what he is doing regarding debt. He won't even let her know when he takes on more debt or why. Many times I have been in meetings with a couple and as we are going through the assets and liabilities, the wife will exclaim, "I didn't know we owed that." He stops communicating with her regarding debt because he is concerned about her response. He knows her response will normally be negative. Rather than try to explain "why," he just says nothing.

Third, the husband usually responds to debt by exhibiting ups and downs in his spiritual life. (He gets on a spiritual roller coaster.) As I have worked with couples over the last several years I've noticed that if things (income, job, promotions) are going well, then the debt is not a big issue. They seem to do well spiritually. However, if there is a glitch in their income or the debt load becomes too great, then they tend to go into a spiritual tailspin. This is to be expected. They work harder and thus have less time to spend with God. Their provision drive is being hindered. They can't get ahead vocationally because they must put all their energy into paying debt and not in being able to be creative and add to their asset base. Their options and flexibility are reduced.

This should not be a surprise because debt does restrict the "freedom" of our income to fluctuate. Prov. 22:7 is true—the borrower does become the lender's slave. Therefore, debt can throw the spiritual leader into an up-and-down mode based on his income and the corresponding debt. (I might add that the debt does not cause the spiritual roller-coaster. If the individual is "walking in the Spirit," he will be able to work through it. Debt does, however, add additional pressure to the individual, and if he is not spiritually sharp, this pressure can throw him into a tailspin.)

A fourth way the husband may respond to debt is to take an "it is her fault" attitude and assume no personal responsibility. He concludes that he has been driven to take out an inordinate amount of debt trying to satisfy his wife's desires for things. He may, therefore, not feel any personal responsibility and develop an attitude of apathy toward paying back the debt. He takes on more and more debt and works less. Eventually he doesn't care if the debt is even paid back. The security of the wife is of very little concern to him.

These four responses of the husband to debt need to be understood by the wife. Once they are understood it will be easier for her to know how to pray and to ask God for wisdom in communicating with him and promoting harmony in their marriage.

WIFE'S RESPONSE TO DEBT

The first response that debt causes in the wife is a feeling of anxiety. Because of a woman's basic nurturing instincts, she has a desire to have a secure environment. She likes to move into a house and put down roots. She doesn't like to move around a lot. Debt can threaten this security because she knows that if the income is not there to make the debt payments she may have to relocate or may even lose her home. This anxiety could lead to some devastating consequences. This was made very clear in a recent letter we received at my company from an anonymous writer. The woman stated, "I could not cope with the stress of my husband's attitude toward indebtedness. When I couldn't convince him of the disaster his spending could bring; for *security of my home,* I had to legally cut our ties (my *fear,* of course, was that eventually we could lose it). It was absolutely the most devastating experience ever."

This woman was so fearful of losing her home because of the debt her husband was taking on that she sought divorce as an option to make her environment more secure.

I remember the response of my wife when I casually mentioned that we were establishing a line of credit for the partnership I'm a partner in and that I would be liable for my pro-rata share. Needless to say, I didn't plan on a two-hour discussion! All of her uneasiness came to the surface when a simple comment included the word *debt.* Why did we need the line of credit? Could we handle the debt? What if our income went down? What about our home? What was the difference between having debt on the business and on credit cards?

I quickly realized that Julie's response to debt was very different from my response. I looked at it as a wise business move, a prudent decision based on sound facts. She saw her security threatened and she didn't like it! It was then my responsibility to help her understand. If she was not comfortable, then perhaps I should not take out the debt. After all, is money more important than my marriage?

Out of anxiety comes the wife's second response: nagging. She can continually be pushing her husband on the debt issue. "Why don't you reduce the debt? Why do you have so much debt?" It is my observation, however, that nagging is simply a plea for communication, a request by the wife for her husband to let her in on what he is doing. She needs to hear his thinking on debt—why it is needed and how it will be paid for.

The woman who wrote the letter stated that "when she couldn't convince him . . ." It was obvious that she had been nagging him about the debt to try to get him to think the way she did about it or at least communicate with her. This is a normal response on the part of the wife if the husband will not communicate with her about debt.

Nagging can not only be a cry for communication, but also the result of a poor understanding of how debt is perceived by the husband. This anonymous writer revealed that she did not understand how her husband perceived debt when she said, "I could not cope with the stress of my husband's attitude toward indebtedness. . . ." She obviously didn't realize that her husband's God-given drives would cause him to have a different attitude toward debt than she had. Instead of trying to understand that difference, she nagged him to try to change his perception of debt to be like hers. When his way of looking at it didn't change, she divorced him. It is very important that you and I understand that we will perceive debt differently than our spouses and work to develop clear communication on the subject for the benefit of our marriages.

A third response that the wife could have to debt is one of apathy. She begins to feel that there is no reason for her to watch what she spends if he is going into large amounts of debt. What does her little bit really matter for clothes if the husband is going to spend huge amounts on houses, boats, and investments? It seems pointless to try to watch what she spends and stay within the budget, so she gives up and takes on debt for the things she wants. Basically, this attitude results if the husband does not do a good job of helping his wife understand why and where debt fits into the overall provision plan.

If the wife begins to exhibit an apathetic, noncaring attitude about controlling the use of debt and starts to use the credit card excessively, it should be a warning indicator to the husband. For women to be indifferent about debt should be a sign to us as men that something is not right. Many times a woman will use the credit card to try to buy things to make her happy (to meet her emotional needs) if her husband is not meeting them. As husbands, we need to make sure that is not the case. A woman's use of debt and attitude towards it in many cases will be an indicator as to how her husband is treating her. She will be less apt to want to use debt to get things for herself if he is doing a good job of building her up and esteeming her.

The final response the wife may have to debt is disrespect for the husband. This disrespect results because she does not feel that he really cares about her, since he doesn't listen to her input and is willing to threaten her basic security orientation by taking on debt. She could feel that since he doesn't explain the purpose of the debt to her, he must not know what he is doing. This causes her respect to wane even more, and she may begin to belittle him and tear him down. She reasons that if he really cared for her, he would discuss their debt situation with her and not increase it.

Action Steps

It is obvious that debt does exist in most marriages. It may be there as a result of *wrong thinking* about debt or of *discontent* from one or both of the spouses. Either way, one needs to realize that debt is a very unsettling thing to the wife because it violates her security orientation. Debt can be devastating to the husband because of what it can do to his spiritual life. If he uses debt to improve the way he looks because of pride, it can interfere with good judgment and cause him to take his eyes off God. He can become greedy. Debt can also affect his provision drive as he must focus so much effort on servicing the debt. He may be forced to overwork or be unable to do some things vocationally because of the lack of freedom due to the debt. How does one deal with the various responses to debt in the marriage relationship that we have highlighted? The following solutions are offered for your consideration.

First of all, the wife must be very careful not to destroy the provision drive of the husband. She needs to realize that this God-given drive to provide brings with it a higher risk tolerance than she has. She needs to understand that debt wisely used in the establishment of a business and the growth of a husband's capital base will probably be a part of his life. She needs to be careful not to nag him about debt as he tries to provide for her.

Second, the husband needs to sit down with his wife and really help her understand the differences in debt. Basically, there is the business-type debt or investment debt where the after-tax return is greater than the after-tax cost. This use of debt, as already indicated, can be a viable part of a person's financial situation. However, the consumptive-type debt for furniture, cars, boats, etc., where the after-tax cost is greater than the after-tax return (i.e., depreciation-type debt) can be devastating in a marriage relationship. This was the topic of my two-hour discussion with Julie. As you recall, she was concerned about the line of credit. She was anxious about the impact of debt, wanting to know why and where it fit into our plan. It was my responsibility to help her be comfortable with these issues or at least clearly understand so she could give me input . . . which brings us to the third solution, getting and valuing the wife's input. Remember, we are after harmony in the relationship. Whether I take out the debt or not is secondary to including her in the thought process and getting her input. After making sure she understands and getting her input, I may still take out the debt. After all, I am ultimately responsible to God to provide for my family (1 Tim. 5:8) and for the decision I make. But I am also wise to get and weigh my wife's input.

Regarding the wife's input, it is important to look at a side issue here that is close to the heart of all women: the home. Since the home is the wife's territory, the way it is perceived is key to marriage harmony. It needs to be established that debt on the home is personal debt and not business or investment debt. The home should not be looked at as an investment. Although the home will likely appreciate and have a good investment return when sold, it is also the wife's territory. *A way to show that the house is not really an investment is to see how agreeable your wife is to selling the house every two years when you have a small appreciation in value (i.e., a strategy of selling houses and moving every two years to realize inflation gains!).* You'll likely find that the security factor outweighs the potential investment return. Your home is not really an investment in the way we define investment (capital employed to realize a gain).

Note: Concerning the home a good scenario to think through as husband and wife when deciding how much debt, if any, to take on with the house is to ask the following: Would we be more anxious and frustrated (a) if we lived in a smaller house and our income went up to support a larger house or (b) if we lived in a larger house and our income went down to the point that we might not be able to pay the mortgage payments and might lose the house? Your answer to these two scenarios will give you some insight into your risk tolerance regarding debt on the house.

The house should not be risked in the pursuit of other business and investment objectives (second mortgages and home equity loans, etc.) unless it is agreed upon by both husband and wife.

I remember vividly the look on the face of a client's wife when she realized that her home was lost. All the investments he had made had gone bad and the home had been leveraged. What she cared about was being ripped away. Yes, they would have been worth a lot more had the investments worked, but was that worth the risk of losing the home? My observation was that it was not! The family home is a place of memories and security, and should not be risked. As a matter of fact, I strongly recommend that a debt-free house should be pursued aggressively. Paying off your home may be an un-American thing to do. It is, however, a great thing to do for your marriage.

A fourth way to avoid the problems that debt can bring is to have a strategy to handle major purchases. A plan for handling these is critical because if they are not planned for, debt is usually the method used to purchase them. It will be up to each individual couple to define what constitutes a "major purchase" for them, but in the general sense a major purchase is any purchase that is not a part of the normal living expenses we looked at in chapter 9. They are typically more expensive items like furniture, cars, golf clubs, and so on.

Julie and I have found that a simple plan is to define major purchases for us and then be committed to communicating about them before any purchase is made. What this does is keep us out of a potentially impulsive situation where we are responding to a request over the phone or a sales gimmick or a good deal. A lot of conflict in marriage over debt is a result of money being spent that was not agreed upon between husband and wife. This is illustrated by the angry response of the wife when the husband comes home with a $500 set of golf clubs and proudly tells his wife how much he needed them. It's not the golf clubs that caused the anger but rather her exclusion from a large-ticket decision. The same thing occurs when the wife proudly displays an expensive new coat to her husband. It's not the coat that upsets him but rather the lack of communication. Having a plan for major purchases will eliminate much potential conflict in the marriage because it will promote discussion and in most cases limit the use of debt.

The fifth solution to this whole problem of debt in the marriage is for husband and wife to sit down periodically to make a list of all they have to be thankful for. This is a practical way in which they can learn to be content. It helps to get their focus off the world (the lust of the eyes) and back on God and what He has blessed them with. We need to quit thinking about what we don't have. We come into this world with nothing, and we leave with nothing

(1 Tim. 6:7). We are not entitled to a certain amount of material possessions. In today's society, however, debt has allowed us to purchase a lot of "things." They become albatrosses around our necks and barriers to a positive, harmonious marriage relationship because of the debt they carry with them. Therefore, the challenge is to "learn" to be content as Paul did (Phil. 4:11, 13). It's important to get off the treadmill of getting more and keeping up appearances or keeping up with the Joneses. It's necessary to limit the use of debt on consumer goods in order to do this.

My wife and I have recently decided to move closer to the office where I work. As we have looked for a different home we have found that it is very easy to get caught up in the upward mobility spiral and be tempted to buy something bigger and bigger and take on more and more debt. In order to overcome this we have had to step back and get things in proper perspective and realize all that we have to be thankful for. We do have shelter, we do have food, and we do have clothing (Matthew 6) and with these we are to be content.

We have also reflected on the risk of too much debt. Debt brings longer work hours, less flexibility with the income we do have, stress on the marriage, and less savings. We have determined that the risk of too much debt is not worth the harmony in our marriage. The things we could buy with the debt pale in comparison to marital harmony.

GETTING OUT OF DEBT

This chapter would not be complete without a word on how you should tackle an existing debt problem. In general, you need to take the following practical steps:

1. Evaluate your income and the four uses of money (living expenses, taxes, giving, and debt payments) to ensure that you have a positive margin. Many people continue to go deeper in debt because they have no plan. They have never determined if they were living within their income. The first step, then, is to make sure that you're not just accumulating additional debt.

2. Implement a cash-flow control system that enables you to accomplish your spending plan. (See chapter 9.) A control system will ensure that you accumulate the positive cash-flow margin indicated by your plan.
3. Once you have a positive cash-flow margin, those funds can be used to reduce your debt. As your debt reduces, you have more margin, and the positive cycle continues.
4. As well as the three preceding steps, you may need to do something drastic:
   - Sell an asset. This might be a car, a stereo, a television, or some similar item. This *is* drastic, but you have to control your debt, and in some cases this liquidation of assets may be necessary.
   - Cut up your credit cards. If you cannot use them (as prescribed in chapter 9), then get rid of them. Credit cards encourage overspending. Remove the temptation and enhance your positive cash-flow margin (as described in steps 1 and 2 above).
   - Do not consolidate your loans. This does not solve the problem. Consolidation reduces your monthly debt payment. Without a plan, the extra money that was being used for debt repayment is spent in other ways, and the problem grows. It is far better to "bite the bullet" and address your debt problem rather than making it easier through loan consolidation. Debts need to be paid—the sooner the better.

In summary, the way to tackle a debt overload is simple in theory, yet difficult in practice. You need to have a plan to spend less than you make. You then need a system to control that plan and apply the positive cash-flow margin to your debt payments. That positive cash-flow margin eventually eliminates your debt. The reality, however, is that it is difficult to be content to spend less than you earn. Unfortunately, there is no other way to get out of debt.

GAME PLAN POINTS OF HARMONY

Make a list of all you have to be thankful for. (This will help you learn to be content and less apt to take on consumptive debt.) Make a separate list of things you have that money can't buy.

Are the things you would buy with more debt worth it in light of your marriage harmony?

Are you communicating before purchasing?

Why do you have the debt you have?

What steps can you take to accelerate paying off your home?

Do I really need this?

Chapter 11

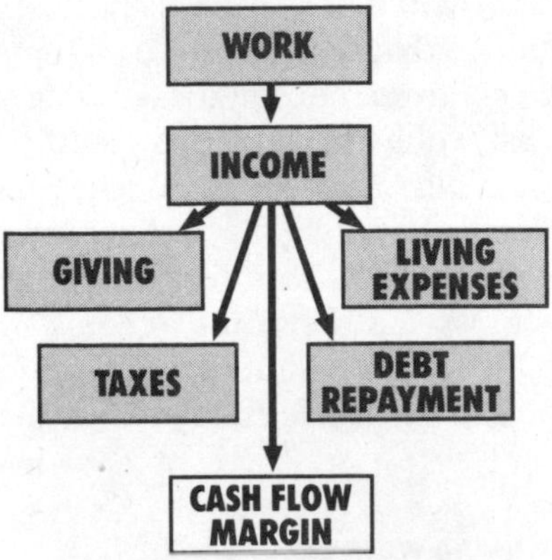

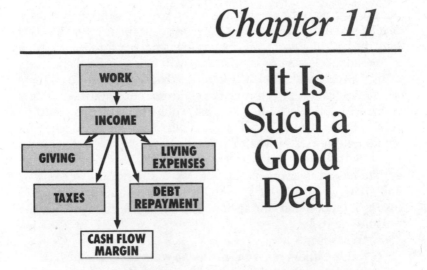

It Is Such a Good Deal

"Hello, Bob? This is Sam. Do you have a few minutes?"

"Sure, Sam. What is it?"

"Bob, I've just come across a super deal that I feel you'd be interested in. For an investment of only $10,000 you can earn $40,000 in the next two years. I've done a lot of research on it, and the concept and people both seem to be sound. It sure looks to me like a no-lose situation."

"Sam, I'm always interested in anything that can make me money. What is it?"

"It will take me some time to explain the ins and outs of the deal. Could I come by and talk to you and Sally tonight?"

"I don't think we've got anything going. That would be fine."

"How does eight o'clock sound?"

"Sounds good."

"OK. I'll see you at eight."

As Bob hangs up he can hardly wait to call Sally. He has been a friend of Sam's for a long time and knows that if Sam has something that he is excited about it must be a good deal. As Bob muses to himself he gets more and more excited. He has been working hard at the plant as a manager, but it has been difficult to save much extra money. He has been able to accumulate about $15,000 over the past four years. The money is earmarked for the education of the kids and for a new car that they will need within the year. As Bob thinks about it, though, he realizes that they could get two cars with $40,000 and still educate the children. He could use $10,000 of the $15,000 to get $40,000. That would make Sally's day if he could replace her car, too. He could also do some remodeling on the house. Wow! Sally would be thrilled!

"Sally, this is Bob. I've got great news. Sam just called me and he has an investment opportunity that he wants to come by and show us tonight. It sounds like a fantastic deal. We could invest $10,000 from our savings and earn back $40,000 in the next two years."

"What is it?"

"I don't know yet. That is why he wants to come by."

"I'm not sure we should dip into our savings. Do you really think we should waste his time? What if the deal doesn't work out?"

"Before we do anything I'll make sure the numbers all make sense."

"I'm not sure—even if the numbers make sense—that I'd be comfortable dipping into our savings. That money is for the kids' education and for a new car this year."

"I know. But just think, we could have more than twice as much if things work out."

"Well, you can have him come by if you want to, but I'm not sure I like the idea. Even if it is a great deal, I don't want to dip into our savings."

"I don't understand how you can say that. You've not even seen the deal. How can you draw any conclusion without seeing the numbers and hearing about the deal?"

"That is just the way I feel. But it is up to you. You can meet with him if you want to."

"OK. I'll be home at six and Sam is coming at eight. See you tonight."

Investments! Apart from debt, there is no area of a couple's finances that can evoke more conflict than this one. I cannot recount how many times the above scene has been played out among the people I meet with. What are the reasons for the conflict over investments and investment decisions?

Reasons for Conflict

Investments more than any other area of one's finances bring to the surface the *foundational differences* between male and female that we discussed in chapter 3. If a couple does not understand these differences, then investments become a tremendous source of conflict. Using the above case study, let's analyze what drives and differences were manifested by Bob and Sally.

First of all, Bob is exhibiting his God-given drive to provide. Like most men, he is attracted to investment because it is another way to generate income and provide for the family. This is why men almost always have their antennae up and are continually coming up with one good deal after another. In all my counseling I have never had a woman bring a "deal" to her husband and say, "Honey, here is a good deal. I think we should look at it."

If a man like Bob, however, is not careful, the drive to provide (which is good) can easily be replaced by greed. Greed is an inordinately covetous drive or longing to have something. It is the desire to have something for nothing. It is the underlying motivation that makes all of the "get rich quick" schemes so popular. It is the motivation that blinds a man to the real facts of the deal. It is also the barrier that causes him to shut out the counsel of his wife when she is sending him loud and clear warning signals.

We see this happening to Bob. Instead of questioning the return on investment, which should be a warning sign (to receive $40,000 in two years, an annualized return of 72 percent would be required), he begins to rationalize in his mind why it must be a good deal. Sam is his friend and he respects him. If Sam feels it is good, it must be good, and so on. Even though Sally is uncomfortable, he doesn't put much credence in what she is saying because she doesn't know the facts.

What about the facts? This is another difference that investments bring out. Men tend to be logical. They look at all the numbers and analyze and calculate and do risk analyses and probabilities. A man figures that the numbers are all there is to the investment. Then his wife, like Sally, gives some response about not liking the investment because she "just doesn't feel good about it." It blows the man's circuits. He doesn't understand what she means when she says she doesn't "feel" good about it. He demands to know why she feels that way. She, of course, doesn't know why. She just does. This is her God-given intuition. Bob would be well advised to give credence and weight to Sally's concern even if she has no "factual" reason. I like the comment by Frontier Airlines Captain Chick Stevens:

> I am for example, nonplussed by their ability to understand things without having a knowledge of those things. A sort of swift and sure instinct which leaps directly from problem to conclusion without being confused by facts. We males are bound by our inherent natures to cope with facts—great bespatterings of facts—wending our way to conclusions brings these facts into regimented order. We are pushed just a bit off center when, after performing our labors of sorting, analyzing, weighing, assigning degrees of importance, we reach our conclusion to find our women already there, smiling sweetly.[1]

Another difference that is obvious in our case is the woman's security orientation. Sally is dragging her feet primarily because she does not want to lose the security of the $15,000 in savings. Bob needs to realize that his risk-taking mind-set is foreign to his wife. So instead of trying to make her think the same way he does, he should try to understand her concerns before making a decision.

Another difference is the long-term versus short-term time horizons of the male and female. Sally is dragging her feet because she likes seeing the cash in the bank *now.* It is difficult for her to feel as comfortable with a *potential* $40,000 in the bank in two years. Her orientation is more for the here and now. It goes against her nature to want to take $10,000 and invest it now to maybe have more in the future. She just is not interested.

I have found that because of both her desire for security and her short-term orientation the wife is usually more interested in cash and liquid investments (easily converted to cash) than in nonliquid investments. I vividly recall the discussion Julie and I had about rental real estate properties. I spent a couple of hours explaining to her the benefits of tax savings, appreciation, and income from the investment. Her response was one of extreme caution and questions like: "*What if* the renters don't pay and we need to make the mortgage payment?" "*What if* we have a lot of repairs and upkeep that take our cash?" It became obvious as we talked that she was much more comfortable with liquidity and cash than with the unknowns and illiquidity of the rental property. Did I go ahead and buy it? You'll find out later in this chapter.

Before leaving this discussion of differences, let me add that even though my illustrations presuppose that women are not interested in investments, which is typically the case, there are situations that may pique a woman's interest in investment.

If her husband is slothful and not meeting his family's needs, she may be apt to be assertive with investments. If she is not sure of her role as a homemaker, she may desire to work outside the home. As a result, her interest in investments may rise. If she is not content to live within her husband's income, she may become interested in investments as a vehicle to get more of the things she wants. If she is detail oriented, she may be attracted to investments and the challenge of understanding them. Her family background may also contribute to a heightened interest level as well. If her family has an interest in investments, chances are that, as she grew up, she was involved in the decision making behind her family's investments.

A second reason for conflict regarding investments is a *lack of communication*. At least Bob called Sally and talked to her about the investment. More often than not the husband does not want to talk to his wife about the investment and just goes ahead and does it. He feels that he knows more about the numbers than she does and therefore is more qualified to make the decision. So why even bother her? He has also learned that when he does talk to her he cannot get her to think the way he does. So he would just as soon not fight the battle to try and explain it to her. Instead of trying to make her think the way he does, he should just talk to her and get her input. It is an understatement to say that much conflict results when the man doesn't communicate with his wife and just calls up and says, "Honey, I just made this great investment for $10,000. We'll get $40,000 in two years." The fact that the husband wants his wife's input and gives her a chance to tell him what she thinks honors her and goes a long way toward promoting marital harmony.

The final reason for conflict regarding investments is the *underlying pressure on the husband that drives him to turn to investments to provide more income.* The pressure can come from his wife or from himself. If the wife is not content with the family income, she can put pressure on him to provide more and more income. This pressure will cause him to be inclined to look for the "deals" that will generate a lot of money very quickly. At the same time he tends to withdraw from her and not discuss the deals with her. He does not want to let her in on what he is doing because she may not like it or because openness may make him too vulnerable to failure. He's afraid he'll hear "I told you so" from her. His self-image may be damaged if he cannot make enough to please her and he seeks more and more deals. Conflict and tensions at home are increased because husband and wife are not communicating and the pressure is mounting.

Isn't it interesting that when a wife pressures her husband to make more money than he can make from his vocation he will resort to taking more risk in the investment area? When he does this, the very things she covets—security and support—are threatened. It is my observation that a lot of the conflict in the marriage regarding investments could be avoided with an attitude of contentment on the part of the wife.

The husband could put pressure on himself to make more money because of a wrong perspective of success. He could take more risk to try and have more reward (more money) to feel better about himself. Self-image is not enhanced by money, and success is not defined by money.

SOLVING THE CONFLICT

To overcome the conflict that investments can bring to the marriage several steps should be taken. Some relate to the husband and some to the wife, but all require a clear understanding by both husband and wife of the basic differences of male and female and how these are manifested. Once the differences are understood, the type of communication that must take place to promote harmony and overcome the conflict is obvious. Let's look at some specific areas in which action can and should overcome the conflict.

WIFE'S CONTENTMENT

Since the husband has a strong drive to provide, the wife should recognize that any discontent on her part stands the chance of causing him to be more willing to take high risk on investments to meet her needs and expectations and wants. She should be very careful to communicate to him that she is content with his income and willing to live within it. As we have seen in earlier chapters, God promises to meet our needs, and the key to contentment is living within what our vocation provides. If the wife sends signals that she wants more, then she runs the risk of jeopardizing the very things that are dearest to her—security and protection. Wives, what signals are you sending to your husbands? Could that risky investment he bought be because of your discontent?

CLEAR COMMUNICATION

Men, it is crucial that you get your wives' input before making any investment decision. Even though her intuitive comments about the investment will more than likely not make sense to your way of thinking, you need to listen to her. My observation is that in most cases your wife just wants to make sure she has had input and that the two of you are communicating. I am convinced that your final decision regarding the investment is much less of an issue to her than whether you took the time to get her input. I have found that once I get Julie's input I have much greater freedom to make the decision. Without her input it seems we're always at a point of conflict.

I remember showing up for a client meeting that I assumed would be just with the husband. Much to my surprise, when I walked into his office his wife met me. When I expressed my surprise that she was there for the meeting, she exclaimed, "This is the only way I can get filled in on what is going on. He talks to you!"

The tendency of most wives to avoid risks makes it important for the husband to clearly understand the risks himself so he can communicate them to his wife. *A general rule of thumb about investments is that if you do not understand it well enough to help your wife understand it, then don't do it.* You must be able to explain it to her so that she understands it.

Another part of helping your wife understand the investment is to help her see the long-term perspective on the investment. Sound investing requires diversification and a long-term perspective, and thus mandates a move into vehicles other than cash. This perspective is natural for you, but not for your wife. Most women will follow their short-term focus and will be most content with cash. It is your job to help her see the long-term benefits of the investment and where it fits in your overall financial plan—all the while, however, being quite sensitive to the short-term needs that must be met.

It is these short-term needs that the man so often overlooks. In his zeal for providing for the future—education, retirement, payment of debt, and so on, he neglects the drapes. Who needs them? For the sake of your marriage any investment decision needs to factor in the short-term needs. You will be well advised not to ignore the pressures your wife is feeling in the short term. Most wives, I have found, would rather take less risk and have less in the future and more short-term security. This is why communication is critical.

I have found one of the most effective ways to ensure that Julie and I are communicating regarding finances and to balance her short-term focus with my long-term focus is to ask her for her priority uses of margin. In other words, what does she want to do with the difference between our earnings and our expenses? Because of my long-term mentality I am naturally thinking of investments and savings, to the potential exclusion of all of the other uses of money. Julie, on the other hand, is likely thinking of shorter-term uses that are perhaps more practical. She responded to my question, for instance, by saying that she would like to have more in the vacation category (her parents live in Phoenix and she'd like to take the boys to visit the grandparents more often) and would like to get a different car sooner than I was planning. It is not that she is right and I should do what she says or that I am right. The point is that I need to factor in what she is thinking to my decision making. If I have a margin of $3,000, I may have more harmony in my marriage if I put $1,000 of it in the vacation category of our budget and only invest $2,000 than if I invest it all. (On the other hand, there are times I feel I should invest the entire $3,000 and help Julie see the purpose for it and the reasoning behind it.) This is the way communication should take place.

So how does one make an investment decision? With all the differences is it possible? Sure. After explaining it to your wife and getting her input, you then weigh the risk. After weighing the risk you decide for or against. How does one weigh the risk? There are two types of risk: financial risk and marriage risk.

Let's look at Bob again. Sally is uncomfortable because she knows they are using education and car money to make the investment. The financial risk Bob faces is the same as anyone faces with a 72 percent projected return. He stands a good chance of losing the money because risk and reward go together regarding investments. The return with the least risk is the rate of short-term CDs and money market funds. Any return higher than that has a greater risk. You can see that 72 percent carries an inordinate amount of risk. There are also tax risks, audit risks, and time involvement risks.

If Bob has the money to lose, he could probably stand the financial risk. However, he does not have the extra money. He is dealing with auto and education funds. The marriage risk is much greater than the financial risk. If he loses the money (as we saw, this is a high probability), he has to face Sally and tell her he lost the money for her new car and that it will be tougher to educate the kids. He will also likely need to work harder to try to recoup the losses, which could tend to put more stress on the marriage. If he is wise, he will discern that Sally is saying to him that she would rather have the $15,000 in hand than the potential $40,000 in the bush. He would deduce that the stress on their marriage if the deal doesn't work is probably a greater risk than the reward of $40,000 in the bank. At their current savings level he would pass on the investment.

In any investment there is always a trade-off and risk. The question is whether or not the risk is worth the reward. Too often, though, we ask that from a strictly financial sense and forget that the greatest risk could be to our marriage relationship. "What does it profit a man if he gain the whole world and amass a lot of investments but lose his marriage and children?" Not only should the investment be evaluated from a financial standpoint but also from a marriage harmony standpoint.

Remember the rental property decision I discussed with Julie. I decided not to do it primarily because of the time it would demand to manage and keep the place up and because of the risk of depleting cash reserves. I already have many demands on my time and that investment would require me to be on call twenty-four hours a day to fix things and deal with tenants. (I have three young sons, and they need my time more than I need an investment.) Even though I potentially could earn more money with appreciation, tax benefits, and income with the rental property than I could on my savings account, the risk of the property not being rented and beginning to deplete our reserves was too great at this stage in our financial lives. I determined that the worst-case scenario with the property would put too much stress on our marriage and was not worth the potentially greater return.

This does not mean that a man always has to do what his wife says regarding investments. She is to have input, and then he has the final decision. I would just comment, however, that it seems that they are right more often then they are wrong. Julie and I have also found that the simple policy of not committing to an investment without talking keeps us from responding to the lure of the moment and potentially making a decision we would later regret. I have also found that if I will just answer her question "Can we afford to lose this money?" I will have a lot more freedom in making the decision. If the answer is yes her worries are reduced and comfort increased.

Once the decision is made, both husband and wife must resist the urge to say, "I told you so!" The husband will be tempted to do this if he does not make the investment and it turns out to be a real winner. The wife will be tempted to utter this comment if he makes the investment and it loses all their money. Remember, we are after harmony and communication. Investments are only a tool. They should not become a source of arguing and of tearing down each other.

MOTIVE EVALUATION

Men, you should take time to evaluate your motive. Are you pursuing the investment because of greed? The Bible contains two very clear warnings about the outcome of your investment if greed is your motive.

> A faithful man will abound with blessings, but he who makes haste to be rich will not go unpunished.
>
> Prov. 28:20

> A man with an evil eye hastens after wealth, and does not know that want will come upon him.
>
> Prov. 28:22

SOUND KNOWLEDGE ABOUT INVESTMENTS

Many times the correct decision about investments will be made for you if you are thinking correctly. Let's look at some truths about investments to begin to think right about them.

1. Keep in Mind Realistic Returns (8–12 percent) and the Purpose of Investments

In my business of financial planning I deal a lot with individuals who have been making investments for thirty to forty years. What has become obvious is that a person does not become wealthy from his investments. He gets wealthy by spending less than he makes from his vocation over a long period of time and preserving that surplus through his investments. In other words, investments are vehicles used for preservation of capital and not dramatic increases in capital. This being the case, you should be content with reasonable rates of return (8–12 percent) and not be pursuing the really high rates of return except with a small amount of funds you can afford to lose.

Note: You may be thinking that my comment is not true. You may be thinking about the guy you know who bought a piece of land for $1,000 an acre and sold it for a return of 200 percent, or about the guy whose stock doubled three weeks after it went public. Although these individuals may appear to get rich quick using investments, in reality they did not. Let me explain. The man that makes a lot of money in land, for instance, is usually the guy who deals in land. That is his business. Therefore, he is generating income as a result of his vocation, not as a result of an investment. He just happens to be in a business that uses investment vehicles (land). It is easy to confuse vocation with investment. As a result, we go out and buy land to try to make as much money as that fellow did and we don't. The same is true with the man who has the publicly traded company. Stock is an investment vehicle, but his return from it was the result of his vocation. Here again we may incorrectly assume the individual got rich because of the stock when in reality it was his vocation that did it.

Contrary to what most people feel, 8–12 percent rates of return are historically very acceptable. The decade of the 1980s with the high interest rates of 17–18 percent of the five-year bull stock market elevated our expectations of return to unrealistic levels. These unrealistic expectations cause us to take unrealistic risks. Referring to chart 11.1, you can see what are realistic rates of return over time for various investments. You can also see that a "high rate" of return is anything in excess of 15 percent. The more realistic expectation of returns should be in the 8–12 percent range. Make sure you have realistic expectations about your investments.

CHART 11.1

COMPOUND ANNUAL RATES OF RETURN (FOR PERIOD ENDING 6/1/88)

	20 Years	10 Years	5 Years	1 Year
Coins	15.1% (1)	13.4% (2)	10.1% (4)	14.0% (3)
U.S. Stamps	12.9% (2)	10.5% (3)	0.2% (12)	1.4% (13)
Gold	12.8% (3)	9.6% (7)	2.2% (11)	3.1% (10)
Oil	9.9% (5)	3.7% (12)	−10.7% (14)	10.5%E (2)
Diamonds	9.9% (6)	9.6% (6)	7.5% (7)	24.9% (1)
Stocks	9.5% (7)	15.8% (1)	14.8% (1)	−4.9% (14)
T-Bills	8.5% (9)	10.1% (5)	7.6% (6)	6.0% (8)
Bonds	8.1% (10)	10.3% (4)	13.4% (2)	6.2% (7)
Housing	7.7% (11)	6.2% (10)	5.0% (9)	2.0% (12)
CPI	6.3% (12)	6.1% (11)	3.3% (10)	3.1% (9)
Silver	5.9% (13)	2.8% (14)	−11.6% (15)	7.4% (15)
Farmland	5.9% (14)	0.6% (15)	−6.5% (13)	3.1% (11)
Foreign Exchange	4.7% (15)	3.2% (13)	9.5% (5)	8.6% (6)

( ) Number shows ranking.

Source: Salomon Brothers, Inc. "Stock Research—Investment Policy." Used by permission.

2. Risk and Reward Go Together
You should only invest in high return/high risk investments with money you can afford to lose. Getting rich quick does not work. He who gathers little by little will prosper (Prov. 13:11).

3. Investments Are Only a Tool
They should not be purchased at the cost of harmony between the husband and wife. If the investment discourages unity in the marriage, don't do it.

4. Sequential Investing Is Best
In Ron Blue's book, *Master Your Money,* he highlights a simple strategy that is profound and will help you as a couple avoid a lot of mistakes. The steps are as follows:[2]

> Step 1: Eliminate all credit card and consumer debt. This provides an immediate investment return of 12–21 percent depending on the interest rate you are paying. This is the first use of any excess margin.
>
> Step 2: Set aside one month's living expenses in the checking account.
>
> Step 3: Invest between two and six months' living expenses in an interest-bearing money market fund account. This is your emergency fund and is the critical step to ensure that you have an amount to "prime the pump" in your budget control system.
>
> Step 4: Save in an interest-bearing account for major purchases such as automobiles, furniture, and home down payments.
>
> Step 5: Accumulate to meet long-term goals.

5. Diversification Is Essential for Preservation of Capital
After you have implemented step 4 in Ron Blue's list you are ready to "invest." At this point you should seek expert advice that will help you develop a diversified investment plan in keeping with your goals, temperament, income, tax bracket, and age.

Any plan should include fixed income investments (bonds, CDs, money market funds, and treasury bills); equities (mutual funds and stocks); and real estate (raw land, income properties, etc.). The percentages will depend upon the previously mentioned factors. The biblical imperative for diversification is found in Eccles. 11:1–2: "Cast your bread on the surface of the waters, for you will find it after many days. Divide your portion to seven, or even to eight, for you do not know what misfortune may occur on the earth."

6. Investments Must Make Economic Sense

In other words, does it have a good chance of generating income or appreciation for you? Is it an investment that will still be a strong asset for you ten to fifteen years from now? In my business I have the privilege of observing financial statements of men and women who have been in business and invested for thirty to forty years. It has become quite obvious to me that there are tried and true investments that stand the test of time and remain a viable long-term economic investment. I typically see stocks, bonds, cash, CDs, and real estate of all kinds on balance sheets. I typically do not see cattle deals, opal mines, energy deals, and the like that have value three or four years after the investment was made. The reason for that is that most of them were tax motivated and not economic value motivated. As a general rule, you should not make tax-motivated investments. Your investment may have tax benefits, but that should not be the motivation. The investment should make economic sense first and foremost; the tax benefits are secondary. If you save $1,000 in taxes but lose your $10,000 investment, how smart was that?

7. Do Not Borrow for an Investment

Even if it is a great deal, it is not worth borrowing for it. "If you can't afford to take the trip, don't buy the ticket." Nothing is worse than paying off the loan on a worthless investment. Furthermore, if you borrow you must be able to earn more on the investment than you are paying for the loan and that requires additional risk. For example, why should I borrow at 10 percent from the bank to try to earn more than 10 percent when if I just didn't borrow I would have the 10 percent return risk-free?

8. Never Co-Sign
"He who is surety for a stranger will surely suffer for it, but he who hates going surety is safe" Prov. 11:15. "Do not be among those who give pledges, among those who become sureties for debts" Prov. 22:26. In all my consulting I have yet to see these verses not come true. Without exception those clients I have consulted with who have co-signed have "suffered for it." If an investment needs a co-signature, that is a sure indication that you shouldn't be doing it.

9. Do Not Get Involved in a Matter Too Great for You (Ps. 131:1)
In other words, don't invest in something you don't know anything about. This gets a man in trouble in two ways. If he knows nothing about it, he must violate the principle of being able to explain it to his wife before doing it. Second, he will likely not be able to ask the pertinent questions necessary to do an effective evaluation. There are enough quality investments that you understand to keep you from pursuing the ones you don't. A friend of mine recently found this out to the tune of $300,000. Instead of keeping his money in areas he was familiar with, he ventured into areas he knew nothing about. This mistake cost him dearly. (Let me add that if you do go into an area like this, it should always be with money you can afford to lose. That is usually what happens.)

In summary, you should understand where investments fit in your overall financial plan and the tremendous potential they have to contribute to conflict rather than harmony in your marriage. You should make every effort to understand your spouse and the distinct differences between men and women as they relate to investments. You should think correctly about investments so as not to be lured by the lies of the world. You should strive for close communication and value it more than a larger net worth. You may miss some great deals, but in the long run the greatest deal is a marriage that works. Don't let investments mess that up!

GAME PLAN

Use this page to list your priority uses of margin as husband and wife. This will provide you with a good starting point for communication as you develop your investment plan as a couple:

Husband's priority	Wife's priority

Chapter 12

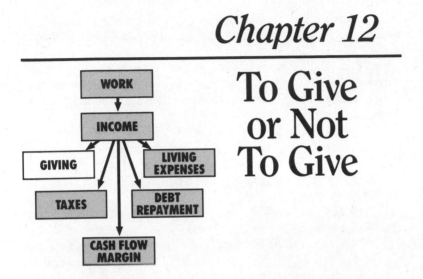

To Give or Not To Give

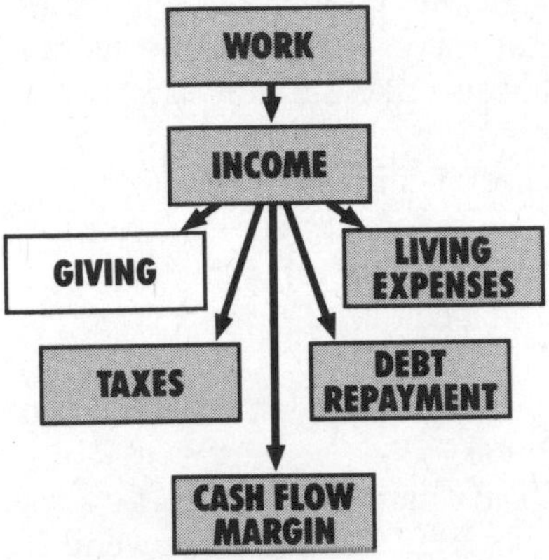

Giving is an act whereby one conveys something to another. The something could be time, a service, a good, or even advice. Giving is also one of the uses you and I have for our money. Is all giving good? How does one determine where to give and how much to give? Is there ever a time one should not give? This chapter will address these questions and others. First, though, let's eavesdrop on conversations that two couples were having about this issue of giving.

It was almost nine o'clock as Bob and Sally slid into the car to drive home after the Sunday evening service. The pastor had talked about the new building program and had challenged everyone to consider prayerfully how much they could give.

"Bob, what did you think about the pastor's comments on giving?"

"Oh, I don't know. It always seems like they never have enough money. If it isn't one thing, it is another. It is hard for me to get too excited about giving. . . . It is like a bottomless pit."

"They really do need the new education wing to meet the needs of all the children. You know, our children will benefit from it too."

"I know. I know. It just seems like so much money. I'm not sure my little bit would help that much . . . and besides, I'm a little uncomfortable giving. It seems like the money is so hard to make. . . ."

"Didn't you hear what the pastor said about giving? How it is for our benefit, and how God commands it?"

"Yeah, I heard him. I still don't really want to give any more. We already give to the general fund a couple of times a year. That should be enough."

"Honey, I really think we should give some more. Don't you think maybe we could pledge $3,000?"

"You've got to be kidding! I just said I really don't want to give any more and you want to give $3,000. I don't believe it! Do you think this money just grows on trees? This always seems to happen. Every few months you start getting on me about giving more. If it's not the building fund, it's the general fund or something else. Can't you see that I really don't want to give very much? I work too hard for it."

"Well, I'm sorry! I didn't know this would make you so upset. I just don't understand why you don't want to give like I do."

"Well, I don't—okay? So let's drop it."

It had been a tough day as Bill started his car to drive home from work. Not only had the boss been pressuring him, but he couldn't get his lunch discussion with Sam off his mind. Sam had been a friend of his for a long time, and it really troubled him to see Sam in such a financial bind. If he didn't help Sam out with $10,000 within the next two days, he could lose his house.

As he drove into the driveway, Bill had decided he would give the money to Sam. After all, he had had a good year at the business and God seemed to continue to bless him and Betty. As he walked into the house he was confident that he should give the money to Sam. He decided he'd wait till after dinner to tell Betty. He was sure she would understand and agree though.

"Honey, I had lunch with Sam today."

"Oh? What did he want?"

"Not much. He and Susie are going through a tough time right now. The new business he got into has taken a little longer than he had anticipated to get off the ground."

"I never was sure he should have quit his old job and started that new one. It seemed too risky to me."

"I think it is a good concept. And according to Sam it's real close to making it. That's why $10,000 should get him over the hump and . . ."

"What did you say?"

"Sam needs $10,000 right now or else he'll lose his house. I decided on the way home that we would give it to him."

"You decided what!"

"Sam is a good friend and so is Susie. I just couldn't stand to see them lose their home. Especially when they are this close to getting the business going. I figured you would understand and agree with me."

"But $10,000! That is a lot of money. What about all the things we need to do—new curtains, microwave, and this carpet has just about had it. Don't you know we need money to do these things?"

"Yeah, I know you've mentioned them, but I just felt like meeting Sam's need was more important now. Don't you?"

"Well, not really. If he hadn't started that stupid business, he wouldn't have this problem. He had a good job before and then he gets some wild idea to press flowers and sell them. I think he should get himself out of this problem. Maybe he should lose his house."

"I really don't understand where you're coming from. We can give him the $10,000 and within the next couple of years do the things you want. . . ."

"That's the problem. It is always 'next year.' Well, I'm tired of next year. . . ."

"Sorry, I guess I shouldn't have brought it up. . . ."

In both conversations it is obvious that there is some disagreement about the issue of giving. Although on the surface it appears that the conflict may be the result of the amount being given, or the reason it's being given, or the person or organization it is being given to, I feel there may be some deeper issues involved.

Let's look at what the root reasons may be and then discuss potential solutions to alleviate the conflict.

In the first conversation we have a situation where the wife wants to give and the husband is not real excited about it. In the second conversation the husband wants to give and the wife doesn't really want to give. In my counseling I have observed both scenarios. There are some reasons that are unique to each situation and some reasons that are germane to both. Let's look at why one spouse may be gung ho about giving and the other spouse more hesitant or totally resistant.

Hesitant Husband

First, the husband may be hesitant to give because his God-given drive to provide makes it more difficult for him to want to give. Giving cuts across the grain of provision. It is easy for a man to reason "how can I provide if I give it away?" or "I can provide better if I don't give so much away." If a husband does want to give, in many cases he may not want to give as much as his wife does.

A caution to you men: The provision drive should never be used as an excuse not to give. If you do not have a desire to give, now is the time for you to evaluate some things. Are you tight with your money? Are you greedy? Do you have a poor self-image that you're salving with your money? Do you have a lack of appreciation for what God has done in your life? Are you hesitant to acknowledge God's hand in your life and in your finances? Giving is a good barometer of all of these things.

Tied in with the provision drive is the financial principle that it takes money to make money. Men understand very well that if they give away capital it will be harder to generate income and create capital because their investment base is reduced. Since most couples have not settled the question, how much is enough? as it relates to their finances, it is especially hard for the breadwinner to want to give much away.

Second, a man may be hesitant to give because of his long-term perspective. He is typically looking down the road and knows he needs to have some money saved for some contingencies the wife may not be inclined to think about because of her "now" orientation. He may see a move coming up that will require funds or he may know that education costs for the kids will be more than originally thought or that the house is going to need painting or that more will be needed for retirement because of inflation. I've observed that many times it is something like this that makes the husband hesitant, but too often he doesn't tell his wife. To avoid conflict over giving he needs to tell her what he's thinking and what potential occurrences in the future have caused him to be resistant to giving now.

Third, the husband may be more hesitant than the wife to give because in most cases he is not as sensitive as she is to the needs. Since women tend to be more emotional and people-centered than men, they are likely to be more tuned in to the needs than men. A man's abstract, calculated, and somewhat insensitive makeup tends to make him less sensitive to needs. Since much giving is in response to an appeal to the emotions that is, in most cases, made by a person, the wife may be more inclined to give than her husband. I know this is true with Julie and me. If someone asks us for money, she is typically more inclined to feel for the individual asking or the need expressed than I am. My first response is to figure out why the need exists and whether it is legitimate.

Hesitant Wife

The first reason the wife may be hesitant when her husband starts talking about giving money away is that it is easy for her to see her security going with it. Just as the man saw money as a source of capital and income, the wife sees it as security and comfort. How can she be taken care of if he is giving money away?

Second, the wife typically sees a lot of uses of cash that the husband may not see. In our case, Betty knew about the carpet, curtains, and microwave. These items were important to her and probably a long way from Bill's mind. Cash is more important to the wife because she is responsible for more of the day-to-day items for which the cash is needed. She may be hesitant to give the money away. I have observed, however, that women who are hesitant to give are not nearly as hesitant if a noncash asset is given away (real estate, stock, mutual fund).

I vividly remember a meeting with a couple where the importance of cash was the issue in the giving decision. Their net worth was $5 million, but most of it was tied up in land. The husband had a very sensitive heart to giving needs and wanted to help a friend so his friend would not lose his business. He wanted to give his friend $30,000. This was not a large amount in relation to his net worth but was a significant portion of his cash. Also there were some things for the home that his wife had been planning to get. Needless to say, the discussion was tense as she let him know in no uncertain terms that he had better not give that money away. Tension ran high over the lunch table—all because a man wanted to do something good but was not being sensitive to his wife's needs. No matter how great the need for our money, our greatest need is to promote harmony and unity in our marriages. We need to be careful that we are not giving away our marriages as we give away our money.

The third reason that a woman may be hesitant is that her husband does not communicate. He just drops on her his desire to give without helping her see how it will affect the big picture. Most women, I have observed, will not fight giving if they are communicated with and showed that their security is not being threatened with the gift. Communication is also critical to help them understand why you really want to give and where it fits into the overall plan.

Like their husbands, wives must be careful not to use these principles to excuse not giving. Hesitancy about giving should lead a woman to look closely at her attitudes. She may not be appreciative and thankful to God for all that He has done and is doing in her life. She may have a poor self-image and as a result be trying to buy a "position" among her peers. She may be greedy and selfish. She may not be growing spiritually, and as a result her sensitivity to giving is not keen.

Both Hesitant

Three additional reasons relate to both the wife and the husband. First, since giving is not a natural activity but supernatural, it requires spiritual maturity on the part of the giver. Giving results from being in close fellowship with God on a daily basis. If either spouse is not growing spiritually, there may be some hesitation on that person's part when it comes to giving. It is not uncommon in a marriage relationship for one spouse to be farther along on his/her spiritual journey than the other. This can very easily cause conflict as the more spiritual spouse may want to give while the other is more hesitant.

It is important for each spouse to give the other freedom to grow spiritually. With time and prayer, your partner may come to the same level of desire for giving that you are experiencing now.

Second, one spouse may hesitate because he or she has seen poor giving decisions made in the past. For instance, the last time Bill gave money to a friend it really didn't help the friend and instead made the situation worse. Perhaps the charity did not use the money wisely. For any one of a number of reasons, that earlier gift was perceived to have been poorly used. An unwise use of money given by either spouse may cause hesitancy toward future giving on the part of the other.

Third, it is not uncommon for one spouse to have a "heart to give" and the other to not have the same "heart" or zeal. One spouse may have the spiritual gift of giving while the other doesn't. This is not good or bad but needs to be understood as a potential reason for hesitancy on the part of one spouse. If you have not taken a spiritual gifts test, you should do so in order to learn what your spouse's gift is and how it manifests itself.

Finally, both spouses are again strongly influenced by their respective backgrounds. One spouse may have come from a family where giving was an integral part of life; the parents may have invited missionaries to their home and always met any need that came along. The other spouse may have come from a home where the parents really didn't give much, if at all. Giving was something you just didn't do. The key point again is to realize that the different backgrounds could cause hesitancy on the part of one partner.

This is what happened to Julie and me. Early on we didn't give much because I had not really seen giving modeled in my family. Although Julie wanted to give and came from a family that gave, she did not push me to give. Rather she let me grow spiritually to where I really wanted to give and then allowed me to develop our family's own giving plan—the people and organizations that I would support now that we were married.

What good does it do to give a lot of money to others and to charity and have disunity and frustration on the home front?

Julie and I have found that it is critical to communicate about this area just as we do about investments. Just because the issue is giving and giving is thought of as "good" does not mean there will not be potential conflict. We have found that it is critical to communicate about *where we give, how much we give, and why we give.* Let's look at some principles regarding each of these in order to facilitate communication in your marriage and correct thinking about giving.

Why Give?

First of all, we give to *acknowledge ownership.* Since God owns all that we have—"What do you have that you weren't given?" (1 Cor. 4:7)—and has allowed us to be a steward of it, our giving is a way of acknowledging God's ownership. It ensures that we are holding all that He has entrusted to us with an open hand. It is impossible to give with a closed hand. The act of giving is a physical, measurable evidence of our belief in God's ownership of all that we have. It shows our love for Him.

When we give, we acknowledge that it is God who ultimately provides our needs. It is He who gives us the ability to make wealth. This fact will help men overcome the fear of giving that stems from their provision drive. When they understand that it is God, not they themselves, who provides what they need, they will be freed up to give. Likewise this truth of God's ownership and ultimate provision will help women realize that no amount of cash can bring ultimate security. Their security is ultimately in the Lord. This will help them be freed up to give. Giving ultimately disarms the power of money.

Not only does giving acknowledge God's ownership, but it acknowledges God and my relationship with Him. "The act of giving best reminds me of my place on earth. All of us live here by the goodness and grace of God—like the birds of the air and the flowers of the field, Jesus said. Those creations do not worry about future security and safety; neither should we. Not even Solomon, the wealthiest man of his time, could outshine a common lily. Giving offers me a way to express my faith and confidence that God will care for me just as he cares for the sparrow and lily."[1]

Second, we give to *meet the needs of others.* In Exod. 16:18 and 2 Cor. 8:15 we see that he who has been given a surplus has been given it to supply the want and need of another. This does not mean that if you do not have a large surplus (margin or savings), you are exempt from giving. Everyone needs to give something to acknowledge ownership, as stated above. However, many of us have a surplus (especially if we control our living expenses) and with this surplus we are to help those who are in need. All we have to do is look around us, and we will see many who could use our help. As I study the Scripture, I see that the widows, the poor, and the orphans are the responsibility of the "church" you and I (Deut. 15:10–11). That is one of the reasons we have money and one of the reasons we are to give. We need to open our eyes and see where God wants us to help out. Giving to meet the needs of our fellow man shows our love for God. As we give to others people will praise God and also come to know Him (2 Cor. 9:12–14). Since giving is supernatural, it is one way we can be a testimony to the world.

Third, we give because of the *benefit that accrues to us.* In Philippians 4 Paul shares that he does not seek a gift from the Philippians for the gift itself but rather for the profit that increases in the account of the giver (v. 17). In 2 Cor. 9:8 we see that the giver will have all grace abound to him and have all sufficiency in everything and an abundance for every good deed. What is the benefit to the giver?

Many today would have us think that the benefit is more money. If I give money, God will give money back to me. The more I give, the more I'll get. It seems to me, however, that the benefit Paul was talking about that accrued to the giver was much deeper than potential material blessings. The main benefit was the freeing of the giver from the bondage of money. "Giving destroys the aura of worth surrounding money. Instinctively, we hoard money in steel vaults and secret caches; giving flagrantly sets it free. Giving proves to be an effective antidote to the temptations of money idolatry because it brings to money the power of grace."[2] Giving money away helps us keep our focus off it. This is the greatest benefit. It keeps us from longing after it and potentially wandering away from the faith, and piercing ourselves with many a pang (1 Tim. 6:10).

Finally, we give out of *obedience* to God. God commands us to give. In Prov. 3:9–10 we read, "Honor the Lord from your wealth, and from the first of all your produce; so your barns will be filled with plenty, and your vats will overflow with new wine."

God does not need our money. But we need to give it. Giving is for our benefit. It flows from our thankfulness to God for all His blessings to us. What a good exercise workout does to the physical body—tones it, shapes it, and makes it work better—giving does to the spiritual dimension of man. It helps him keep his perspective healthy. It keeps him from depending on money for his happiness. Giving is a good barometer of our spiritual maturity.

WHERE TO GIVE

Your giving can be broken down into three general categories. You can give to charity, family, or others. Let's look at each of them.

In giving to *charity* we find several guidelines in Scripture. We are to meet the needs of those who teach and lead us (Gal. 6:6); we are to meet the needs of the poor and the widows (1 John 3:17); we are to give for the furtherance of the gospel (1 Tim. 5:18); we are to give to the promotion of discipleship (1 Cor. 9:11, 14). These general guidelines can be met through giving to your church, to a parachurch organization, and/or to people involved in each of the areas. Many people I know teach "storehouse giving." It is not the purpose of this book to debate the validity of that concept. Suffice it to say, you should, at a minimum, be meeting the needs listed. If your church does that in a way you are comfortable with, you may be okay with channeling all your giving through the church. If not, you will need to find other avenues to meet the various needs.

As a couple, you may find that you are more inclined to give to one need than to another. Perhaps you have a heart for the poor more than for discipleship. It is up to you to communicate with each other and prayerfully consider where God would have you give. The checklist at the end of this chapter will help you in your decision making.

In giving to *family* you need to weigh carefully the maturity and stewardship ability of the one to whom the money is given. There is much conflict in marriages over how much and when to give to family members, primarily children. It is important for you as husband and wife to communicate regarding such issues as why you are giving money to your children and what you want them to learn. Too often, couples do not ask these questions and just give money to their children without a thought as to the potential consequences. (Ron and Judy Blue have written a book, *Money Matters for Parents and Their Kids,* that addresses a lot of the issues that should be thought through regarding giving to family.)

Giving to *others* is probably the area where I have seen some of the greatest marriage conflict. One reason is that usually it is an urgent need, and one of the spouses gets a burden to give and does so without talking to the other. The other reason is that one of the spouses does not see why the individual needs the money. Remember Betty? She didn't see why Sam couldn't work his way out of the problem.

In giving to others, it is critical to make sure that your giving is not going to short-circuit what God may be trying to do in that individual's life. You can only determine this by much time in prayer to God and communication with your spouse. As with any decision, receiving counsel is wise and where better to get that counsel on a giving decision than from your spouse?

How Much to Give and How to Give It

The "how much" is simple. It is between you, your spouse, and God. It would be nice if the Bible would tell us an exact amount or percentage to give. As a matter of fact, most of us want a flat percentage, so we can feel that that amount is God's and the rest is ours to do what we want to with. As we've seen, however, God owns it all, and part of our training process in obedience is communicating with him in this area of giving.

So how much do I give? A study of the Old Testament reveals that the tithe is in reality 23 percent and not the commonly used 10 percent. (An annual tithe of 10 percent was required for the maintenance of the Levites [Lev. 27:30; Num. 18:21], a second tithe of 10 percent was brought to Jerusalem for the Lord's feast [Deut. 14:22], and every third year an additional 10 percent was to be collected for strangers, widows, and orphans.) The New Testament sets a new standard for giving—the example of Christ—and mentions tithing only in connection with the old covenant. The guideline for giving under grace, not law, is found in 2 Cor. 9:6–7,

"Now this I say, he who sows sparingly shall also reap sparingly, and he who sows bountifully shall also reap bountifully. *Let each one do just as he has purposed in his heart; not grudgingly or under compulsion; for God loves a cheerful giver."* We also see in 2 Cor. 8:12 that we are to give in *accordance to how we have been prospered.* From the one who has been given much, much is required (Luke 12:48).

Since the "how much" is not black and white, it is important to communicate as a couple and have a plan concerning your giving. At my firm we have learned that people don't give because they don't know they can, they don't know how, and they don't *plan* to. Without a plan couples tend to spend all their income on living expenses, leaving nothing to give. Once a plan is developed and living expenses are controlled, couples find out they can give. The plan helps them with the amount they can give and becomes a basis for communication that can help them avoid the impulsive (not well-thought-out) giving we saw in the case studies at the beginning of this chapter. The plan helps giving become a basis of communication rather than a source of conflict.

I remember vividly in one of my earlier consulting appointments uncovering a tremendous lack of harmony as a result of this giving area. The wife wanted to give, and the husband really didn't want to. It was obvious, after looking at their net worth, that they could afford to give. The husband, however, was just reluctant because of background, provision sensitivity, and so on. After I did a financial plan for them and showed them the impact of various levels of giving on their current cash flow as well as on the long-term growth of their net worth, the husband became more comfortable with giving. As a matter of fact, they increased their annual giving tenfold. It has been exciting to see the increased harmony in their marriage, not to mention the significant giving they are now doing. The plan was the impetus.

The parameters, then, for "how much" are on the one hand to give a small amount to acknowledge ownership and on the other hand to give it all away. Anywhere in between is an issue between you and God and a function of your financial position.

The answer to the "how to" question is quite obvious. *Cheerfully!* In Prov. 3:9–10 and 1 Cor. 16:2 we see two other how to's.

We're also to give from the *first* of *all* of our income, and we are to give *periodically as the income is received.*

At the beginning of this chapter we asked whether all giving is good and whether there is ever a time not to give. Giving is good if it is done prayerfully and in harmony with your spouse. It is good if it does not cause a stumbling block for the recipient or for your own relationship with your spouse. It is good if it is done with the right attitude. When should you not give? You should not give if it drives a wedge in your marriage relationship. Remember, God does not need your money. Giving is for your benefit. What good does it do if you build the entire education wing on your church and lose your spouse? What good does it do if you give and never communicate with your children?

GAME PLAN

On the following page is a "giving worksheet" to help you communicate with your spouse about giving. Before doing this sheet, however, make sure you have determined the amount you have available in the giving category by working through the diagram we've used throughout this book. You must have a positive margin. If your giving creates a negative margin (dips into savings), you need to reduce your living expenses, debt, or giving. You cannot have financial peace without a positive margin.

Many of our clients have come to us because of this giving area of their finances. Since it is such a subjective area, it is difficult for a person to see clearly enough to evaluate whether he has his giving in proper order. You may want to find an accountability partner so you can determine if your giving is proportionate to your income or if you've succumbed to the world and allowed living expenses to get too high. Larry Burkett's book, *Your Finances in Changing Times,* contains some helpful criteria for helping you evaluate how and to whom you should give the surplus God has given you.

Plan Your Giving Matt. 28:18–20

What	Where				How Much
	City	State	Country	World	
	(Atlanta)	(Ga.)	(USA)		
1. *Local Church*					
Building					
Teachers/pastors					
Evangelism					
Discipleship					
2. *The Needy*					
Poor					
Widows					
Orphans					
3. *Fulfill Great Commission*					
Evangelism					
Discipleship					
Christian school					
Parachurch organizations					

Chapter 13

A Woman Looks at Finances and the Woman's Role

According to the personality tests Russ and I are both high Ds, which means we are both very bold and determined to get our way. My dad told us before we got married that we wouldn't make it unless the Holy Spirit was in control of both of our lives. The principles that I am going to share have not come easily for me, as I wrestled with obeying God and His Word versus doing things my way.

As a nurse anesthetist, I was well trained, well paid, could change my own tires and oil, and could do everything a man could; I didn't need a man. I wanted it all: sports cars, travel, designer clothes, no cooking, cleaning, or dishes, just a fancy job and an exciting life. This did not include a husband that I would have to submit to, and especially not one that didn't make much money.

Mind you, I had not been raised this way. I came from a very godly home where my mom and dad loved each other very much. Mom was an incredible example of biblical submission, and Dad respected and honored her. You would think that I would be looking for that kind of marriage, but I wasn't.

Then I met Russ. He came from a family where his dad was the authority in the home. It was obvious that Russ thought women should fit the biblical pattern, especially in marriage. Even though he was an "enemy," so to speak, he fascinated me with his strong leadership and desire to walk with God. After we had dated a year, Russ asked me to marry him. I told him there was no way. I finally had to come to grips with why. I did not want to have to submit. Along with submission came the fact that he was a teacher, and I was not going to be poor. I became very confused, and I couldn't sleep at night. It became clear that sin was clouding my ability to think. I asked the Lord to reveal the sin in my life. Selfishness, wanting my own way, pride, not trusting God and His Word, all paraded in front of my mind's eye. I realized that I thought money could make me happy and was unwilling to do without new clothes, jewelry, new cars, eating out, or vacations in order to fit into my husband's income.

I confessed these things one by one, and the effect was like a breath of fresh air; I was able to think clearly again. All of a sudden it dawned on me that Russ had all the qualities that I had prayed for in a husband. That night I made a commitment to God to *submit* to Russ for the rest of my life. No matter what that meant—living on a teacher's income, living in Africa, watching football on Sunday afternoons—I chose to be obedient to God's plan for marriage.

Several years ago, I was asked to do a short talk on the stress of budgeting for women. At first, I thought I would pull together an informative talk about cash flow, debt, investment strategy, compounding interest, long- and short-term perspectives, and so on. As I considered my approach, I was not comfortable because all those things are subject to the husband's final word. If I did educate my audience on the finer points of finances, would I be doing them and their marriages any favor? I began to ask myself questions. What should *I* be doing? Should I read the business page, *Wall Street Journal,* track the NYSE? Should I work vocationally, make investments, deal in real estate, send off to every sweepstakes? Was it important for me to pick mutual funds, do my own taxes, know what FDIC means, understand the federal deficit? What does God want me to do?

Having already studied the Scripture for my role in marriage, I went back to find guidelines for the financial area. I believe

God holds me accountable for finances in three areas of my role. They are:

being *submissive,* financially, to my husband;

being a *helper,* financially, to my husband;

being *content,* financially, where I am.

My understanding of these three areas directly affects how I handle and respond to money issues in my marriage. Learning how to be content with my husband's income, understanding my influence as a helper, and fitting into my husband's plans make for a harmonious marriage.

SUBMISSION

When I think of *submission,* I like the term "fitting in." In 1 Pet. 3:1 (LB), we see, "Wives, *fit in* with your husband's plans." The Amplified Bible says, ". . . adapt yourselves to them." "Adapt" means to make to fit; to knit together; to be properly adjusted to the shape intended. To me, the words "adjust," "adapt," and "fit," mean—in a financial sense—that I do with money what Russ wants. I fit in with his plans by staying within the budget.

This component of fitting in is made clear in Prov. 31:11, Amplified Bible, which says, "The heart of her husband trusts in her confidently. . . . so that he has no lack of honest gain [she doesn't waste his income] or need of dishonest spoil [she doesn't pressure him for things he can't afford]." Any comment, even in jest, that makes him think you are not happy with what you have or with what he provides could make him feel like a failure, thus pressuring him to cheat on his income tax or jump into a get-rich-quick scheme. We know of a wife who told her husband that she would not have people over until he let her do $20,000 worth of redecorating (which they couldn't afford). What pressure was he under? Since his provision wasn't enough for her, dishonest spoil might be attractive. A man's desire to please his wife is very strong.

Matthew Henry's *Commentary* says, "She contributes so much to his content 'that he shall have no need of spoil;' he need not be griping and scraping abroad, as those must be whose wives are proud and wasteful at home. He thinks himself so happy in her that he envies not those who have most of the wealth of this world; he needs it not, he has enough, having such a wife."[1]

"Everything is so carefully and economically managed, (she is careful to be a good steward so that he feels completely relaxed with her in the area of finances) he is never tempted to dishonesty to fulfill his desires, no need to leave his happy home. Her husband's comfort is her interest and her rest. To live for him is her highest happiness."[2] Which is more important: securing my husband's trust or buying what I want and always having conflict over finances?

Titus 2:4–5 instructs the "young women to love their husbands, to love their children, to be sensible, pure, workers [keepers, KJV] at home [homemakers, Amplified], kind, being subject to their own husbands, that the word of God may not be dishonored." There are several things we can draw from this. First, the word *subject* means "placed under." I really like the illustration of president and vice president. We work together as a team for the good of the whole. I am the vice president. I have a responsibility to work hard, give input, handle my areas of accountability, take over in the president's absence, etc. Even the business world accepts the fact that the president is the final decision maker, but that in no way defeats the importance of the vice president. It is the way the system works best.

Second, we see the concept of keeper. The Greek word *oikourgos,* "keeper at home," describes someone as guarding, staying at home, being a good homemaker, having to do with home and family. It combines the root words for "house" and "work." This tells me where my primary focus should be. As a keeper I should have the same standards for excellence and work just as hard at home as when I was a nurse anesthetist.

Third, another important thing in this passage is the reason I am to stay in my God-given role—so the word of God won't be dishonored.

Doing my job as unto the Lord will have untold financial benefits that I may never be aware of! I knew a family where the mother violated several principles of keeping her home and being subject to her husband. She did not guard her daughter from the wrong friends. She refused to move when her husband was transferred because she didn't want to leave her job. Her daughter is now serving a prison sentence because of a crime she committed. Where would her daughter be now if she had been guarding her from wrong friends, if she had been willing to live in a smaller house so she could be home watching for destructive tendencies, if she had been willing to move for her husband's benefit, which would have taken the girl out of a bad environment? The husband lost his job, and they spent every penny they had on court costs.

To me, God's job description for women in marriage is not the easy way out. It takes a strong woman, committed to God and her husband, walking in the Spirit, to do this. To some, this may seem "below" them, but in God's economy unselfishness and servanthood are important.

In order to think correctly about submission, it's important to understand what submission is not. First, submission is not inferiority as opposed to superiority. Men were not given their position of headship (leadership) because they are more intelligent, stronger, better, or any other such thing. Their position was assigned from the beginning by God. The leadership and authority went to the man at the same time the responsibility went to him. Authority follows responsibility. The position of submission is one of protection for us. 1 Tim. 2:14 says, "but the woman being quite deceived, fell into transgression." Eve would have saved herself a lot of heartache if she had stayed under Adam's authority.

Second, submission is not dependent upon who is right. You are to give input—he needs that—but the final decision is his. Don Meredith, in his book, *Becoming One,* states, "Women are to absolutely submit themselves to their husbands without excuses as they entrust themselves to God. No matter how strong the proof of her husband's weaknesses, there are no exception clauses in God's command to her. Peter goes out of his way to make this clear by stating, 'even if any of them are disobedient to the word . . .'"[3]

Are there limits to submission? The answer is yes. God will not absolve you from responsibility just because your husband told you to commit a sin. Submission is not an excuse for sin. If your husband abuses his position of leadership and asks you to go against a moral law of Scripture, you need to submit to the higher law of God. But don't use spirituality as an excuse to get out of something you just don't want to do.

Third, submission is not dependent on the spiritual state of your husband. In 1 Pet. 3:1–2 we read, "In the same way, you wives, be submissive to your own husbands so that even if any of them are disobedient to the word, they may be won without a word by the behavior of their wives, as they observe your chaste and respectful behavior." It seems clear that even if our husbands are not where they should be spiritually (or where we think they should be), our response is crucial.

Whenever I have spoken to groups of women about a wife's fitting in with her husband's plans, the question, "What about me, what about my fulfillment?" always comes up. Well, what about "me"? Do I want a good marriage, God's way? Fulfillment comes from doing what I was created to do. Do I want peace in my home? Scripture doesn't uphold "me"-ism. 1 Cor. 6:19–20 says, "Do you not know . . . that you are not your own? For you have been bought with a price: therefore glorify God in your body." In Rom. 14:7–8 we are told that "not one of us lives for himself . . . ; for if we live, we live for the Lord . . . ; therefore whether we live or die, we are the Lord's." In 1 Cor. 7:34 we read, ". . . but one who is married is concerned about the things of the world, how she may please her husband." As Christians, none of us has the right to live for self. As a Christian woman, getting married committed me even further to not living for myself but for my husband and family.

Even the secular world is beginning to see the need for the woman to fill her role. In the Atlanta paper there was an article entitled "Individualism Now Seen as Divisive to the Family." A conference of leaders of labor, management, government and academia met to discuss work and family. This is what they said: "Individualistic tradition has been one of our greatest strengths. . . . it is becoming in its present undisciplined forms one of our greatest liabilities. Gone are the days when family concerns were left at the front door of the house in the capable hands of the mother at home. Today, there's often no one at home and family worries are another part of the daily workload. If work and family are inseparable, if they are both essential to make individual lives meaningful and constructive . . . then let's stop fooling around. Families have to be first because if they don't, work does not only become second-best, it becomes second-rate."[4] We need to restore the honor back to the wives and mothers at home, don't we?

Personally, I like being in submission to Russ. It takes all the pressure off me for the big, heavy decisions. I tell him, here's my input, now I'm trusting God with your decision. I am amazed at how a woman's position of influence can be more powerful than a man's position of leadership when her attitude is right.

HELPER

The second component is that of being a *helper.* Let's go to Gen. 2:18, for it is there that we will find why God created woman. "Then the Lord God said, 'It is not good for the man to be alone; I will make him a helper suitable for him.'" The one word that defines my existence as a married woman is helper—but what does it mean and how do I apply it to finances? I went to the dictionary to find out. For each definition of *help,* I jotted down a completion or extension or rewording that would bring out my purpose. Perhaps my notes (in parenthesis) will be useful to you.

> *to be responsible for* (husband, children, home).
>
> *to make it easier for him to do something* (taking carc of the home front so he's free to concentrate on work).
>
> *to ease or share his labor* (letting him know I am happy and will stay within the budget no matter what the income).
>
> *to make it easier for him to exist, develop, happen, improve* (make him a success by taking the pressure off him for more money).
>
> *to cause improvement in him* (my contentment with his income allows him to feel that he is a success, he is happier with himself, me, and his job).
>
> *to make him more effective, larger; to aid his growth* (by not spending our money unnecessarily).
>
> *to promote him* (may literally mean a raise or promotion for him because I am easing his load at home, allowing him to be effective at work; speak positively about him).
>
> *to serve or wait on him* (make sure his needs are met; make him the most important thing in my life).

to give assistance, be cooperative, useful, beneficial to him (I am on his team, united in producing the same effect; my efforts are concurrent with his).

to supply another with whatever is necessary to accomplish his ends or relieve his wants (I take care of my job description and create "peace at home").

The antonym of the word "help" is "hinder": to get in the way of, make difficult for, obstruct. "To obstruct" means "to retard progress by placing obstacles in the way." If I'm not helping him I will:

hold him back (by not trusting God for him or me; by refusing to move if his vocation relocates him).

restrain him (by taking things in my own hands or nagging him).

get in his way (by overspending, making him unhappy).

make it difficult for him (undermine his efforts to save money; insist that he come home early so I can do my thing).

thwart him, impede his progress (forcing him to take a second job to pay off my credit cards).

frustrate him (by my discontent and comparisons).

slow up his progress (because he has to come home early and help me with my job, he can't concentrate 100 percent on work).

retard his progress by putting obstacles in his way (refusing to live on less in a new or better job for him).

What if a presidential campaign manager, in the heat of an upcoming election, gets a second job as a shoe salesman in order to "find" himself? Or the assistant head coach, during the Super Bowl, goes to work at a fast-food place because no one notices all that he has been contributing to the game? We would all agree that these people just didn't understand their job description nor their importance and contribution in filling that description. If we think working outside the home is helping because we are more fulfilled, then we don't understand our God-given job description. A letter my dad wrote me when I quit work has been of great benefit. Here is a portion of it:

> Now then—work. I have some thoughts to submit for your perusal. Namely—I think it is very good for you *not* to work! In my opinion you were right on to go ahead and get the training and do the job—and you did it extremely well. [Dad was an anesthesiologist, and I worked for his group.] But now, you are married. That changes things. The anesthesia thing is *completely* separate from Russ—and you spend *most* of your waking life in it. Whereas, no work—spend most of your time being *wife* and involved in Russ's life. That's much better! Further, a nurse anesthetist *must* be a *strong, independent, stand-up-to-the-men* type person. . . . Those are not exactly qualities to be developed in marriage. Anyway, it just this week dawned on me that I hope you *don't* go back to it. How about that! Rather, you can be full-time wife and homemaker—which is a *real* and Godly calling, and very, *very* wonderful. You will have plenty to do—with being available to people and to Russ.

I am convinced that God does not hold me responsible to help my husband afford a larger house, a nicer car, and more expensive clothes. He will ask me how I did on His job description for me. Did I submit and love my husband, love my children, work at home, train my children, extend hospitality, help Russ, and ease his load? One of the best ways for me to help my husband is to be content.

CONTENTMENT

The third component is *contentment.* Contentment is an attitude: realizing that God has provided everything I need for my present circumstances. I'm reminded of the story of the two little boys that were given shovels and pointed to a room full of manure. The one boy grumbled the whole time. The other went to work very excited. The reason? With all that manure, there had to be a pony in there somewhere. One day, while complaining to myself about all the laundry, cleaning, cooking, ironing, and other thankless jobs, I ran across Prov. 14:4, which says, "Where no oxen are, the stable is clean." It hit me that all my work meant I was blessed with a husband and children! Attitude is key, isn't it? Contentment means having a mind at peace, satisfied with what you have and your circumstances; it means not demanding more. A mind centered on the Lord doesn't have to be buying things to be happy. Dr. Sam Peoples has a saying that gets right to the point. "The circumstances of life and the people around me in life do not make me the way I am but reveal the way I am."[5] Are your circumstances revealing a heart of contentment?

When I married Russ, I vowed before God to love, cherish, honor, obey him for richer or for poorer. That meant that I committed myself to be content with his income for the rest of my life. God takes our vows very seriously, and so should I. Because contentment is a spiritual issue, the more I understand what God says about contentment, the easier it becomes to be content where He has me.

In 1 Tim 6:7–10, verse 8 says, "And if we have food and covering, with these we shall be content." Do we have food and clothing? Are we content? We should be.

I feel the best way for a woman to learn contentment is to live frugally, because this takes the pressure off her husband. I also think it helps if a woman learns to be content with little, making it possible to be content with a lot if that happens. My mom calls it having a "do-without" mind-set. In watching her, I realized that because of this she was always content, didn't pressure Dad for things, and was happy just being with him; she allowed Dad to change careers when he felt it was time.

Being content with what we have is a lost art today. Luke 3:14 says, ". . . be content with your wages." That's easy to interpret, isn't it? Heb. 13:5 says, "Let your character be free from the love of money, being content with what you have, for He . . . will never forsake you." Eccles. 5:10 says, "He who loves money will not be satisfied with money." Since content means being satisfied with what we have, love of money is not the answer. The point is to trust God, give up expectations, and be content. In Phil. 4:11–13, Paul tells us that he *learned* contentment in all circumstances. Does that explain why we are to consider it all *joy* when we encounter various trials (James 1:2)? We are learning contentment! Credit cards are certainly no help. They take the joy out of waiting. One year we decided to buy a dining room table that we liked. We had to save for another year to be able to pay cash for it. I appreciate that table so much more than if we had just charged it. There are many benefits of doing without, even though we all prefer the benefits of plenty. I ran across a little poem that I really like[6]:

Use it up,
Wear it out,
Make it do,
Do without.

I think that should be a standard feature on every credit card.

Credit cards make it too easy to get around learning contentment and indulge our misdefined "need." Paul also says in Phil. 4:19 that "my God shall supply all your needs according to His riches in glory in Christ Jesus." I've seen two problems with the word *need:* a lack of definition and a lack of honesty. Something you need is necessary to subsistence. I like to compare *need* with *want* and *desire* to help me use the word correctly.

Need	*Want*	*Desire*
hamburger	steak	lobster
VW	Cutlass	Mercedes
apartment	house	mansion
homemade dress	department store dress	designer dress
water	tea	Perrier

Now, it's important to be honest. We almost all have what we need. That's almost a given in our country. We don't all have what we want and desire, but we say the wrong thing. I have told Russ that I need a new outfit for a certain event. That isn't right. I *want* a new outfit; I already have what I need. I cringe when I hear gals say they have to work because they needed a bigger house or car. They have to work because they *wanted* a bigger house or car.

The key here is attitude toward what you have and what your husband is able to provide. A man needs to feel that he all his wife wants and needs. When Black Monday hit during October 1987, I communicated to Russ that I was okay if the economy and business took a downturn. I told him I did not have to have our house, cars, and vacations to be happy. I told him he was all I needed, and I would live anywhere with him. I was willing to do whatever it took to help him be a success in God's eyes. The next day he told me he really appreciated that because it freed him up at work to do his job rather than worrying about what I might think or do if I lost all my nice things. It's very important for me to *verbally* express my contentment to Russ. So many times I will think to myself how fortunate I am to have him, but I don't tell him that. So I try to let him know frequently that I have everything I need. I am happy right where I am. I don't need a bigger house, a fancier car, or new clothes. Most of all, I'm wealthy because I have him and his children. Are you content with your needs being met? Are you able to hold your wants and desires in an open hand, willing for God to take them at any time?

To me, as a woman, the key to finances is contentment, and the key to contentment is thankfulness. I practice thankfulness by making lists of things that I am grateful for that money can't buy (my own children; love; my salvation; a husband who loves me and God with all his heart; my husband's job; a mind that works; a sense of humor; the ability to see, hear, taste, touch; a free country; competent medical care in this country; etc.). It also helps me to read good books (see appendix). It keeps God's perspective before me and helps me realize that others face the same difficulties I do.

DISCONTENT

What is discontent? It means having a disquieted mind, dissatisfaction, uneasiness from the want of gratification or from disappointed wishes or expectations. Discontent keeps us from enjoying what we do have. Discontent shows up when I find myself thinking, "I wish. . . ." I wish I had a dining room set, I wish I had a new car, I wish I had new clothes, I wish I had a fur coat, I wish I didn't have to look for sales or cut coupons.

Discontent can show up in dislike of what I have, or a desire for something different. Two years ago we had a banquet to attend, and I wanted something new to wear. Not only did I wish for something new, I disliked all the nice things I already had. It's not discontent to need a new car, or carpet, or washing machine—the problem is to be discontented with the old until you can afford the new. Men typically desire to please their wives, so the subtle pressure of "I wish . . . I'm tired of . . ." (comparing your husband, your house, and your car with others) puts them under tremendous pressure. (Did you know the Bible talks about comparison to others? In studying Matt. 20:15, ". . . or is your eye envious because I am generous?" I came up with this paraphrase: "God can do what He wants with what is His. Are you envious because He is generous to someone else? Can you be glad for someone driving a BMW when you have a VW?" Envy means a feeling of discontent and ill will because of another's advantages or possessions.) A good measure of dissatisfaction or discontent is consumer debt. "People buy things they don't need with money they don't have to impress neighbors they don't even like"[7] because of their discontent. How much do you use that credit card and carry a balance on it?

The dangerous thing about discontent is that it is the start of covetousness (wanting excessively to have; desiring more than one needs; desiring what another rightfully possesses; being greedy), which Col. 3:5 equates with idolatry. "So kill . . . the evil desire lurking in your members . . . and all greed and covetousness, for that is idolatry" (Amplified). To me, discontent shows an unwillingness to trust God for where you are and what you have, or don't have.

I am convinced that a woman can destroy her husband and her family by her discontent. In Prov. 14:1, the Bible says that "the wise woman builds her home but the foolish woman tears it down with her own hands." This is a slow process either way. I think the "building up" is loving your husband and children and doing what is best for them—devoting your time to raise, encourage, discipline, train, love, and enjoy your children, and pray for, support, and meet your husband's needs. I think that "tearing down" is discontent. A commentary on the Book of Proverbs says that "a wife is either a blessing or a curse to her husband. Her wisdom may make up for many of his defects; while all the results of his care and good stewardship may be wasted by her foolishness. She instructs her children by her example. . . . She educates them for God and for eternity; . . . Who can estimate the worth of a Christian mother? But consider the foolish woman, her idleness, waste, love of pleasure, want of forethought and care, her children allowed their own way, her happiness ruined! It is the undoing of her own hands."[8]

The results of a wife's discontent (for whatever reason) can take many forms. First, a husband can respond by overworking. He feels that if he can make more money, he can please his wife. This can lead a man to not only work longer hours but to also make poor decisions at work or be enticed into poor business deals as he feels more and more pressure from home.

Second, a wife's discontent can make her husband unhappy at work. Whenever Russ comes home and tells me he has been in a bad mood at work, a warning flag goes up. He may be responding to my discontent. Once he was responding to a comment said in jest, about how I didn't like living in Atlanta. He felt he had made me unhappy by bringing me here. Husbands just don't like feeling they can't provide or do enough to keep their wives happy.

Third, some men will get away from the wife's discontent and constant "I wish" by giving up. He may tell her to just go charge it. A man does this to get his wife off his back. This leads to debt pressures, and a vicious cycle is started that adds pressure to the marriage. This husband can begin to lose interest in work because he knows he can't earn enough to keep his wife happy and pay off the debt. I saw this firsthand when we stayed with some new friends. Their home was a mansion! Under the surface was a husband who was despondent. His wife would not stop spending money. He was heavily into debt with no hope of repaying all she had spent, and she continued to overspend.

Finally, some husbands insist that their wives work. This can also be a man's tactic to get the pressure of his wife's discontent off him. A friend of mine recently complained to me that her husband wouldn't let her quit work. I asked her if she had ever expressed her willingness to be content on his income. Grinning, she told me he wouldn't mind her staying home, but he told her she couldn't have the fancy restaurants and vacations that she wants. Clearly, he felt that he couldn't provide enough to keep her happy. Since she wanted the extras, then he insisted that she work.

So how do I apply all this? Basically, I ask the Lord to give me wisdom to communicate the right things to Russ. I communicate to Russ that I want him to be able to accomplish his goals, that he will feel that he is a success in God's eyes. I want him to be free to do his job well, knowing that I am behind him one hundred percent. I want him to know that there is no pressure from me for more money. I am willing to stay on the budget or do without—whatever it takes. I try not to miss opportunities to build him up and let him know that I need him. I tell him "thank you" for working so hard and providing for all my needs. I tell him I don't want more, I have everything I need. I'm wealthy because I have him and his love and faithfulness. I am content right where I am.

In order to do this, my heart has to be right. It is imperative that I let the Holy Spirit control my thoughts, my actions, my words, moment by moment. I like Major Ian Thomas' description of walking in the Spirit. "The One who calls you to a life of righteousness is the One who, by your consent, lives that life of righteousness through you! This is the divine genius that saves a man from the futility of self-effort. You will have become totally dependent upon the life of Christ within you. . . ."[9] "It is only the Spirit of God acting within you, who can ever enable you to behave as God intended you to behave!"[10] In other words, quit trying and let Him do it through you. I also must be spending time in God's Word. It is the only way to renew my mind and get God's perspective. In living the years I have left, what really matters in the face of eternity? A few more things? No, but my marriage and my children and the people God brings across my path do.

Conclusion

My prayer when we were first married was that I would be so frugal and careful with our money that I would eventually win his trust. While we were engaged Russ told me of his concern about our future joint account and especially about putting my name on his credit card. I'm happy to say that as I am learning to submit, help, and be content, things have now come full circle to the point where Russ tells me I *have* to go shopping; he insists that I spend money on myself and on the house. One day we went shopping together, and he insisted I get something. Everything was too expensive, so I just didn't feel right about getting anything. Two weeks later, two dresses that I had really liked, except for the price, arrived at the door by UPS. Russ had gone back and had them sent to me! I chose Prov. 31:12, "She does him good and not evil all the days of her life" as my special verse for my relationship to Russ as his wife. God continues to reinforce my commitment to His Word as Russ tells me often how grateful he is for me and that he couldn't be happier. Not only that, but he credits me with his accomplishments in the work world. There are many benefits from doing things God's way!

We enjoy going over our finances, because we are a team. We don't have to fight. Russ thanks me for fitting in and being a good steward; he is pleased with how I handle our finances. At the end of the year when we go over the budget, I thank him for providing for us and managing our finances so well. He thanks me for not putting him under pressure and being happy to stay on the budget. We both thank the Lord for our wonderful marriage and for His faithfulness to us. "Now to Him who is able to do exceeding abundantly beyond all that we ask or think, according to the power that works within us . . ." (Eph. 3:20).

PRACTICAL HOW-TO'S

I think it's important to realize that there is no magic in methods. Just because you *do* all the right things doesn't mean God is pleased. The important thing is that you do the things that please God and your husband because your heart is set on Him and you are walking in the Spirit. You are to be *the* expert on your husband. You need to find out what makes him feel that you are on his team and what helps him the most; then make *that* a priority. I like to view finances as a challenge. I enjoy taking what I have and seeing what I can do with it. These are just some ideas and helps that I have found workable for me to stay on the budget and fit in with Russ's plans.

WAYS TO SAVE

children's clothes: semiannual neighborhood sales and garage sales.

children's toys: garage sales and secondhand stores.

clothes for me: I make a list of what I have and what I could use and then I watch for sales. Sometimes just a few accessories will stretch what I have.

eating out: Limit this and use two-for-one coupons or specials in the paper.

long-distance calls: only on bargain times, very infrequently, or write.

alert to sales: Keep an eye on sales in the paper so if something comes up I already know the best place to go.

gift closet: This has been a real breakthrough for me. In a small notebook, I keep a list of people that I buy for, and a list of the things purchased and for whom. We have predetermined on our budget what we can spend per person, per type of gift. (For instance $10 per Christmas gift, maximum). So, taking advantage of sales, I buy gifts all through the year. My goal is to be done with Christmas shopping by the summer. I also keep on hand several baby, birthday, and wedding gifts —all picked up at sales (after Christmas, end of season, going out of business, etc.).

controlled shopping: Don't go shopping unless there is a definite need or a planned item is on sale. Don't shop a great sale if you don't have the money.

haircuts: If you don't have the money, skip it. Can use coupons, wait till next month.

cut socializing costs: Have friends over for lunch, dinner, dessert; or popcorn and a video (decent, of course).

have a do-without month: We had neighbors who didn't buy anything that they could do without one month per year.

papers, magazines, monthly clubs: should be stopped if money is tight.

greeting cards: Make them or get them at half off through sales or mail order.

film: mail order is much cheaper; pictures make good gifts.

double coupons: only if I compare or buy that certain item anyway.

meals: Plan weekly menu, use store sales to help plan menu, and use coupons. Only grocery shop once a week.

gifts for Russ and me: We decide ahead of time what we will spend on each other and agree on what to do for the boys' birthdays and Christmas gifts.

QUESTIONS TO ASK BEFORE BUYING

The purpose of these questions is to help you make a wise decision and promote harmony in your marriage.

Is this a need? want? or desire?

Am I getting the best deal I can for the money?

Does it reflect the Lord in me?

Will it accomplish God's purpose?

What is my goal?

Will this purchase require extra time for upkeep?

Will it hold its value?

Is this an instant decision? an unplanned item? Wait.

Is this a get-rich-quick thing?

Have I prayed about this?

Did Russ request this?

Chapter 14

A Game Plan to Communicate

As we have made our way through these practical chapters, it has become quite obvious that a key step in solving the various problems that money can cause in a marriage is a plan to communicate. You need a plan to communicate not only about specific money issues but also about your priorities and purpose as a couple. To say, "Honcy, I just wanted you to know that I'm planning on betting our whole paycheck next week on the Super Bowl," is clcar communication but probably won't promote harmony!

Communication is key because even though the problems related to money may appear to be money problems, they may be nothing more than communication problems. Many times I havc heard a wife explain, "If he would only talk to me and let me know what is going on." The husband often says, "She just doesn't understand how hard I work and how difficult it is right now, and all she does is spend."

The issue of money is so volatile that many "blow up" at each other when discussing it. How do you go about discussing it without disrupting the harmony?

It is the purpose of this chapter to take a look at a game plan of communication that can help you communicate about money in all the various areas—giving, investments, etc.—and thereby promote a harmonious marriage relationship.

MOTIVATION FOR COMMUNICATION

Motivation is nothing more than that which inspires people to action and encourages them to follow through to completion. What motivates husbands and wives to communicate? They will only be motivated to communicate if they understand and hold in high esteem their marriage relationship. They must be committed to it. Hopefully, you are as convinced as Julie and I are that marriage is important. If you value your marriage highly, you'll do what it takes to communicate and not allow money to disrupt it.

In our world today this motivation to communicate can only come from a clear understanding of God's Word. Many passages discuss communication (see chart 14.1). Let's focus on a few verses, however, from the Amplified Bible to set the foundation for why we should communicate.

In 1 Cor. 1:10 Paul writes, "But I urge and entreat you, brethren, by the name of our Lord Jesus Christ, that all of you be in *perfect harmony,* and *full agreement* in what you say, and that

CHART 14.1

THE BIBLE ON COMMUNICATION

Read these passages thoughtfully:

- Gen. 2:18, 21–24
- Ps. 34:3
- Ps. 128:1–4
- Prov. 5:18
- Prov. 17:1
- Prov. 17:14
- Eccles. 9:9
- Mal. 2:16
- Matt. 19:3–8
- 1 Cor. 13:4–7
- Col. 3:8–9
- Col. 4:6
- 1 Tim. 3:4–5
- Titus 1:6
- James 1:19–20

there be no dissensions or factions or divisions among you; but that you be perfectly united in your common understanding and in your opinions and judgments." Our motivation for communication, whether it be about finances or any other area, should be to create harmony and agreement.

Eph. 4:29 admonishes us, "Let no foul or polluting language, nor evil word, nor unwholesome or worthless talk [ever] come out of your mouth; but only such [speech] as is good and beneficial to the spiritual progress of others, as is fitting to the need and the occasion, that it may be a blessing and give grace (God's favor) to those who hear it."

Phil. 2:2 adds, "Fill up and complete my joy by living in harmony and being of the same mind and one in purpose, having the same love, being in full accord and of one harmonious mind and intention."

And 1 Pet. 3:8–9 says, "To sum up, let all be harmonious, sympathetic, brotherly, kindhearted, and humble in spirit; not returning evil for evil, or insult for insult, but giving a blessing instead; for you were called for the very purpose that you might inherit a blessing."

It's clear that the God of the universe desires that we live harmoniously and be of one mind. This should be our motivation for desiring to communicate. We need to purpose in our hearts to cooperate and not let a temporal tool, such as money, disrupt or ruin this God-ordained relationship, our marriage.

What are some practical ways to go about implementing a plan for communication? The following plan has worked very well for Julie and me.

MECHANICS OF COMMUNICATION

As you read through this section, refer to the communication flowchart (chart 14.2). The first step you should take to begin the communication process is to make sure you really understand how your spouse responds to frustrating circumstances. Each of us has a certain set of "indicators" we exhibit when we are frustrated or upset about something in our life.

You need to take the time to become a student of your spouse. Make sure you know how your spouse responds and what indicators he or she exhibits when frustrated. This is why a clear under-

CHART 14.2
COMMUNICATION FLOWCHART

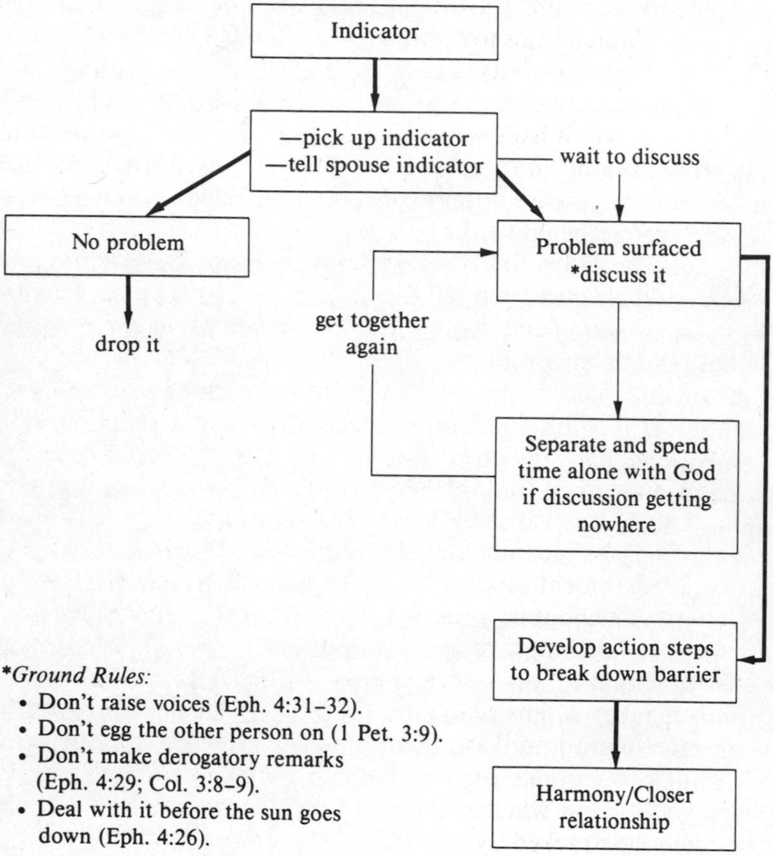

Ground Rules:
- Don't raise voices (Eph. 4:31–32).
- Don't egg the other person on (1 Pet. 3:9).
- Don't make derogatory remarks (Eph. 4:29; Col. 3:8–9).
- Deal with it before the sun goes down (Eph. 4:26).

standing of the differences between you and your spouse is so critical. It will help you be more perceptive to the indicators.

I have found over the years that my wife consistently exhibits certain indicators when she is frustrated—she becomes very silent and loses her sense of humor. Whenever I am frustrated, I usually respond by changing the subject and talking about side issues.

When either of us exhibits these indicators, Julie and I know that we need to communicate about something.

Once those indicators have been observed, it's important to be sensitive to them. Too often they are ignored (especially by the husband), which leads to a greater frustration later. There are two ways to show sensitivity. First, you respond to the indicator you see in your spouse's behavior with a question such as, "Is anything bothering you? What's wrong?" This shows that you have picked up on something and are being sensitive to it and want to discuss it. Second, if you are upset and your spouse is not picking up on the indicator, then it's your responsibility to tell him or her. If I'm not being sensitive to my wife in picking up on her frustration, she should go ahead and tell me that something is bothering her. As you can see from the flowchart, one of our basic "ground rules" is that any problem must be discussed before the sun goes down (Eph. 4:26). This avoids potentially greater problems that can occur if small frustrations are not dealt with. *The primary point is that the issue must be discussed before the sun goes down.* I know many men find this especially hard since they don't tend to talk much anyway. Now there is a time limit!

Once the indicator has been brought out in the open and there is agreement that a problem needs to be resolved, you can begin to talk about it. In most cases it is very easy for one spouse to ask, "Is anything wrong?" and the other to say "no" when the answer is really "yes." "No" is the normal first response every time. It takes a sensitive, consistent, and perceptive spouse to continue to prod until the frustration is actually communicated. If you know (or take the time to find out) your spouse's indicators, you'll know whether there is a problem or not. You will not be easily sidetracked by the "no" that is first uttered.

Let me illustrate the situation this way. The husband comes home from a tough day at the office. Unbeknownst to him, his wife has had trouble balancing the checkbook and there appears to be an overdraft. She's not in a very good mood. He picks this up as he walks in the house, so he asks her if anything is wrong. She says, "No, it's nothing." Now, he can believe that and really catch it later—husbands often accept the "no" and grab the paper and head for the television, then wonder why she is in such a foul mood—or he can take more time to get her to "come out with it."

If he's read her indicator correctly, he knows something is wrong. The issue is, does he want to take time to discuss it? Is the TV more important than your spouse?

You will also note on the flowchart that in some cases it is appropriate to wait to discuss the problem. If I am at a party and I notice that my wife is upset about something, that is probably not the appropriate time to have a heavy discussion about the problem. Or, if I pull out the checkbook to pay for dinner and notice a lesser balance than I thought should be there, that is not the time to question my wife about where the money went. It's better to wait until we are in private. Given the ground rule that frustrations must be discussed before the sun goes down, it is important that this take place as soon as possible. (You don't want to be up all night!)

Here is where the other three ground rules come in—and they're not always easy! (1) Don't raise your voice; (2) don't egg on or be antagonistic; (3) don't make derogatory remarks. Many times when I notice that my wife is frustrated, my first thought is to say something like, "That is the stupidest thing I have ever heard!" That kind of remark will only disrupt the harmony and break down the communication lines even more. Therefore, if the discussion is going nowhere, you should separate for a set amount of time (no longer than one hour). The purpose is for each of you to spend some time alone with God praying as David did in Ps. 139:23–24, "Search me, O God, and know my heart; / Try me and know my anxious thoughts; / And see if there be any hurtful way in me; / And lead me in the everlasting way," before getting together to discuss the problem again. During this time of separation you will often find that the dispute is really your problem as much as it is your spouse's problem.

Take the time, be persistent, and talk out the problem. It's worth the effort. My wife and I have been up several nights very late working through a problem, but it is such a joy to know that the problem has been resolved before we go to bed. Over the years we have found that when conflicts are worked through and resolved, they become stepping-stones to a stronger marriage. As I said earlier, if problems are allowed to fester and continue to grow day after day, the oneness and unity of the relationship is disrupted.

As you discuss the problem try to determine some specific action steps to solve it. In the area of finances, for example, many frustrating problems are caused when there is no cash-flow control system. A specific action step to promote harmony, as we have seen, is to set up a budget and—with the input of both spouses—assign specific areas of responsibility. If investments are the frustration point, then perhaps a commitment is needed to communicate options before any final decision is made.

Hopefully, as you have read this book you have learned more about why your spouse may respond the way he or she does to certain financial situations. Also, you should have some idea of appropriate steps you can take to promote harmony and avoid conflict. You will find yourself in fewer and fewer discussions or fights about money if you have a plan for your money.

The bottom-line goal in communicating is to establish a closer and more harmonious relationship. To that end there are two other issues to be discussed.

First, *don't settle for a stalemate.* It is not healthy for the relationship for a couple to leave an issue unresolved or for husband and wife to remain on opposite sides of an issue. I know some would say that it is okay to agree to disagree. How much harmony can result from that? I would propose that there should never be a stalemate on an issue. The purpose of communication is to make sure each spouse has clearly stated his or her position on an issue. Once this is done, if there is an impasse (disagreement regarding the correct answer or action), then the husband has the final say. As we have seen in 1 Cor. 11:3, the man has been given the responsibility to make the decisions in his family—not because he is smarter or better than his wife, but because God knew someone had to be the final decision maker and He appointed the husband.

Men, this position is not to be taken lightly. The husband should take great care to make sure he gets his wife's input and weighs it carefully before making any decision, especially a decision that directly opposes his wife's desire. Wives, you may need to exercise faith and trust God for the decision your husband will make, especially if it is different from what you think is the right decision. It is his responsibility to make the decision and your responsibility to submit to the decision and trust God for the outcome. You need to resist the urge to come back to your husband later and say "I told you so" if his decision doesn't work out. Money is a tool and nothing more. How the husband and wife handle the decision-making process is more important than the actual outcome of the decision.

Julie and I have had several occasions in our married life to test this way to avoid a stalemate. It really does work. If we are faced with a decision where we do not appear to have agreement, I will listen to Julie's input and weigh it carefully before making the final decision. Her input is always followed with the words, "That is my input; now I am trusting God with you to make the decision. I am with you no matter what you decide." With those words she gives me the freedom to make the decision but also encourages me to spend time with God to make the decision.

Second, *never take revenge.* In 1 Peter 3, we see that we are not to repay evil for evil, but rather to give a blessing instead. Therefore, if the husband makes a decision that the wife is not comfortable with (a bad investment, for instance), she should not frivolously spend his money just to get even with him. Harmony is much more important than the money, which is simply a tool.

HOW TO HAVE A PLANNING WEEKEND

One of the practical ways we have found to facilitate communication in the marriage relationship is to have a planning weekend regularly. This is simply a weekend set aside for us as husband and wife to get away (without children) for the purpose of communicating and taking inventory of our relationship. During this weekend we can take the time to discuss issues such as finances, children, work, goals, and dreams.

Here is a suggested format for the weekend. Although this does not have to be adhered to, it illustrates that there should be a balance between work and play.

Planning Weekend Agenda

Topics: Finances, children, church (spiritual), social, work, major decisions, dreams, etc.

Friday	2:00–4:00	Arrive
	4:00–6:00	Rest and unwind
	6:00–	Dinner and discuss a topic
Saturday	8:00–10:00	Breakfast and time alone with God
	10:00–12:00	Discuss a topic or continue discussion
	12:00–5:00	Lunch, shop, recreation, etc.
	6:00–	Dinner and discuss a topic
Sunday	8:00–10:00	Breakfast and time alone with God
	10:00–12:00	Discuss action steps to promote and enhance marriage

A caution is in order here: When you go on a planning weekend, expect to do some work and come away with one or two specific action steps that will enhance your relationship. Usually both spouses have been busy with the children or job and, when they get away for the weekend, see it as a great opportunity to relax, watch football games, and shop—to do anything except plan. They run the risk of never accomplishing the desired end of discussing the issues they set out to resolve. Therefore, it's important to set an agenda beforehand and commit yourselves to accomplishing the desired goals. In some cases, if you bring to the surface a very strategic issue that must be discussed at length, you may decide to stay on that issue for the entire weekend. The important thing is that you accomplish one or two specific things that will make your relationship better as a result of the weekend.

To illustrate what can happen if expectations are not adjusted before the planning weekend, let me share a story that happened to Julie and me. We had scheduled a planning weekend several weeks in advance, and I had anxiously looked forward to our time together to discuss some key issues in handling our finances and raising the kids. Being the planning type, I saw no reason to wait until we arrived at our destination to begin discussing some of the issues that I knew we were going to talk about over the weekend. We hadn't driven more than twenty-five minutes (it was a two-hour drive) when I began to ask Julie some questions to get her input.

Needless to say, she didn't respond with much enthusiasm, and after a short period of time, she blurted out, "I can't believe it! We just left home, and you are already wanting to plan and be organized and haven't even given me a chance to relax. I have been with the kids all day, and you want to start planning before we even get a chance to relax and get where we're going."

That was when we realized that a planning weekend could only be a success if both husband and wife had the right expectations about it. It is neither a weekend of fun and games nor a weekend of intense, unrelenting work, and you can do your marriage more harm than good if you don't agree on a reasonable balance. Julie and I soon overcame our problem, and we had a very productive weekend.

The marital intimacy checklist (chart 14.3) is a practical tool that can be a good way to start the communication process at the outset of your planning weekend. Julie and I typically answer each of the questions individually and then get together and compare them. If in any one of the areas we have a tremendous difference in how we perceive unity, then that is where we start talking. For example, on financial intimacy, if she has a 1 and I have a 5, then obviously we are perceiving it dramatically differently, and there is a tremendous potential for conflict. If we have basically the same numbers in an area, then we do not focus in on it as much as other areas.

THE MEANS OF COMMUNICATION

If communicating along these guidelines seems impossible, then you need to know that it is impossible! Without walking closely with God and asking His Holy Spirit to give wisdom and insight, it is impossible to be truly sensitive to your spouse and tune in to his or her concerns and feelings. By nature we are selfish. We want our own way. Therefore, we need to ask God to give us His wisdom and the sensitivity we need to communicate properly.

As we have seen throughout these pages, money is simply a tool, but our marriages have eternal significance. We have also seen that being sensitive to each other encourages harmony in our marriages. It is impossible to be sensitive without experiencing the power source of the Holy Spirit as a reality in our lives. It is my prayer that before you close this book you will deal seriously with the four steps highlighted in the conclusion of this book. These steps are the key to eternal life and also the key to an abundant, fruitful, and harmonious marriage now.

CHART 14.3

MARITAL INTIMACY CHECKLIST

A Good Way to Begin the Communication Process

As you review your marriage from your vantage point, how would you evaluate your degree of satisfaction or dissatisfaction with the following items?

Circle the number which best describes your feeling about each item.

	Very Dissatisfied	Somewhat Dissatisfied	Neutral	Somewhat Satisfied	Very Satisfied
1. Spiritual Intimacy (oneness before God)	1	2	3	4	5
2. Work Intimacy (sharing common tasks)	1	2	3	4	5
3. Intellectual Intimacy (closeness in ideas)	1	2	3	4	5
4. Recreational Intimacy (relating in fun and play)	1	2	3	4	5
5. Emotional Intimacy (being on same wavelength)	1	2	3	4	5
6. Crisis Intimacy (closeness in problems and pain)	1	2	3	4	5
7. Conflict Intimacy (understanding in facing and struggling with differences)	1	2	3	4	5
8. Creative Intimacy (sharing in acts of creating together)	1	2	3	4	5
9. Commitment Intimacy (common benefits from shared efforts)	1	2	3	4	5
10. Aesthetic Intimacy (sharing experiences of beauty)	1	2	3	4	5
11. Sexual Intimacy	1	2	3	4	5
12. Communication Intimacy (feeling of openness in every area)	1	2	3	4	5
13. Financial Intimacy (communication on finances)	1	2	3	4	5

After each spouse responds separately, get together and discuss why you responded the way you did—especially if you respond to the same issue differently (for example, one spouse puts a 1 and the other a 5).

Chart reproduced by permission of Ron Blue & Co., Atlanta, Ga.

GAME PLAN

Get your calendar, sit down with your spouse, and do the following:

1. Decide when you're going to have a planning weekend. Mark it on the calendar.
2. Decide how you want to structure the weekend: how long it will be, where you'll go, what is a reasonable schedule.
3. Discuss what you want to accomplish on the weekend: budget, discipline of children, etc.
4. Decide if there is anything you need to do as preparation for the weekend: get babysitters, make reservations, save the money.

Now, get away and communicate!

Conclusion

Hopefully, as you have made your way through this book you have been made aware of the tremendous potential your marriage has to make a positive impact for the Lord now and, through your posterity, after you are gone. You should also be aware of the devastation that money can bring to your marriage if it is not kept in proper perspective.

God's Design

If you desire harmony in your marriage, it is important to order your marriage as closely as possible to the design that God has made so clear in Scripture. I want to summarize here the essence of that design:

- The husband has the ultimate responsibility to provide for his family.
- The husband provides by working hard at a vocation that God has equipped him for and that he enjoys.
- The husband is careful not to overwork as he provides, and constantly strives to keep balance in his life between work, family, and his other responsibilities.
- The husband understands his responsibility and is not lazy or slothful.
- As the husband works he generates a certain amount of income. The income is a function of his vocation and may be a little or a lot.

- The husband then makes sure he promotes communication with his wife regarding the income he does generate so they are in agreement about how the funds should be allocated.
- Both husband and wife are in agreement on a plan that will ensure that they live within the income generated by the husband. They realize that more income is never the answer and are committed to make it on the husband's income.
- They are both committed to live within the husband's income because they have a clear understanding of the awesome responsibility inherent in their respective job descriptions: the wife as help-meet and the husband as provider and leader.
- The wife's primary responsibility is within the home. She should only work vocationally outside of the home if she is fulfilling excellently her God-given responsibilities within the home. She does not work simply in the pursuit of income.
- Both the husband and the wife understand that lifestyle is not a function of material possessions but a function of spiritual maturity and depth. To that end they are both committed to growing spiritually day by day.
- They both understand that the key to harmony in their marriage is communication. They therefore strive to develop good communication skills, especially in relation to specific money areas.

A FINAL NOTE TO MEN

Men, work hard at what God has equipped and called you to do vocationally, all the while keeping balance in your life by living according to time priorities rather than income priorities. Realize that you are successful as you do what God has made you to do and that money is not the barometer for success. Be committed to communicating with your wife, both in the area of money and also by way of encouragement to her in her role as help-meet and companion. Make sure she knows that she is valued as she works "in the home" nurturing your posterity. This communication won't come naturally for you, and therefore you need to cultivate your relationship with God so you'll be filled with His supernatural power. Make it your overriding life's desire and focus to leave a godly posterity that will carry on into the next generation and beyond. You can only do this as you fulfill your God-given job description and thereby maximize harmony in your marriage.

A Final Note to Women

Women, be committed to live within the income generated by your husband. Make sure he knows you are content with what he makes and with him and that you are rich even though you may not have much money. Think correctly about the awesome responsibility God has given you, that of being the primary teacher and trainer of your posterity. It will not be natural to submit and fit in with your husband's plans and his income, and therefore you need to cultivate your relationship with God so you'll be filled with His supernatural power. Make it your life's overriding desire to fulfill your God-given job description and thereby maximize harmony in your marriage so that you can leave a godly posterity that will carry on into the next generation and beyond.

The Source

You may have read this entire book and been struck with the realization that you do not have the power source within you to enable you to do what's been noted. You may be sitting there about to finish this book, thinking that there have been some good ideas shared but that they are basically impossible to implement. I know, in my life, that if it were not for my relationship with the Lord God of the universe through His son, Jesus Christ, I would not be able to be sensitive to Julie and experience the joy and harmony that we have in our marriage. It is God, working through the power of the Holy Spirit in my life, that allows me to be sensitive to her. The principles that follow can plug you into that power source.

Just as there are financial principles that are true related to our money, there are also spiritual principles that are true related to our spiritual condition. Those principles are as follows:

Principle 1: Man is separated from God. The Bible teaches that God loves all men and wants them to know Him. But man is separated from God and His love because of man's sin. The Bible says in Isa. 53:6, "All of us like sheep have gone astray, each of us has turned to his own way; but the Lord has caused the iniquity of us all to fall on Him." In Rom. 3:23 it says, "All have sinned and fall short of the glory of God." You may be thinking that "all men" does not include you, but we find in Psalm 14 that God looked to and fro throughout the land to see if there was anyone who did good, and He found no one. "All" means *all,* and that means you and me. We are separated from God. This leads us to principle 2.

Principle 2: We owe a penalty for our sin. Heb. 9:27 says that man is destined to die once and after this comes judgment. 2 Thess. 1:8–9 says, "Those who do not know God will be punished with everlasting destruction and shut out from the presence of the Lord." Our sin has separated us from God, and we will be judged for our sin. We owe a penalty for our sinfulness that must be paid. The only problem is, we are not worthy to pay that penalty. No amount of good works can put us back in right standing with God. There is a solution, however, and this is principle 3.

Principle 3: Christ paid the penalty. Rom. 5:8 says, "But God demonstrates His own love toward us in that while we were yet sinners, Christ died for us." 1 Pet. 3:18 says, "For Christ also died for sins once for all, the just for the unjust, in order that He might bring us to God, having been put to death in the flesh, but made alive in the spirit." Jesus Christ was born at Christmas to die at Easter, to pay the penalty for your sins and for mine. It is not enough just to believe these principles. We must go on to principle 4.

Principle 4: I must individually accept Christ's payment. We can believe that Christ died for our sins, but if we do not appropriate that for ourselves through faith, then we will perish in our sins. Only those who personally receive Jesus Christ into their lives, trusting Him to forgive their sins by faith, can be put in right standing with God and receive the power that only He can give. John 1:12 says, "But as many as received Him, to them He gave the right to become children of God, even to those who believe in His name." John 5:24 says, "Truly, truly, I say to you, he who hears My word, and believes Him who sent me, has eternal life, and does not come into judgment, but has passed out of death into life."

But how does a person appropriate the reality of Jesus Christ in his or her life? Very simply, he or she does that by faith. Jesus says, "Behold, I stand at the door and knock. If anyone hears My voice and opens the door, I will come in to him, and will dine with him, and he with Me." If God is knocking on the door of your life, then you need to pray by faith a simple prayer that expresses the desire of your heart. Pray a prayer similar to the one following: "Lord Jesus, please come into my life and be my savior and Lord. Please forgive my sins and give me the gift of eternal life. Thank you for forgiving my sins." This prayer, if it expresses the desire of your heart, is the key to opening the door and allowing Christ to come into your life. We know that He is there because the Bible says in 1 John 5:11–13, "And the witness is this, that God has given us eternal life, and this life is in His Son. He who has the Son has the life; he who does not have the Son of God does not have the life. These things I have written to you who believe in the name of the Son of God, in order that you may know that you have eternal life."

You can know that you have eternal life if you, by faith, have acknowledged that you are sinful and that Christ paid the penalty for your sins, and have asked Him into your heart.

May God bless you and encourage you as you pursue harmony in your marriage together.

Notes

Chapter 1 The Purpose of Money

1. Philip Yancy, "Learning to Live with Money," *Christianity Today,* 14 December 1984.
2. Bill Gillham, *Lifetime Guarantee* (Brentwood, Tenn.: Woglemuth & Hyatt, 1987), 76–77.
3. Ian Thomas, *The Saving Life of Christ* (Grand Rapids, Mich.: Zondervan Publishing House, 1961), 70–71.
4. Yancy, "Learning to Live with Money."

Chapter 2 The Purpose of Marriage

1. Mike Mason, *The Mystery of Marriage* (Portland, Oreg.: Multnomah, 1985), 139.
2. Ibid., 101.
3. George Gilder, *Men and Marriage* (Gretna, La.: Pelican, 1986), 43.
4. James Dobson, *Straight Talk to Men and Their Wives* (Waco, Tex.: Word Books, 1980), 64.
5. *Common Ground,* 1987. Search Ministries, P.O. Box 521, Lutherville, Md. 21093.

Chapter 3 Reasons for Marriage Conflict

1. James Dobson, *Love for a Lifetime* (Portland, Oreg.: Multnomah, 1987), 70.
2. Tim LaHaye, *Spirit-Controlled Temperament* (Wheaton, Ill.: Tyndale House, 1966), 5–6.
3. Gary Smalley, *If Only He Knew* (King of Prussia, Pa.: R. M. Marketing, 1979), 5.
4. Mike Mason, *The Mystery of Marriage* (Portland, Oreg.: Multnomah, 1985). 129.
5. Dobson, *Lifetime,* 44.

Chapter 4 Work: Blessing or Curse?

1. C. H. Spurgeon, *The Treasury of David* (McLean, Va.: MacDonald, n.d.), 88.
2. Used by permission. Life Messengers, 1926 Densmore Ave N., Seattle, Wash. 98133.

Chapter 5 Will He Ever Come Home?

1. Gordon MacDonald, *The Effective Father* (Wheaton, Ill.: Tyndale House, 1983), 35, 44, 50–51.
2. Tim Hansel, *What Kids Need Most in a Dad* (Old Tappan, N.J.: Fleming H. Revell, 1984), 30, 165, 28.

Chapter 6 The Myth of the Working Mother

1. National Family Foundation, *Daycare: Hard Realities—Tough Choices* (Naples, Fla.: National Family Foundation, 1988). Available from the foundation at 440 Spinnaker Dr., Naples, Fla. 33940.
2. "Weathering the Stress," *Atlanta Constitution,* 15 November 1988.
3. George Gilder, *Men and Marriage* (Gretna, La.: Pelican, 1986), 153.
4. "Childcare: A Problem or a Voting Issue?" *Public Opinion* (July-August 1988): 36.
5. Gilder, *Men and Marriage,* 171.
6. Ibid., 44.
7. Ibid., 151–52.
8. Ibid., 152–53.
9. Ibid., 153.
10. "Weathering the Stress," *Atlanta Constitution,* 15 November 1988.
11. "Children of Change," *Atlanta Journal,* 16 November 1988.
12. Ibid.
13. Gilder, *Men and Marriage,* 154.
14. Jack Wilkinson, "Nothing Is Forgotten in Dr. Denmark's Office," *Atlanta Constitution,* 1 April 1986.
15. National Family Foundation, *Daycare.* Used by permission.
16. Sandra Evans, "Study Shows Negative Effects of Full-Time Child Care," *Washington Post,* 23 April 1988.
17. "Children of Change—Unsteady Foundations Shake the Young," *Atlanta Constitution,* 16 November 1988.

Chapter 9 Freedom in Control

1. Philip Yancy, "Learning to Live with Money," *Christianity Today,* 14 December 1984.

Chapter 11 It Is Such a Good Deal!

1. C. A. Stevens, "Women Are Something Else!" *Frontier Magazine,* 1982.
2. Ronald W. Blue, *Master Your Money* (Nashville, Tenn.: Thomas Nelson, 1986), 180–81.

Chapter 12 To Give or Not to Give

1. Philip Yancy, "Learning to Live with Money," *Christianity Today,* 14 December 1984.
2. Ibid.

Chapter 13 A Woman Looks at Finances and the Woman's Role

1. Matthew Henry, *Commentary on the Whole Bible,* ed. L. F. Church (Grand Rapids: Zondervan, 1961), 788.
2. George Santa, *A Modern Study in the Book of Proverbs* (Milford, Mich.: Mott, 1978), 733.
3. Don Meredith, *Becoming One* (Nashville: Thomas Nelson, 1982), 102.
4. Maureen Downey, "Individualism Now Seen as Divisive to the Family," *Atlanta Constitution,* 6 April 1987.
5. Sam L. Peoples, Jr., *A Stress Management Seminar* (Birmingham, Ala.: Christian Ministries, n.d.), 2.
6. George Fooshee, Jr., *You Can Be Financially Free* (Old Tappan, N.J.: Fleming H. Revell Co., 1976), 42.
7. Ibid., 39.
8. Santa, *Proverbs,* 205.
9. Ian Thomas, *The Saving Life of Christ* (Grand Rapids: Zondervan, 1976), 15.
10. Ian Thomas, *The Mystery of Godliness* (Grand Rapids: Zondervan, 1964), 47.

Recommended Reading

Books

Blue, Ron. *The Debt Squeeze: How Your Family Can Become Financially Free.* Pomona, Calif.: Focus on the Family, 1989.

———. *Master Your Money.* Nashville, Tenn.: Thomas Nelson Publishers, 1986.

———, and Judy Blue. *Money Matters for Parents and Their Kids.* Nashville, Tenn.: Oliver Nelson, 1988.

Burkett, Larry. *Your Finances in Changing Times.* San Bernardino, Calif.: Campus Crusade for Christ, 1975.

———. *What Husbands Wish Their Wives Knew about Money.* Wheaton, Ill.: Victor Books, 1977.

Cooper, Darien. *You Can Be the Wife of a Happy Husband.* Wheaton, Ill.: Victor Books, 1974.

Dayton, Howard L., Jr. *Your Money: Frustration or Freedom?* Wheaton, Ill.: Tyndale, 1979.

Dobson, James. *Love for a Lifetime.* Portland, Oreg.: Multnomah Press, 1987.

———. *Straight Talk to Men and Their Wives.* Waco, Tex.: Word Books, 1980.

Fooshee, George, Jr. *You Can Be Financially Free.* Old Tappan, N.J.: Revell, 1976.

Gilder, George. *Men and Marriage.* Gretna, La.: Pelican Publishing Co., 1986.

Hansel, Tim. *What Kids Need Most in a Dad.* Old Tappan, N.J.: Revell, 1984.

———. *When I Relax I Feel Guilty.* Elgin, Ill.: David C. Cook, 1979.

Henrichsen, Walter, and Gayle Jackson. *A Layman's Guide to Applying the Bible.* Grand Rapids, Mich.: Zondervan, 1985.

Howard, J. Grant. *Balancing Life's Demands.* Portland, Oreg.: Multnomah Press, 1983.

LaHaye, Tim. *Spirit-Controlled Temperament.* Wheaton, Ill.: Tyndale House Publishers, 1966.

Laney, J. Carl. *The Divorce Myth.* Minneapolis, Minn.: Bethany House Publishers, 1981.

Mason, Mike. *The Mystery of Marriage.* Portland, Oreg.: Multnomah Press, 1985.

McGuire, Dorothy, Carol Lewis, and Alvena Blatchley. *Submission: Are There Limits?* Denver, Colo.: Tri-R Ministries, 1984.

Meredith, Don. *Becoming One.* Nashville, Tenn.: Thomas Nelson Publishers, n.d.

Packer, J. I. *Knowing God.* Downers Grove, Ill.: InterVarsity Press, 1973.

Ryken, Leland. *Work and Leisure in Christian Perspective.* Portland, Oreg.: Multnomah Press, 1987.

Sherman, Doug, and William Hendricks. *Your Work Matters to God.* Colorado Springs, Colo.: NavPress, 1987.

Smalley, Gary. *For Better or for Best.* King of Prussia, Pa.: R. M. Marketing, 1979.

———. *If Only He Knew.* King of Prussia, Pa.: R. M. Marketing, 1979.

Thomas, W. Ian. *Saving Life of Christ.* Grand Rapids, Mich.: Zondervan Publishing House, 1961.

Wheat, M. D., ed. *Intended for Pleasure.* Old Tappan, N.J.: Revell, 1977.

———, ed. *Love Life for Every Married Couple.* Grand Rapids, Mich.: Zondervan Publishing House, 1980.

Tape Series

"Philosophy of Christian Womanhood." Denver, Colo.: Tri-R Associates, 1969.

"Challenge of Christian Manhood." Denver, Colo.: Tri-R Associates, 1977.

McLaughlin, David. "The Role of the Man in the Family." Neenah, Wis.